Uva's Guide to Cranes, Dollies, and Remote Heads

Uva's Guide to Cranes, Dollies, and Remote Heads

Michael G. Uva and Sabrina Uva

Focal Press

Boston   Oxford   Auckland   Johannesburg   Melbourne   New Delhi

Focal Press is an imprint of Butterworth–Heinemann.
Copyright © 2002 by Butterworth–Heinemann

R A member of the Reed Elsevier group

∞ Recognizing the importance of preserving what has been written, Butterworth–Heinemann prints its books on acid-free paper whenever possible.

Library of Congress Cataloging-in-Publication Data

Uva, Michael.
    Uva's guide to cranes, dollies, and remote heads / Michael G. Uva and Sabrina Uva.
Sabrina Uva.
    p. cm.
    ISBN 0-240-80487-2 (alk. paper)
    1. Cinematography—Equipment and supplies—Handbooks, manuals, etc. 2. Grips (Persons)—Handbooks, manuals, etc. 3. Photographic assistants—Handbooks, manuals, etc. 4. Stage machinery—Handbooks, manuals, etc. I. Uva, Sabrina. II. Title.

TR850 .U95 2001
778.5′3—dc21

2001040636

British Library Cataloguing-in-Publication Data
A catalogue record for this book is available from the British Library.

The publisher offers special discounts on bulk orders of this book.
For information, please contact:
Manager of Special Sales
Butterworth–Heinemann
225 Wildwood Avenue
Woburn, MA 01801-2041
Tel: 781-904-2500
Fax: 781-904-2620

For information on all Focal Press publications available, contact our World Wide Web home page at: http://www.focalpress.com

10 9 8 7 6 5 4 3 2 1
Printed in the United States of America

DEDICATION

This book is dedicated to my wife, Sabrina. She has put up with, and still puts up with, the long hours and trips out of town and all the meetings. She is my rock. This dedication is a repeat of my first book, but this woman—my equal partner in this life and my eternal partner in Christ—deserves the lion's share of the credit.

Table of Contents

Contributing Companies

Advanced Camera Systems, Inc.
Megamount
16117 Cohasset St.
Van Nuys, CA 91406
(818) 989-5222
www.advancedcamera.com

Aerocrane USA, Inc.
Remote Heads, Cranes, Jibs
16139 Wyandotte St.
Van Nuys, CA 91406
(818) 705-5681
Fax (818) 705-5683
and
21704RJ Heerhugowaard
The Netherlands
(31) 2207-46410
Fax (31) 2207-46510
aerocraneusa@aol.com

Anytime Production Rentals
SR-71 Sliding Plate
755 N. Lillian Way
Hollywood, CA 90038
(323) 461-8483
www.ragtimerentals.com

Backstage Equipment, Inc.
8052 Lankershim Blvd.
North Hollywood, CA 91605
(800) 69-CARTS
(818) 504-6026
Fax (818) 504-6180
www.backstageweb.com

Barber Tech
The Barber Baby Boom and Barber Boom 20 foot

14803 Otsego St.
Sherman Oaks, CA 91403
(818) 986-4831

Barbervision
9148 Exposition Dr.
Los Angeles, CA 90034
(213) 280-0363
Fax (213) 280-0367

Birns and Sawyer, Inc.
The Porta-Jib
1026 N. Highland Ave.
Los Angeles, CA 90038
(213) 466-8211

Cablecam Systems, Ltd.
(818) 601-6333,
Fax (818) 601-6333
jr@cablecam.com

Camera Support Systems
4725 Lagoon Dr.
Mound, MN 55364
(612) 474-9246

Chapman Studio Equip, Inc.
Chapman Crane Arm, Lenny Mini, Lenny 2 and 3 Arms
12940 Raymer St.
North Hollywood, CA 91605
(888) 883-6559
(818) 764-6762
www.chapman-leonard.com

Egripment USA Inc.
Mini Seven Wedge, Pearson Head, Liberty Range Jib, Mini-Jib, Maxi-
    Jib/Super Maxi-Crane/Jib, Javelin Crane/Jib, Piccolo Crane/Jib, Sky-
    king/Skymote Crane/Jib, V.I.P. Four-in-One Crane and more
7625 Hayvenhurst Ave., #27
Van Nuys, CA 91406
(818) 787-4295
Fax (818) 787-6195
Egripment@egripment.com

Eurogrip Grip Equipment
The Euro Jib
Hantverkarvagen
25 C S-136 44 Haninge, Sweden
46 (0) 8 745 00 45
or
Cartoni USA
960 Enchanted Way, #104
Simi Valley, CA 93065
(805) 520-6086

EZ Float, Inc.
7625 Sunrise Blvd., #1202
Citrus Heights, CA 95610
(916) 726-2819
www.ezfloat.com

EZ FX
324 Maguire Rd.
Ocoee, FL 34761
(800) 541-5706
Fax (407) 877-6603
www.ezfx.com

Filmair
51 Auckland Street, Paarden Eiland
Cape Town, South Africa
P.O. Box 537, Milnerton
7435 (021) 511-5579
Fax (021) 511-2812

Geo Film Group
Remote Heads, Cranes, Jibs, and Arms
7625 Hayvenhurst Ave.
Van Nuys, CA 91406
(818) 376-6680
Fax (818) 376-6686
www.geofilm.com

Grip House
5-11 Tauton Rd.
Metropolitan Centre, Greenford
Middlesex UB6 8UQ
(0181) 578-2382
Fax (0181) 578-1536

Gyrosphere
7625 Hayvenhurst Ave., #49
Van Nuyes, CA 91406
(818) 787-9733
www.gyrosphere.com

International Camera Systems/Continental Camera Rental
7240 Valjean Ave.
Van Nuys, CA 91406
(818) 989-5222
Fax (818) 994-8405

Isaia and Company
4650 Lankershim Blvd.
North Hollywood, CA 91602
(800) 5-Camera
(818) 752-3104
Fax (818) 752-3105
www.movies@isaia.com

J.L. Fisher Inc.
Four-Way Plates, Dollies, Arms
1000 Isabel St.
Burbank, CA 91506
(818) 846-8366
Fax (818) 846-8699
www.jlfisher.com

Louma L.A.
Louma Crane and Akela Cranes
8536 W. Venice Blvd.
Los Angeles, CA 90034
(310) 558-7890

Mathews Studio Electronics
6910 Tujunga Ave.
North Hollywood, CA 91605
(818) 623-1661
Fax (818) 623-1671
www.camerasystems.com

Matthews Studio Equipment
2405 Empire Ave.
Burbank, CA 91504
(818) 843-0831

Media Logic
The Seven Jib
17 West 20th Street, Suite 5E
New York, NY 10011
(212) 924-3824
Fax (212) 924-3823

Microdolly Hollywood
3110 West Burbank Blvd.
Burbank, CA 91505
(818) 845-8383
Fax (818) 845-8384
www.microdolly.com

Micron Tool & Manufacturing
Cam Mate Crane
2026 West Campus Drive
Tempe, AZ 85282
(602) 438-1245

Modern Studio Equipment
various rig plates, leveling heads, rigs, mounts
7428 Bellaire Ave.
North Hollywood, CA 91605
(818) 764-8574
Fax (818) 764-2958

Movie Tech/ABC Products
2150 Northmont Pkwy., Suite A
Duluth, GA 30096
(678) 417-6352
Fax (678) 417-6273
www.movietech.de
www.abc-products.de

Nebekers Motion Picture Video
Remote Heads
1240 E. 2100 South, Suite 300
Salt Lake City, UT 84106
(801) 467-1920
Fax (801) 467-0307
www.nebekers.com

Panavision
6219 De Soto Ave.

Woodland Hills, CA 91367
(818) 316-1080
Fax (818) 316-1081

Panther Corporation of America
4242 Lankershim Blvd.
North Hollywood, CA 91602
(818) 761-5414
Fax (818) 761-5414
contact@panther-gmbh.de
www.panther-gmbh.com

PDM MFG. Co.
7309 Kentland Ave.
West Hills, CA 91307
(818) 340-9376

Porta-JIB™ by Losmandy
Hollywood General Machinery, Inc.
1033 North Sycamore St.
Los Angeles, CA 90038
(323) 462-2855
Fax (323) 462-2682
www.porta-jib.com

Precision Camera Supports, Inc. (PCS)
7625 Hayvenhurst Ave., #12A
Van Nuys, CA 91406
(818) 785-5681
Fax (818) 785-5683

Redman Movies and Stories
Giraffe Crane
1240 East 2100 South
Salt Lake City, UT 84106
(801) 467-6671

The Shotmaker Co.
Camera Cars, Lightweight Jib, Aerocrane, Pegasus Crane, Super Jib,
    Shotmaker Elite
10909 Van Owen St.
North Hollywood, CA 91605
(818) 623-1700
Fax (818) 623-1710

info@shotmaker.com
www.shotmaker.com

Sorenson Design International
1040 Benson Way
Ashland, OR 97520
(541) 488-5466
Fax (541) 488-5526

Spacecam
31111 Viaduct Colinas
Thousand Oaks, CA 91362
(818) 889-6060
Fax (818) 889-6062

Stanton Video Services Inc.
The Jimmy Jib (Jr./Giant)
2223 East Rose Garden Loop
Phoenix, AZ 85024
(602) 493-9505
Fax (602) 943-2468

Strada Unlimited, Inc.
6062 Tollgate
Sisters, OR 97759
(877) 632-8444
Fax (541) 549-4226
www.stradacranes.com

Swiss Crane
11925 Wilshire Blvd., Suite 221
Los Angeles, CA 90025
(213) 955-1712

TCC (Super Techno)
7277 Hayvenhurst Ave., #87
Van Nuys, CA 91406
(818) 787-0277
(818) 787-2447

Technocrane, Ltd.
Echnocrane
7618 Woodman Ave., #1
Van Nuys, CA 91402
(818) 782-9051

Trovato Manufacturing, Inc.
Trovato Tote Jib, The Trovato Tote Jr.
P.O. Box 18188
Rochester, NY 14619
(716) 244-3310

Tyler Camera System
ZG Arm, models 6-200, 8-130, and 11-100
14218 Aetna St.
Van Nuys, CA 91401
(818) 989-4420
Fax (818) 989-0423
www.tylermount.com
or
Ken Hill Manufacturing
3104 Bewley St.
Fort Worth, TX 76117
(817) 831-3011
Fax (817) 838-7374

Weaver-Steadman
Fluid Head
1646 20th St.
Santa Monica, CA 90404
(310) 829-3296
Fax (310) 828-5935

Wescam USA, Inc.
7150 Hayvenhurst Avenue
Van Nuys, CA 91406
(818) 785-9282
Fax (818) 785-9767
www.wescam.com

Wolfe Air (Gyron)
39 East Walnut St.
Pasadena, CA 91103
(626) 584-8722
Fax (626) 584-4069
www.danwolfe.com

About the Author

Michael Uva is a highly motivated self-starter. He created one of Hollywood's largest privately owned fleet of rental trucks for grip equipment in just a few years and then sold it off. He learned his business strictly through on-the-job experience, having never attended any formal motion picture or cinema-related schools or classes.

When Michael began his career as a grip, no specialty books related to his craft were available. After several years of learning his craft from other key grips and grips, Michael wrote the first edition of this book to share his knowledge. He teaches at the University of California at Los Angeles on occasion. Michael's goal in writing this book is to help new students, other grips, and production members by providing a firsthand, fingertip reference guide to grip equipment used in the industry.

Warning/Disclaimer

This book was written to provide pictorial information only on the subject matter that is covered. It was not sold to give legal or professional service. If you need a legal expert for assistance, then one should be sought. Also before you try to grip, find someone (*a grip*) who is qualified to train you properly.

This book is a great "aid" but is in no way the final word on this subject. This book has not reprinted all the information that is available to the publisher and author. It is written to complement and/or supplement other text. This text is only a guide to help the reader identify a piece of equipment by sight and by the manufacturer's proper name. This book was written as completely as possible without trying to train you to do this sort of work. There may be mistakes either typographical or in its content.

This book is intended to be used as a pictorial reference only. This book will not and does not accept any liability or damage caused by this book. It is *highly suggested* that the reader work with a *highly skilled, highly trained* motion picture film technician *first*. The sole purpose of this book is to entertain and educate.

Safety is the number one concern of all persons who work on a movie set. Take it personal! Make it personal!

NOTE: It is advised that the user of Chapman/Leonard Equipment or any other vendor's equipment should check with the manufacturer on the latest updates, specifications, and changes that may have occurred. Do not attempt to use any studio equipment without being trained by either the manufacturer or a fully qualified studio technician. Do not attempt to figure it out on your own. *Get trained first!*

T.O.T.: I will use the acronym T.O.T., standing for "Tricks of the Trade" throughout this book. These pointers may help you out some day.

Cranes and Communication Systems

I highly recommend that when you get a mobile crane, jib, or arm that will keep you some distance from the camera operator (e.g., the camera operator on a Titan crane or a Lenny arm with a remote), you ask production to rent you a communication system so that you can hear the operator's requests.

Any good sound department will set up a one-way system for you. The operator will have an open microphone and transmitter that will probably be an omnidirectional microphone. The operator will request movement in whichever direction is desired. He or she can speak in a normal voice, even so much as a whisper during a sound take. You and the other grips will have the receiver system (headsets) on so that the grip operating the crane or arm knows what is requested. I use a system that a mixer (soundperson) designed for my jobs.

The company I use is Roll Sound, (800) 468-7970. I provide this information because if you cannot get the perfect piece of equipment to do the job right, you might as well use two tin cans and a string. So I give full credit to Bob Dreebin, president of Roll Sound, for my rental system. Call him, and he will set you up.

Here is the basic system he has designed for this book:

SM58 microphone or equivalent
XLR-F to XLR-M cable
Sony headphone amplifier with volume control or equivalent
1/4 inch phono mong to sub M-mini mall
Comtec M-72 transmitter or equivalent (comes in various frequencies a, b,
    c, d, e, f, etc.) [Note: Mike must be kept in a clear area from the
    operator monitor (sweet spot) to prevent static.]
1 to 4 mono headsets and Comtex R-736 personal receivers

Cranes, Jibs, and Arms

The following pages list descriptions and specifications of the cranes, jibs, and arms used in the industry. The following guidelines are recommended for usage of this equipment:

1. Cranes, jibs, and arms can be set lower or higher depending on which base, dolly, tripod, or other crane they are being used.
2. Some of these cranes, jibs, and arms may look short, but they may be the type that have kits or extensions to lengthen their reach or change from remote operation to carrying a cameraperson and/or assistant. *Read the manufacturers' specifications carefully!*
3. The manufacturers' specs from their brochures are their recommended dolly, base, or tripod. Please call the manufacturer or supplier if you have any questions about a crane, jib, or arm.

CAUTION!!!

1. Do not operate any of these cranes, jibs, or arms without *first being instructed on the proper operation of each unit.*
2. Remember! The reach (length of arm) past the pivot point determines the actual height/plus base height (plus risers, if any).
3. See the manufacturers' instructions for full details on each piece of equipment.
4. These rigs are *not* meant to support personnel, unless there is a note to the contrary.
5. Call the manufacturer of the arm or jib if the weight of the camera is in question.

Seno's Over/Under Jib Arm (Modern Studio Equipment)

This arm can be used on an overhead tracking system, which is perfect for product shots, buck (roof removed from car) interior car shots, rock videos, and many other filming needs.

Specifications

Lens height	2 ft.
Lens lowest	−2 ft
Horizontal reach	2 ft.
Arm's capacity	100 lbs. (maximum weight of camera and head combined)
Dollies recommended to be used with	All
Arm's attaching base (to dolly or crane)	Mitchell
Arm's receiving base	Mitchell
Heads that can be used on arm	Gear, remote, and fluid
Cameras that can be used on arm	Most
Weight of arm (empty)	50 lbs.

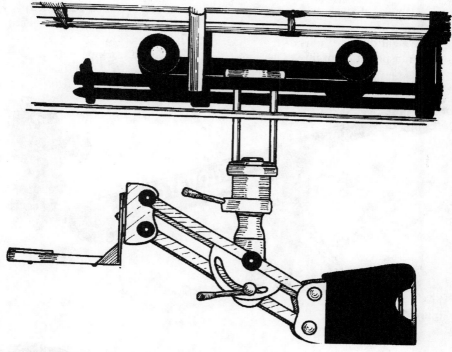

Figure 1 Seno's over/under jib arm.

Shipping weight	50 lbs.
Transportation of arm	Small truck

Trovato Jr.

Specifications

Lens lowest	Ground
Vertical travel	4 ft.
Horizontal reach	46 in.
Jib capacity	100 lbs. (maximum weight of camera and head combined)
Dollies recommended to used with	All
Jib's attaching base (to dolly or crane)	Mitchell (can be replaced with a special adapter plate)
Jib's receiving base	Double-sided Mitchell plate (can be replaced with a special adapter plate)
Heads that can be used on jib	Standard fluid heads and underslung heads

Cameras that can be used on jib	Most (100 lbs. combined weight of camera and head)
Weight of jib	50 lbs.
Transportation of jib	Small truck or van

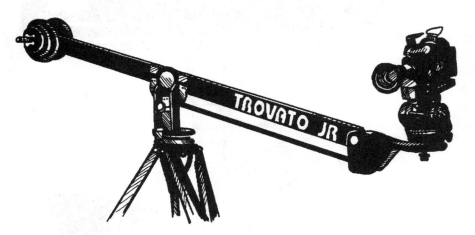

Figure 2 Trovato Jr.

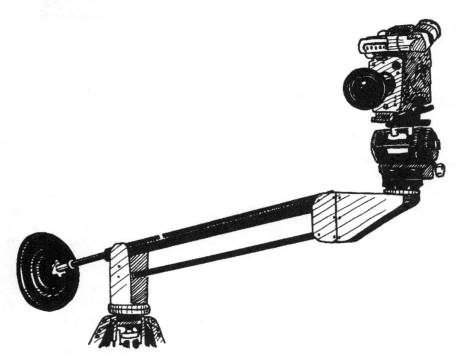

Figure 3 Trovato Tote jib.

Trovato Tote Jib

Specifications

Lens height	4 ft.
Vertical travel (Model 36)	4 ft.
Lens lowest	Camera to ground if underslung

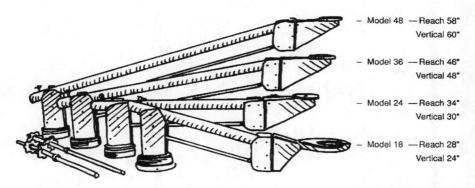

- Model 48 — Reach 58"
  Vertical 60"

- Model 36 — Reach 46"
  Vertical 48"

- Model 24 — Reach 34"
  Vertical 30"

- Model 18 — Reach 28"
  Vertical 24"

Figure 4 Tote jib. Model 18 shown with optional lower plate and receiver head.

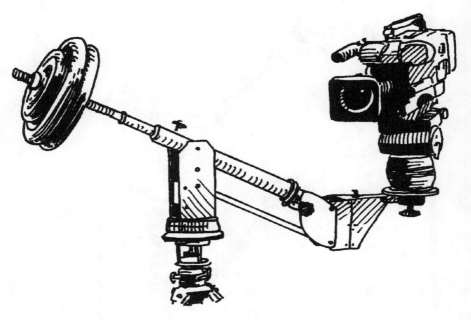

Figure 5 Tote jib.

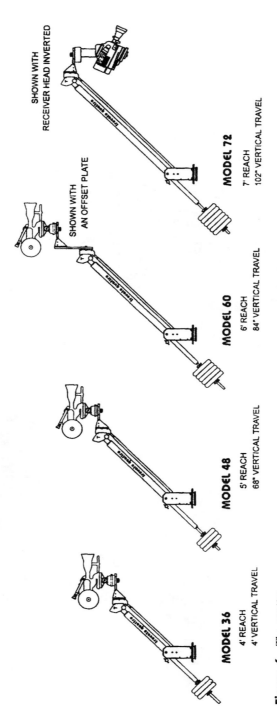

Figure 6 The quattro.

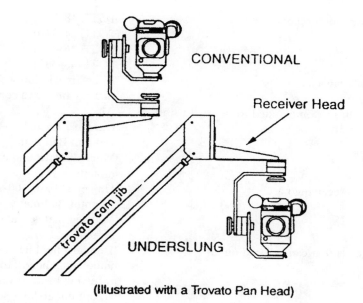

(Illustrated with a Trovato Pan Head)

Figure 7   The cam jib.

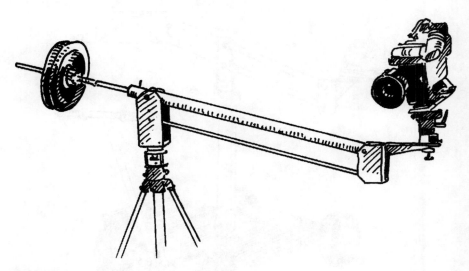

Figure 8   The cam jib.

Horizontal reach	TOTE 18–28 in.
	TOTE 24–34 in.
	TOTE 36–46 in.
	TOTE 48–58 in.
Jib's capacity	75 lbs. (maximum weight of camera and head combined)
Dollies recommended to be used with	All
Jib's attaching base	Universal base, 100- and 150-mm Ball plates, Mitchell plate, and custom mounts
Jib's receiving base	Universal base, 100- and 150-mm Ball plates, Mitchell plates, and custom mounts
Heads that can be used on jib	Standard fluid head and underslung heads; tote jib receiving heads invert to accept underslung heads
Cameras that can be used on jib	Most (75 lbs. combined weight of camera and head)

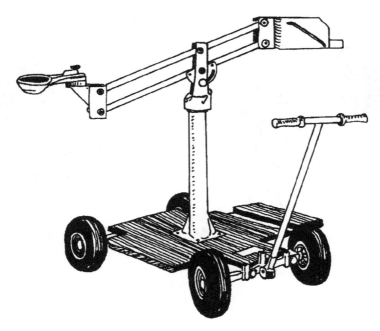

Figure 9   Liberty range jib.

Weight of jib without weights (Model 36)   30 lbs.
Transportation of jib   Small car

Liberty Range Jib

Specifications

Lens height	5 ft. 8 in.
Lens lowest	−10 in.
Horizontal reach	3 ft. 9 in.
Jib capacity	99 lbs. (maximum weight of camera and head combined)
Dollies recommended to be used with	Most
Jib's attaching base (to dolly or crane)	Euro-style
Jib's receiving base	Euro-Ball
Heads that can be used on jib	Fluid
Cameras that can used on jib	Most
Weight of jib (empty)	57 lbs.
Transportation of jib	Small truck or van

Egripment Mini-Jib/Arms (Models 124 and 124/60 Long)

Specifications

Lens height	5 ft. 8 in. and 7 ft.
Lens lowest	10 in. and floor (above ground level)
Horizontal reach	3 ft. 9 in. and 5 ft. 3 in.

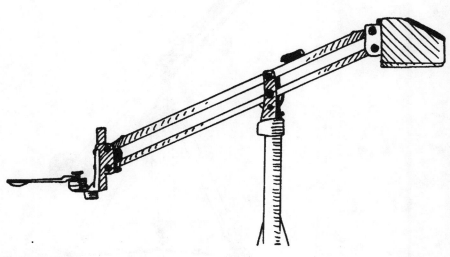

Figure 10 Egripment mini-jib/arms.

Jib's capacity	99 lbs. (maximum weight of camera and head combined)
Dollies recommended to be used with	Most
Jib's attaching base (to dolly or crane)	Euro-style
Jib's receiving base	Euro-Ball
Heads that can be used on jib	Fluid with ball adapter
Cameras that can be used on jib	Most
Weight of jib (empty)	57 lbs. and 61 lbs.
Transportation of jib	Truck or van

Porta Jib

Specifications

Lens height	6 ft.
Lens lowest	Ground

Figure 11a   Porta jib.

Figure 11b Porta jib with track wheels.

Horizontal reach	About 4 ft.
Jib's capacity	90 lbs. (maximum weight of camera and head combined)
Dollies recommended to be used with	All
Jib's attaching base (to dolly or crane)	Mitchell
Jib's receiving base	Mitchell
Heads that can be used on jib	Fluid
Cameras that can be used on jib	Most
Weight of jib (empty)	46 lbs.
Transportation of jib	Small truck

Weaver-Steadman Five-Axis Fluid Crane

This crane features full fluid movement with a weightless camera. The head allows a 360-degree pan, a 360-degree tilt, and a 360-degree roll.

Specifications

Lens height (with secondary arm)	6 ft.
Lens lowest	−2 ft. (below ground level)
Horizontal reach	18 ft.

Figure 11c Porta jib traveller.

Arm's capacity	90 lbs. (maximum weight of camera and fluid head combined)
Dollies recommended to be used with	Fisher 10 (with Fisher center mount), Chapman (with a Chapman center mount), Hybrid, the Panther, or the Spider Dolly
Arm's attaching base (to dolly or crane)	Mitchell
Arm's receiving base	Mitchell
Heads that can be used on arm	Weaver-Steadman fluid
Cameras that can be used on arm	Most
Weight of arm (empty)	154 lbs.
Transportation of arm	Small truck

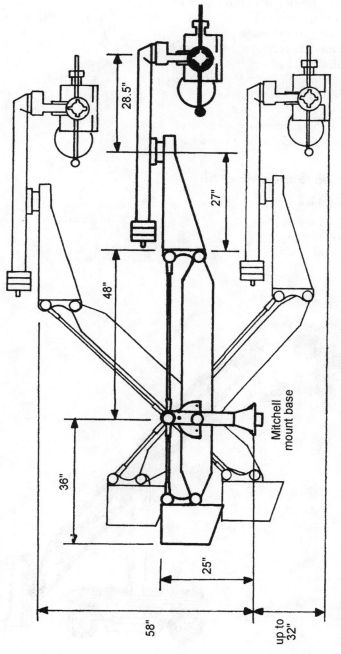

Mitchell
mount base

28.5"

27"

48"

36"

25"

58"

up to
32"

Figure 12   Weaver-Steadman five-axis fluid crane.

Additional Specifications

Maximum reach from center of dolly column to camera	9 ft.
Maximum vertical range	5 ft. 6 in.
Minimum distance between camera body and horizontal surface	1.25 in.
Minimum aperture dimensions through which a 35 BL-3 with support will pass	22 in. (height) by 14 in. (width)
Crane weight	154 lbs.
Total shipping weight for crane, secondary arm, counter weights, and container	451 lbs.

Maxi-Jib/Super Maxi-Jib

Specifications

Platform height	16 ft. 8 in.
Platform lowest	–5 ft. 4 in.
Horizontal reach	15 ft. 4 in.

Figure 13a   Maxi-Jib.

Crane's capacity

Dollies recommended to be used with

77 lbs. (maximum weight of camera and head combined)
Dino Dolly (designed to operate with all internationally recognized dollies that will support the weight of the fully assembled system)

Figure 13b Super Maxi-Jib and jib on track.

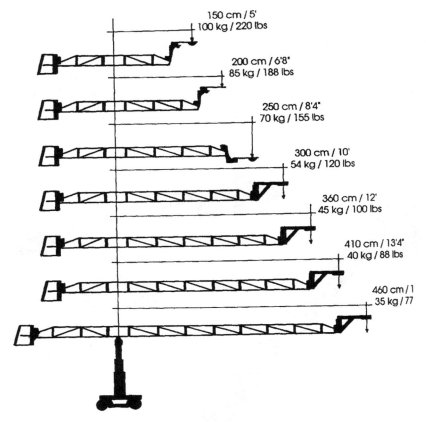

Figure 13c Maxi-Jib and Super Maxi-Jib—reach and weight capacity.

Crane's attaching base (to dolly or crane)	Euro-style
Crane's receiving base	Euro-Ball, Mitchell
Heads that can be used on crane	Remote and fluid
Cameras that can be used on crane	Most
Weight of crane (empty)	152 lbs.
Transportation of crane	Truck or van

NOTE: Remember, the heights given are a maximum, but the crane may be used in several shorter configurations. Check the manufacturer's specifications.

Additional Specifications for the Super Maxi-Jib

Minimum arm reach	240 cm	8 ft.
Maximum arm reach	740 cm	24 ft. 8 in.
Minimum platform height	−294 cm	−9 ft. 10 in.
Maximum platform height	880 cm	29 ft. 4 in.
Maximum load (at maximum length)	100 kg	220 lbs.

Lift range	1,174 cm	39 ft. 2 in.
Length operational	980 cm	32 ft. 8 in.
Length transportational	250 cm	8 ft. 4 in.
Weight Javelin crane arm	250 kg	550 lbs.
Section width	25 cm	10 in.
Section length	<250 cm	<8 ft. 4 in.
Section height	30 cm	1 ft.
Length variations	7	7
Minimum doorway clearance height	235 cm	7 ft. 10 in.
Minimum doorway clearance width	125 cm	4 ft. 2 in.
Maximum amounts of weights with full load at maximum length	51	51
Dolly steering	4 wheel	4 wheel

Seven Jib

The heads may be inverted on this jib.

Specifications

Vertical lift	6 ft. 4 in.
Horizontal reach	4 ft. 6 in.

Figure 14   Seven jib.

Jib's capacity	45 lbs. (maximum weight of camera/head/accessories combined)
Dollies recommended to be used with	Most
Jib's attaching base (to dolly or crane)	100-mm bowl or Mitchell, 150-mm bowl with screw-on adapter plate
Jib's receiving base	Supplied
Heads that can be used on jib	100-mm, 150-mm, or O'Connor bowl
Cameras that can be used on jib	Most
Weight of jib (empty)	26.5 lbs.
Transportation of jib	Car

T.O.T
When asked for a pancake or quarter apple to raise a person, bring both.

ZG Arm (Model 6-200)

Specifications

Lens height	7 ft.
Lens lowest	−2 ft.
Horizontal reach	6 ft.
Arm's capacity	200 lbs. (maximum weight of camera and head combined)
Dollies recommended to be used with	Fisher #10 (with center mount)
Arm's attaching base (to dolly or crane)	K. Hill (supplied)
Arm's receiving base	K. Hill (supplied)
Heads that can be used on arm	Gear, remote, or fluid
Cameras that can be used on arm	Most
Weight of arm (empty)	98 lbs.
Shipping weight	380 lbs. (barbell weights not included)
Transportation of arm	Small truck

NOTE: Training and demo reels available. Call K. Hill Manufacturing.

Figure 15   ZG Arm 6-200 on Fisher 10.

Javelin Crane Arm

This crane can be assembled in seven different lengths and variations.

Specifications

Platform height	29 ft. 4 in.
Platform lowest	−9 ft. 10 in.
Horizontal reach	24 ft. 8 in.

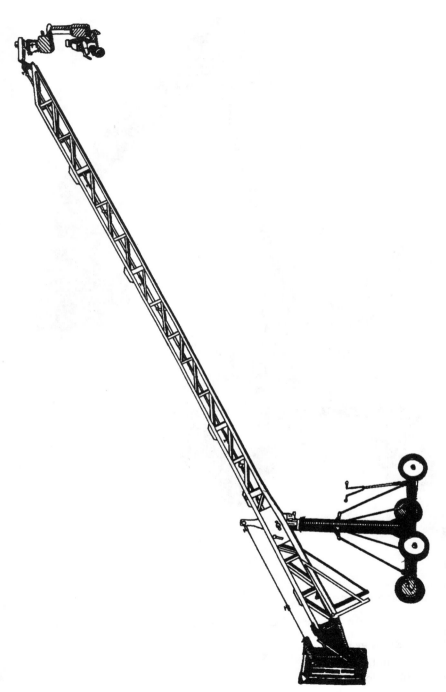

Figure 16a The Javelin crane arm.

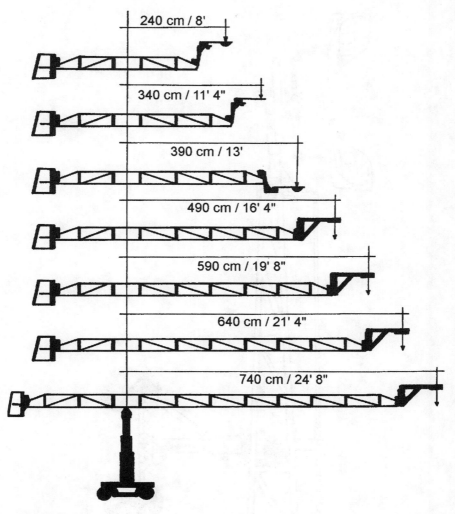

Figure 16b   The reach of the Javelin crane arm.

Crane's capacity	220 lbs. (maximum weight of camera and head combined)
Dollies recommended to be used with	Javelin base
Crane's attaching base (to dolly or crane)	Euro-style
Crane's receiving base	Mitchell mount
Heads that can be used on crane	Gear, remote, or fluid
Cameras that can be used on crane	Most
Weight of crane (empty)	550 lbs.
Transportation of crane	Truck or van

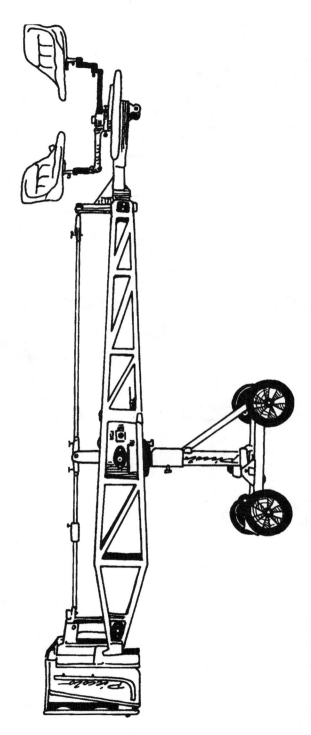

Figure 17 The Piccolo crane.

Piccolo Crane

This crane will work on straight or curved track, supplied by Equipment. It has its own integral track wheels.

Specifications

Platform height	14 ft.
Platform lowest	−3 ft. 4 in.
Horizontal reach	15 ft.
Crane's capacity	145 lbs. (maximum weight of camera and head combined)
Dollies recommended to be used with	Piccolo base, but may be mounted on certain cranes (call for information)
Crane's attaching base (to dolly or crane)	Euro-style
Crane's receiving base	Euro-Ball
Heads that can be used on crane	Remote, gear, or fluid
Cameras that can be used on crane	Most
Weight of crane (empty)	325 lbs.
Transportation of crane	Truck or van

Lightweight Jib

Specifications

Lens height	8 ft. 8 in.
Lens lowest	1 ft. 6 in.
Horizontal reach	About 3 ft.
Jib's capacity	About 65 lbs. (maximum weight of camera and head combined)
Dollies recommended to be used with	Panther (but can be used on any dolly using a center mount)
Jib's attaching base (to dolly or crane)	Elemack-style receiver
Jib's receiving base	Euro-Ball
Heads that can be used on jib	Fluid
Cameras that can be used on jib	Most
Weight of jib (empty)	About 50 lbs.
Transportation of jib	Small truck

Specifications for the Panther Lightweight Jib

Maximum lens height with Mini Panther Dolly	2.74 m	9 ft. 0 in.
Minimum lens height with mini low rig	0.91 m	3 ft. 0 in.
with low shot plate	0.99 m	1 ft. 3 in.

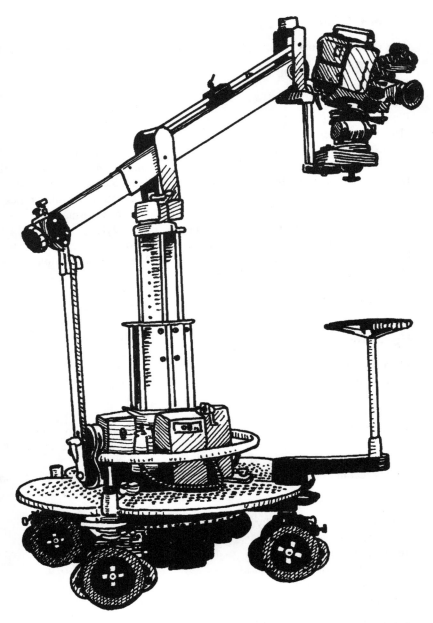

Figure 18a The Lightweight jib.

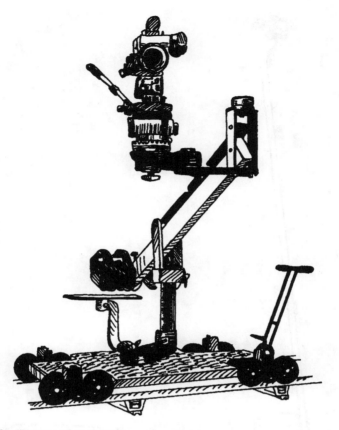

Figure 18b   The Lightweight jib with track wheels.

Maximum arm travel	1.14 m	3 ft. 9 in.
Maximum arm reach	1.27 m	4 ft. 2 in.
with offset camera mount	0.91 m	3 ft. 0 in.
Total overall length	1.9 m	6 ft. 3 in.
Dry weight	20.4 kg	45 lbs.

NOTE: Jib arm has telescoping back section for trimming.

Jimmy Jib (Junior to Giant)

This jib can be adjusted to seven different configurations with some additional accessories.

Specifications

NOTE: The specifications for the Junior are listed first, followed by a slash, and then the specifications for the Giant.

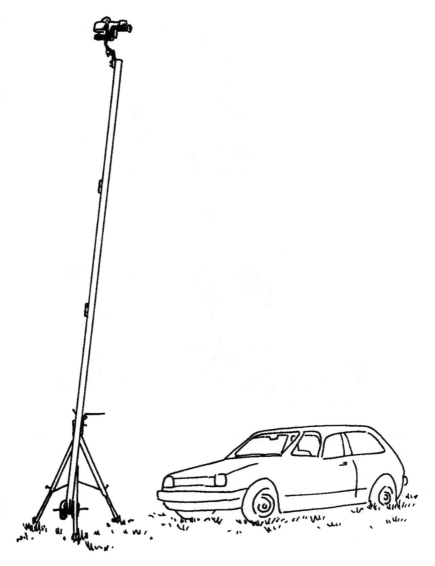

Figure 19a The Jimmy jib.

Lens height	9 ft./30 ft.
Lens lowest	−2 ft./−24 ft.
Horizontal reach	3 ft. 5 in./18 ft.
Jib's capacity	70 lbs. (maximum weight of camera and head combined)
Dollies recommended to be used with	Elemack-type dollies or most center-mount dollies

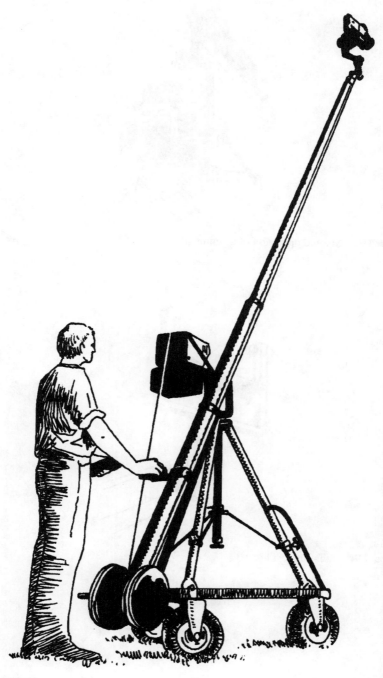

Figure 19b Operating a Jimmy jib.

Figure 19c Manual operation of a Jimmy jib.

Figure 19d Stanton post head.

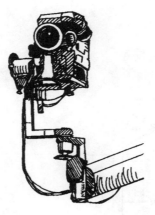

Figure 19e Stanton single post head with remote kit.

Figure 19f Operating the Jimmy jib.

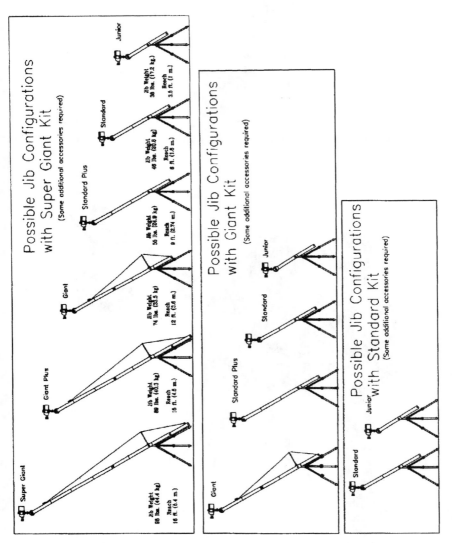

Figure 19g Reach and height capacity of the Jimmy jib.

Maximum elevation at camera lens

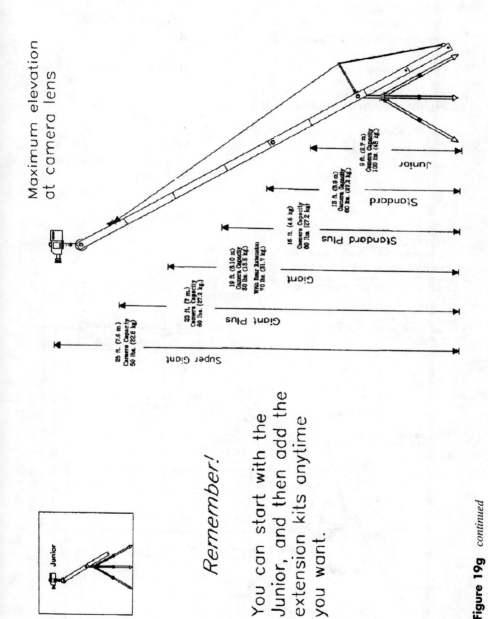

9 ft. (2.7 m)
Camera Capacity
100 lbs. (45 kg.)

Junior

13 ft. (3.9 m)
Camera Capacity
60 lbs. (27.2 kg.)

Standard

16 ft. (4.8 kg)
Camera Capacity
60 lbs. (27.2 kg)

Standard Plus

19 ft. (8.10 m)
Camera Capacity
30 lbs. (13.6 kg.)
With Rear Extension
70 lbs. (31.7 kg.)

Giant

23 ft. (7 m.)
Camera Capacity
60 lbs. (27.2 kg)

Giant Plus

25 ft. (7.6 m.)
Camera Capacity
50 lbs. (22.6 kg)

Super Giant

Junior

Remember!

You can start with the Junior, and then add the extension kits anytime you want.

Figure 19g *continued*

Jib's attaching base (to dolly or crane)   Mitchell mount
Jib's receiving base   Double cradle
Heads that can be used on jib   Jimmy jib (supplied)
Cameras that can be used on jib   Most
Weight of jib (empty)   38 lbs./124 lbs.
Transportation of jib   Trunk of car or backseat

Fisher Jib/Arm (Model 20)

Specifications

Lens height (on beam)   9 ft. 5 in.
Lens lowest   −3 ft. (below ground level, on beam)

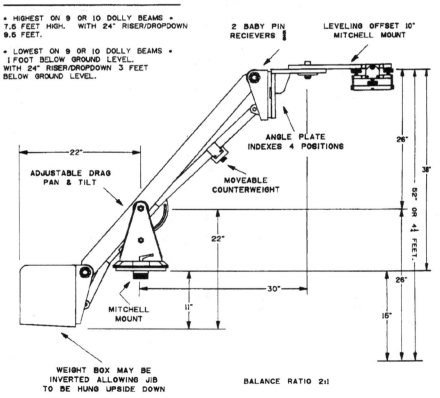

MINIMUM AND
MAXIMUM HEIGHT

• HIGHEST ON 9 OR 10 DOLLY BEAMS •
7.5 FEET HIGH. WITH 24" RISER/DROPDOWN
9.5 FEET.

• LOWEST ON 9 OR 10 DOLLY BEAMS •
1 FOOT BELOW GROUND LEVEL.
WITH 24" RISER/DROPDOWN 3 FEET
BELOW GROUND LEVEL.

2 BABY PIN RECIEVERS

LEVELING OFFSET 10"
MITCHELL MOUNT

ANGLE PLATE
INDEXES 4 POSITIONS

ADJUSTABLE DRAG
PAN & TILT

MOVEABLE
COUNTERWEIGHT

MITCHELL MOUNT

WEIGHT BOX MAY BE
INVERTED ALLOWING JIB
TO BE HUNG UPSIDE DOWN

BALANCE RATIO 2:1

Figure 20a   Fisher jib arm.

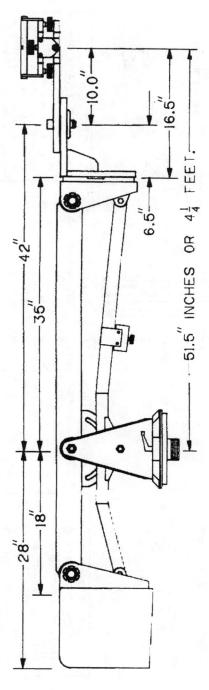

Figure 20b Fisher jib arm features.

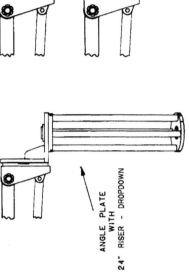

EXAMPLES
OF OTHER
MOUNTING OPTIONS

OPTIONAL
ACCESSORIES

•BABY ANGLE PLATE
 USE WITH RISER
•24" RISER - DROPDOWN
•1-1/8 LIGHT PIN ADAPTER
•EXTENDED ANGLE PLATE
•150MM CLAW BALL ADAPTER
•EXTRA WEIGHTS

ANGLE PLATE
WITH
24" RISER - DROPDOWN

FEATURES

•100 LBS. WITH BASIC ACC. MOUNTED
•SUPPORTS UP TO 150 LBS.
•WEATHERPROOF
•ULTRA SMOOTH PAN & TILT
*** RELIABLE ***
•FRONT END IS SUBMERSIBLE

FOR LOADS OVER 100 LBS THE
USE OF A J. L. FISHER INC.
CENTER MOUNT IS
RECOMMENDED.

STANDARD
ACCESSORIES

•LEVELING OFFSET 10"
•ANGLE PLATE
•DETACHABLE WEIGHT BOX
•18 LARGE WEIGHTS 15 LBS. EA.
•4 SMALL WEIGHTS 4 LBS. EA.
•PLATE WASHER HANDSCREW
 AND ALLEN WRENCH.
•RISER NUT

FOR BEST RESULTS WITH REMOTE CONTROL
PAN AND TILT HEADS DO NOT APPLY PAN
AND TILT DRAG ON JIB.

FOR SAFETY REASONS THIS EQUIPMENT IS
NOT EQUIPPED WITH A POSITIVE TILT
BRAKE. ONLY A DRAG MECHANISM.

NOT DESIGNED TO SUPPORT PERSONNEL

Figure 20b *continued*

Figure 20c   Fisher jib arm shown on Fisher #10 dolly.

NOTE: These heights or depths can be achieved only with the use of a 24-inch riser.

Horizontal reach	4 ft. 3 in.
Jib's capacity	210 lbs. (maximum weight of camera and head combined)
Dollies recommended to be used with	Fisher #9 and #10
Jib's attaching base (to dolly or crane)	Mitchell mount
Jib's receiving base	Mitchell mount

NOTE: The Mitchell (receiver) mount will rotate from top to bottom, also sideways, on an angle plate. The weight bucket also inverts. The Fisher center mount is recommended for loads over 100 lbs.

Heads that can be used on jib	Fluid, gear, and remote
Cameras that can be used on jib	Most
Weight of jib (empty)	100 lbs. (uses plastic/rubber-coated lead weights; 27 weights @ 12.5 lbs. each)
Total weight of lead	324 lbs. (weights only)

NOTE: Additional weight package totaling 96 lbs. is for full-capacity use.

Transportation of jib	Truck or van

Additional Specifications for the Fisher Jib Arm (Model 20)

Maximum lift beam elevation	160 cm	63 in.
Minimum elevation (standard head)	41 cm	16 in.
Minimum elevation (long low-level head)	13 cm	5 in.

Vertical beam travel	119 cm	47 in.
Lift capacity	227 kg	500 lbs.
Lifts per system charge	7	
Length	137 cm	54 in.
Width	68 cm	$26^5/_8$ in.
Height (operating)	98 cm	$38^1/_2$ in.
Height (folded)	64 cm	25 in.
Minimum turn radius (round steering)	56 cm	22 in.
Minimum turn radius (conventional steering)	112 cm	44 in.
Carrying weight	190 kg	420 lbs.
Maximum dolly load capacity	408 kg	900 lbs.

Chapman Crane Arm

Specifications

Lens height	
Titan Crane	38 ft.
Olympian	22 ft. 6 in.
Hybrid or Hustler dolly	9 ft. 6 in.
Lens lowest	
Olympian	−3 ft.
Hybrid or Hustler	−2 ft.

Figure 21a   Chapman crane arm on Titan.

Figure 21b   Chapman crane arm on Olympian.

Figure 21c   Chapman crane arm on Hybrid.

Figure 21d   Chapman crane arm on Olympian with extension.

Figure 21e   Chapman crane arm on Olympian only.

Figure 21f   Chapman crane arm on Hybrid.

Horizontal reach	About 7 ft.
Arm's capacity	600 lbs. (maximum weight of camera and head combined)
Dollies recommended to be used with	Chapman Hybrid or Hustler
Arm's attaching base (to dolly or crane)	Mitchell mount
Arm's receiving base	Mitchell mount
Heads that can be used on arm	Fluid, gear, and remote
Cameras that can be used on arm	Most
Weight of arm (empty)	About 80 lbs.
Transportation of arm	Small truck

NOTE: This arm *is* designed to support personnel!

Aerocrane Jib/Arm

Specifications

Lens height	9 ft. 6 in.
Lens lowest	−3 ft. (below ground level)

NOTE: These heights or depths can be achieved with the use of a Sachtler head and a Panther dolly.

Horizontal reach	7 ft.

NOTE: Because of the variations of lengths between short and long versions, almost every combination is possible, with 1-foot increments on the arm's length. Finer increments are possible using an adjustable front bracket.

Jib's capacity	75 lbs. (maximum weight of camera and head combined)
Dollies recommended to be used with	Panther (but most other dollies can be used)
Jib's attaching base (to dolly)	Euro-Ball or Mitchell mount
Jib's receiving base	Euro-Ball or Mitchell mount
Heads that can be used on jib	Sachtler preferable, but most fluid or remote heads can be used
Cameras that can be used on jib	Most
Weight of jib (empty)	About 90 lbs.
Transportation of jib	Small truck or van

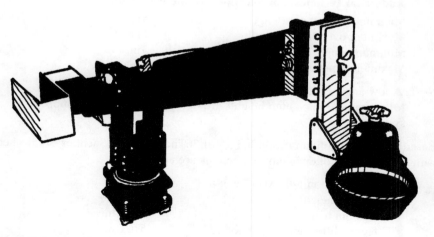

Figure 22a The Aerocrane.

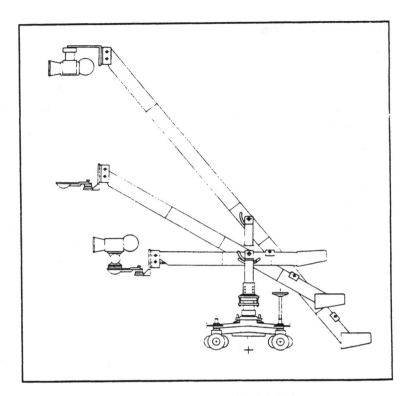

Figure 22b   The Aerocrane topslung and underslung positions.

Additional Technical Specifications for the Aerocrane

Minimum overall arm length	5 in.
Maximum overall arm length	11 in.
Minimum length from center post	3 in.
Maximum length from center post	7 in.

NOTE: A low-angle bracket will add 1 foot to these length measurements. Minimum and maximum heights are determined by camera support system.

Based on a dolly column/tripod height of 36 inches and a Sachtler Studio head with Arm BL, the following measurements are applicable.

Short Conversion 5-ft. Arm Length

Minimum height	14 in.
Maximum height	6 ft. 6 in.
Effective lift range at one go	5 ft. 6 in.

Long Conversion 11-ft. Arm Length

Minimum height	36 in.
Maximum height	9 ft. 6 in.
Effective lift range at one go	12 ft. 6 in.

NOTE: Because of many variations of lengths between the short and long version, almost every combination is possible within the above perimeter with 1-foot increments on arm length and finer increments with adjustable front bracket. A low-angle front camera bracket is available with the 150-mm bowl or Mitchell.

Barber Baby Boom

Specifications

Lens height	10 ft.
Lens lowest	−2 ft. (below ground level)
Horizontal reach	7 ft.
Boom's capacity	75 lbs. (maximum weight of camera and head combined)
Dollies recommended to be used with	Barber dolly

NOTE: This boom will fit any center-mount dolly when using a converter.

Boom's attaching base (to dolly or crane)	Supplied with dolly
Boom's receiving base	Supplied with boom
Heads that can be used on boom	Supplied with boom
Cameras that can be used on boom	Most (no I-Max or Vista Vision)
Weight of boom (empty)	About 90 lbs.
Transportation of boom	Small truck or van

WARNING: Use only qualified operators!

Additional Specifications for the Barber Baby Boom

Maximum radius	7 ft.
Maximum turning diameter	14 ft.
Overall length	13 ft.
From fulcrum to monitor	5 ft.
Vertical span	9 ft.
Maximum height	10 ft.
Minimum height	1 ft. (above ground level)
Horizontal boom span	12 ft.
Boom radius	360 degrees
Camera pan radius	360 degree
Camera tilt radius	180 degree
Maximum camera load	70 lbs.

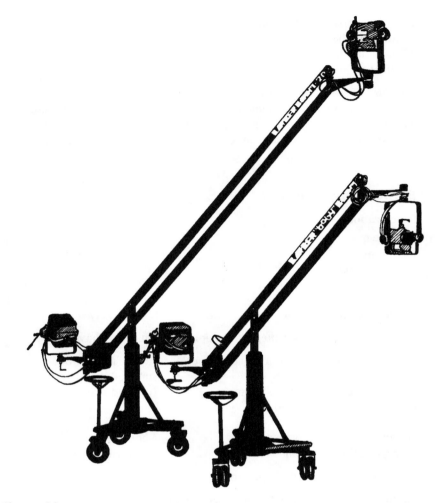

Figure 23a Barber Baby Boom.

Dimensions	
Length	118 in.
Width	18 in.
Height	34 in.
Setup time	15 to 30 min.
Cable connections	
Video monitor	Built-in
Camera power	Built-in
Video power	Built-in

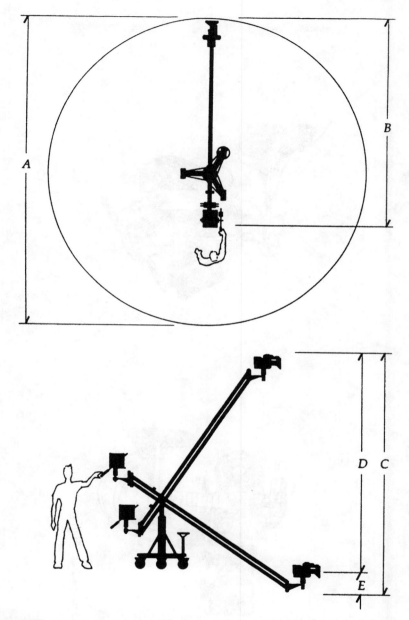

Figure 23b Maximum turning diameter, vertical span, and height of Barber Baby Boom.

Figure 23c Barber Boom head.

Remote Connection
   Video monitor   Built-in
   Camera focus   Accessory
   Camera zoom   Accessory

Specifications for the Barber Dolly

Length	38 in.
Width	38 in.
Height	45 in.
Maximum weight	350 lbs.

MC-88 Crane

Specifications

Platform height	24 ft.
Platform lowest	−4 ft.

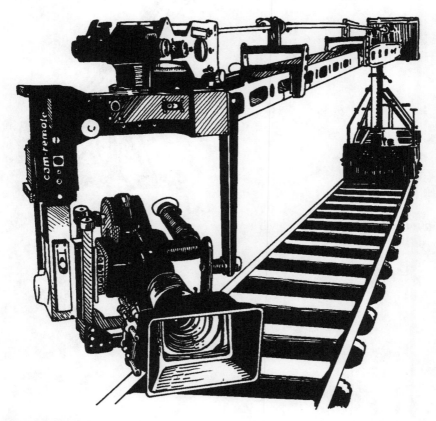

Figure 24a   MC-88 crane on track.

Figure 24b MC-88 crane on dolly.

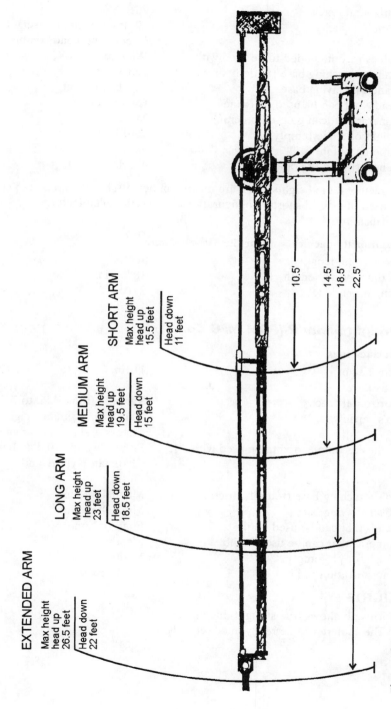

EXTENDED ARM

Max height
head up
26.5 feet

Head down
22 feet

LONG ARM

Max height
head up
23 feet

Head down
18.5 feet

MEDIUM ARM

Max height
head up
19.5 feet

Head down
15 feet

SHORT ARM

Max height
head up
15.5 feet

Head down
11 feet

10.5'

14.5'

18.5'

22.5'

Figure 24c Maximum height of various arms for the MC-88 crane.

Horizontal reach	20 ft. 8 in.
Crane's capacity	105 lbs. (maximum weight of camera and head combined)
Dollies recommended to be used with	Wide-based dolly
Crane's attaching base (to dolly or crane)	Euro-style
Crane's receiving base	Mitchell mount
Heads that can be used on crane	Cam-Remote
Cameras that can be used on crane	Most
Weight of crane (empty)	180 lbs.
Shipping weight	450 lbs.
Transportation of crane	Truck

NOTE: Remember, the heights given are maximum heights, but the crane can still be used in several shorter configurations. Check the manufacturer's specifications.

Additional Specifications for the MC-88 Crane

Short boom length	10 ft.
Medium boom length	18 ft. 5 in.
Long boom length	24 ft.

Straight Shoot'R (PDM MFG Co.)

Specifications

Lens height	110 in.
Lens lowest	−3 ft.
Horizontal reach	Variable from 51 in. to 77 in.
Jib's capacity	100 lbs. (maximum weight of camera and head combined)
Dollies recommended to be used with	Fisher #9 and #10, Panther, Chapman Hybrid, and Hustler
Jib's attaching base (to dolly or crane)	Mitchell mount
Jib's receiving base	Mitchell mount
Heads that can be used on jib	Fluid or remote
Cameras that can be used on jib	Most
Weight of jib (empty)	110 lbs.
Transportation of jib	Small truck

HIGHLIGHTS

1. This jib allows true straight-line moves.
2. The camera can be ready in 60 seconds.

Figure 25a Straight Shoot'R.

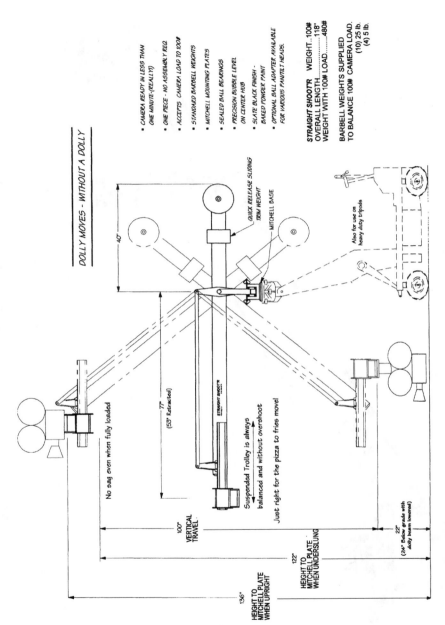

- CAMERA READY IN LESS THAN ONE MINUTE-(REALLY!)
- ONE PIECE - NO ASSEMBLY REQ.
- ACCEPTS CAMERA LOAD TO 100#
- STANDARD BARBELL WEIGHTS
- MITCHELL MOUNTING PLATES
- SEALED BALL BEARINGS
- PRECISION BUBBLE LEVEL ON CENTER HUB
- SLATE BLACK FINISH - BAKED POWDER PAINT
- OPTIONAL BALL ADAPTER AVAILABLE FOR VARIOUS PAN/TILT HEADS.

STRAIGHT SHOOT'R WEIGHT ..100#
OVERALL LENGTH ....118"
WEIGHT WITH 100# LOAD ......480#

BARBELL WEIGHTS SUPPLIED
TO BALANCE 100# CAMERA LOAD.
(10) 25 lb.
(4) 5 lb.

DOLLY MOVES - WITHOUT A DOLLY

40"

QUICK RELEASE SLIDING TRIM WEIGHT

MITCHELL BASE

Also for use on heavy duty tripods

No sag even when fully loaded

77"
(53" Retracted)

STRAIGHT SHOOT'R

Suspended Trolley is always balanced and without overshoot

Just right for the pizza to fries move!

100"
VERTICAL TRAVEL.

122"

HEIGHT TO MITCHELL PLATE WHEN UNDERSLUNG

136"

HEIGHT TO MITCHELL PLATE WHEN UPRIGHT

22"
(24" Below grade with dolly beam lowered)

Figure 25b Specifications for the Straight Shoot'R.

Fisher Jib/Arm (Model 21)

Specifications

Lens height	11 ft. 5 in. (on beam)
Lens lowest	−4 ft. (below ground level, on beam)

NOTE: These heights or depths can be achieved only with the use of a 24-inch riser.

Horizontal reach	5 ft. 7 in.
Jib's capacity	210 lbs. (maximum weight of camera and head combined)
Dollies recommended to be used with	Fisher #9 and #10

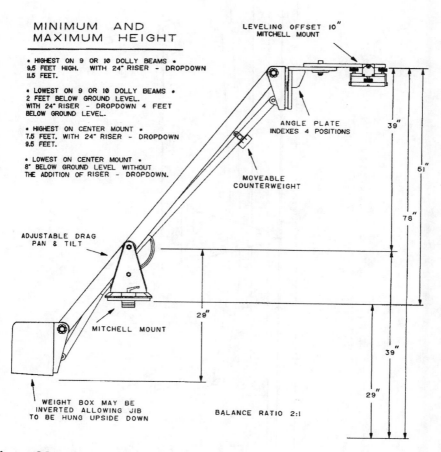

MINIMUM AND MAXIMUM HEIGHT

• HIGHEST ON 9 OR 10 DOLLY BEAMS • 9.5 FEET HIGH. WITH 24" RISER - DROPDOWN 11.5 FEET.

• LOWEST ON 9 OR 10 DOLLY BEAMS • 2 FEET BELOW GROUND LEVEL. WITH 24" RISER - DROPDOWN 4 FEET BELOW GROUND LEVEL.

• HIGHEST ON CENTER MOUNT • 7.5 FEET. WITH 24" RISER - DROPDOWN 9.5 FEET.

• LOWEST ON CENTER MOUNT • 8" BELOW GROUND LEVEL WITHOUT THE ADDITION OF RISER - DROPDOWN.

LEVELING OFFSET 10" MITCHELL MOUNT

ANGLE PLATE INDEXES 4 POSITIONS

MOVEABLE COUNTERWEIGHT

ADJUSTABLE DRAG PAN & TILT

MITCHELL MOUNT

39"

51"

78"

29"

39"

29"

WEIGHT BOX MAY BE INVERTED ALLOWING JIB TO BE HUNG UPSIDE DOWN

BALANCE RATIO 2:1

Figure 26a Fisher jib arm (model 21).

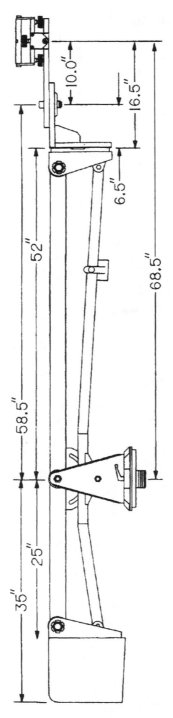

Figure 26b Features of the Fisher jib arm (model 21).

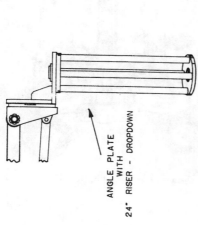

EXAMPLES
OF OTHER
MOUNTING OPTIONS

ANGLE PLATE
WITH
24" RISER - DROPDOWN

FOR BEST RESULTS WITH REMOTE CONTROL
PAN AND TILT HEADS DO NOT APPLY PAN
AND TILT DRAG ON JIB.

FOR SAFETY REASONS THIS EQUIPMENT IS
NOT EQUIPPED WITH A POSITIVE TILT
BRAKE. ONLY A DRAG MECHANISM.

NOT DESIGNED TO SUPPORT PERSONNEL.

FEATURES

•100 LBS. WITH BASIC ACC. MOUNTED
•SUPPORTS UP TO 150 LBS.
•WEATHERPROOF
•ULTRA SMOOTH PAN & TILT
*** RELIABLE ***
•FRONT END IS SUBMERSIBLE

FOR LOADS OVER 100 LBS THE
USE OF A J. L. FISHER INC.
CENTER MOUNT IS
RECOMMENDED.

STANDARD
ACCESSORIES

•LEVELING OFFSET 10"
•ANGLE PLATE
•DETACHABLE WEIGHT BOX
•18 LARGE WEIGHTS 15 LBS. EA.
•4 SMALL WEIGHTS 4 LBS. EA.
•PLATE WASHER HANDSCREW
 AND ALLEN WRENCH.
•RISER NUT

Figure 26b *continued*

Figure 26c   Fisher jib arm (model 21) shown on pedestal dolly.

Jib's attaching base (to dolly or crane)	Mitchell mount
Jib's receiving base	Mitchell mount

NOTE: The Mitchell (receiver) mount will rotate from top to bottom or side to side on the angle plate. The weight bucket also inverts. The Fisher center mount is recommended for loads over 100 lbs.

Heads that can be used on jib	Fluid, gear, and remote
Cameras that can be used on jib	Most
Weight of jib (empty)	115 lbs. (uses plastic- or rubber-coated lead weights; 27 weights @ 12.5 lbs. each)
Total weight of lead	324 lbs. (weights only)

NOTE: Additional weight package totaling 96 lbs. is for full-capacity use.

Transportation of jib	Truck or van

ZG Arm (Model 8-130, Ken Hill MFG)

Specifications

Lens height	12 ft.
Lens lowest	−4 ft.
Horizontal reach	8 ft.
Arm's capacity	130 lbs. (maximum weight of camera and head combined)
Dollies recommended to be used with	Fisher #10 (with center mount)
Arm's attaching base (to dolly or crane)	K. Hill (supplied)
Arm's receiving base	K. Hill (supplied)
Heads that can be used on arm	Gear, remote, or fluid
Cameras that can be used on arm	Most
Weight of arm (empty)	125 lbs.

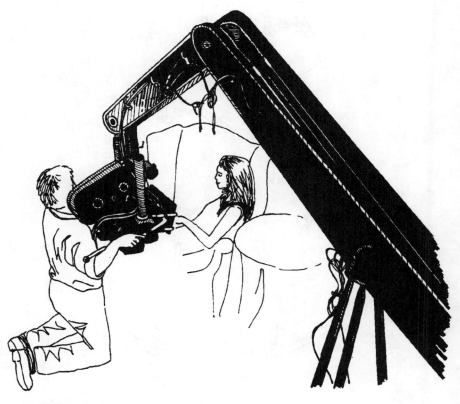

Figure 27a ZG arm.

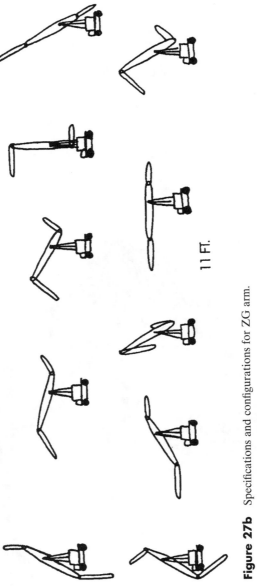

11 FT.

Figure 27b Specifications and configurations for ZG arm.

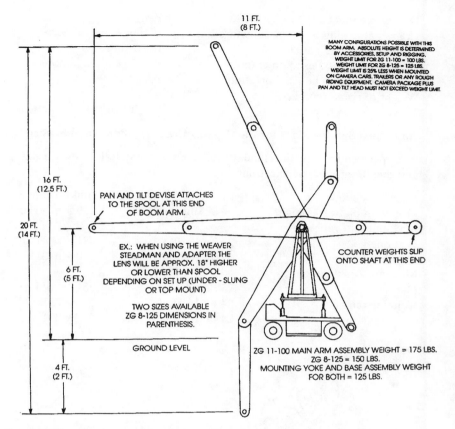

Figure 27b *continued*

Shipping weight	420 lbs.
Transportation of arm	Small truck

NOTE: Training and demonstration reels available. Call K. Hill Manufacturing.

Pegasus Crane (Standard and Super)

Specifications

NOTE: The specifications for the standard crane are set first, followed by a slash, and then the super specifications.

Lens height	12 ft. 8 in./20 ft. 3 in.
Lens lowest	−2 ft. 4 in./−3 ft. 4 in.
Horizontal reach	About 10 ft./20 ft.
Crane's capacity	551 lbs. (maximum weight of camera and head combined)

Dollies recommended to be used with	Panther
Crane's attaching base (to dolly or crane)	Elemack-style receiver
Crane's receiving base	Euro-Ball
Heads that can be used on crane	Fluid, gear, or remote
Cameras that can be used on crane	All
Weight of crane (empty)	980 lbs.
Transportation of crane	Small truck

Additional Specifications for the Pegasus Crane (Standard and Super)

NOTE: The specifications for the standard crane are set first, followed by a slash, and then the super specifications.

Longest section	(unknown)/1.60 m	(unknown)/63 in.
Minimum platform height	−0.075 m/−1.05 m	−29.5 in./−41 in.
Maximum lift range		
at one go	2.50 m/4.80 m	98 in./189 in.
with conversion	5.60 m/7.90 m	220.5 in./311 in.
Maximum payload on		
platform	250 kg/250 kg	551 lbs./551 lbs.
Counterweights	24 by 16.5 kg/	24 by 33 lbs./
	24 by 16.5 kg	24 by 33 lbs.

Figure 28a The Pegasus crane standard mode.

Figure 28b The Pegasus crane remote 1.

Figure 28c The mammoth base for the Pegasus crane.

The Panther Pegasus Crane...

... is the answer for grips, DP's and camera operators who want that little bit more from a crane.

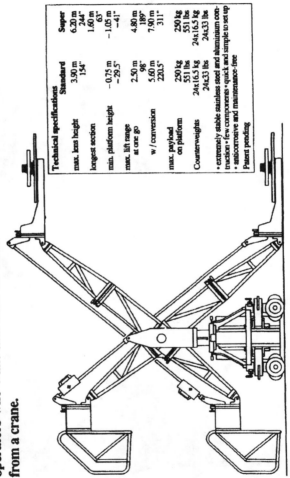

Technical specifications	Standard	Super
max. lens height	3.90 m / 154"	6.20 m / 244"
longest section		1.60 m / 63"
min. platform height	−0.75 m / −29.5"	−1.05 m / −41"
max. lift range at one go	2.50 m / 98"	4.80 m / 189"
w / conversion	5.60 m / 220.5"	7.90 m / 311"
max. payload on platform	250 kg / 551 lbs	250 kg / 551 lbs
Counterweights	24x16.5 kg / 24x33 lbs	24x16.5 kg / 24x33 lbs

• extremely stable stainless steel and aluminium construction • few components • quick and simple to set up
• anticorrosive and maintenance-free
• Patent pending

Panther Pegasus Crane standard version

Figure 28d The Panther Pegasus crane—standard and extended versions.

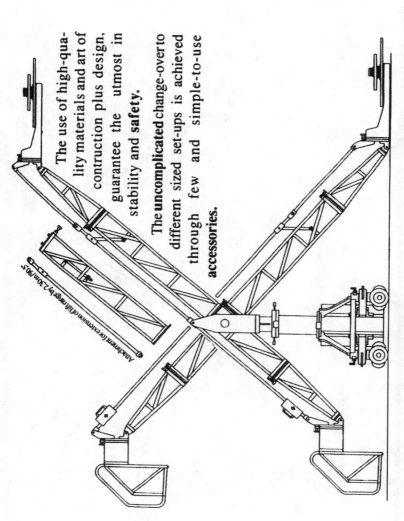

The use of high-qua-lity materials and art of contruction plus design, guarantee the utmost in stability and **safety**.

The **uncomplicated** change-overto different sized set-ups is achieved through few and simple-to-use **accessories**.

Attachment for extension of lift range by 2.30m/90,5"

Panther Pegasus Crane in extended Version

Figure 28d *continued*

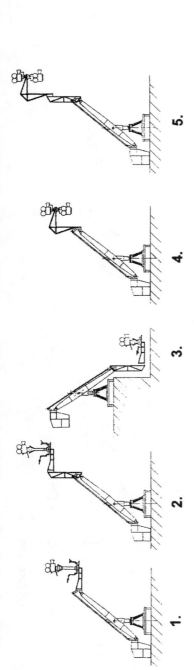
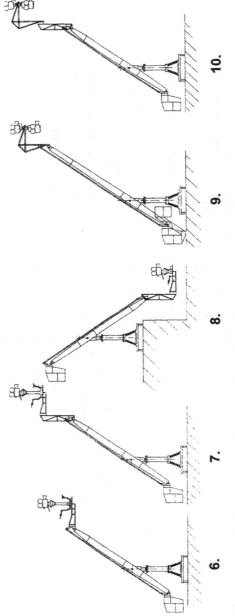

Figure 28e   The Pegasus crane with the Panther Building Block System.

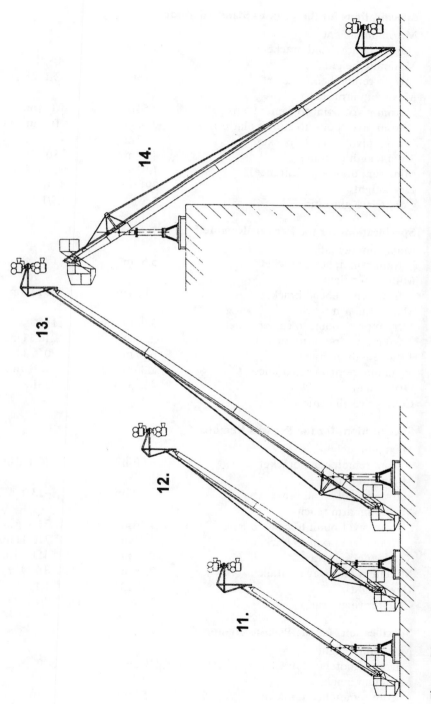

Figure 28e *continued*

Specifications for the Pegasus Standard Mode

Maximum height		
from remotehead bracket	3.96 m	13 ft.
Minimum height		
from remotehead bracket	−0.66 m	−2 ft. 2 in.
Maximum arm reach		
from pivot point to camera lens	2.54 m	8 ft. 4 in.
from pivot point to end of platform	2.79 m	9 ft. 2 in.
from pivot point to bucket	1.82 m	6 ft.
Total length of crane	4.62 m	15 ft. 2 in.
Minimum doorway clearance	1.93 m	6 ft. 4 in.
Dry weight	391.0 kg	840 lbs.
Counterweight ratio	1.5/1	1.5/1

Specifications for the Pegasus Remote I

Maximum height		
from remotehead bracket	5.69 m	18 ft. 8 in.
Minimum height		
from remotehead bracket	−1.04 m	−3 ft. 5 in.
Maximum arm reach		
from pivot point to camera lens	3.96 m	13 ft.
from pivot point to bucket	2.41 m	7 ft. 11 in.
Total length of crane	6.37 m	20 ft. 11 in.
Minimum doorway clearance	2.38 m	7 ft. 10 in.
Dry weight	432.3 kg	953 lbs.
Counterweight ratio	2.2/1	2.2/1

Specifications for the Pegasus Remote II

Maximum height		
from remotehead bracket	8.00 m	26 ft. 3 in.
Minimum height		
from remotehead bracket	−3.96 m	−13 ft.
Maximum arm reach		
from pivot point to camera lens	7.16 m	23 ft. 6 in.
from pivot point to bucket	2.41 m	7 ft. 11 in.
Total length of crane	9.57 m	31 ft. 5 in.
Minimum doorway clearance	2.66 m	8 ft. 9 in.
Dry weight	541.13 kg	1,193 lbs.
Counterweight ratio	3/1	3/1

Specifications for the Pegasus Remote III

Maximum height		
from remotehead bracket	10.36 m	34 ft.
Minimum height		
from remotehead bracket	−5.79 m	−19 ft.

Maximum arm reach		
from pivot point to camera lens	10.36 m	34 ft.
from pivot point to bucket	2.41 m	7 ft. 11 in.
Total length of crane	12.19 m	40 ft. 11 in.
Minimum doorway clearance	2.66 m	8 ft. 9 in.
Dry weight	589.66 kg	1,300 lbs.
Counterweight ratio	4.25/1	4.25/1

Specifications for the Shotmaker/Panther Pegasus Crane

Maximum lens height	5.48 m	18 ft.
(with high/low rig)	6.4 m	21 ft.
Minimum lens height	0.66 m	2 ft. 2 in.
(with high/low rig)	−0.06 m	−2 ft.
Minimum doorway clearance	2.38 m	7 ft. 10 in.

NOTE: Subtract 30 inches from the previous dimensions when not using a 30-inch riser.

Maximum arm reach		
from pivot point to camera lens	3.35 m	11 ft.
from pivot point to end of platform	3.81 m	12 ft. 6 in.
from pivot point to bucket	2.41 m	7 ft. 11 in.
Total length of crane	6.22 m	20 ft. 5 in.
Dry weight	444.5 kg	980 lbs.
Counter weight ratio	1.5/1	1.5/1

Specifications for the Mammoth Base

Length	1.62 m	5 ft. 4 in.
Width	1.62 m	5 ft. 4 in.
Adjustable track wheel widths		
Setting 1	0.62 m	2 ft. ½ in.
Setting 2	0.87 m	2 ft. 10½ in.
Dry weight	158 kg	350 lbs.

Fisher Jib/Arm (Model 22)

Specifications

Lens height	13 ft.
Lens lowest	−3 ft. (below ground level)

NOTE: These heights or depths can be achieved only with the use of a 24-inch riser and center mount.

Horizontal reach	8 ft. 3 in.
Jib's capacity	150 lbs. (maximum weight of camera and head combined)
Dollies recommended to be used with	Fisher #9 and #10

Jib's attaching base (to dolly or crane)   Mitchell mount
Jib's receiving base   Mitchell mount

NOTE: The Mitchell (receiver) mount will rotate from top to bottom or side to side on the angle plate. The weight bucket also inverts. The Fisher center mount is recommended for loads over 100 lbs.

Heads that can be used on jib   Fluid, gear, and remote
Cameras that can be used on jib   Most
Weight of jib (empty)   135 lbs. (uses plastic- or
                                    rubber-coated lead weights;
                                    27 weights @ 12.5 lbs. each)

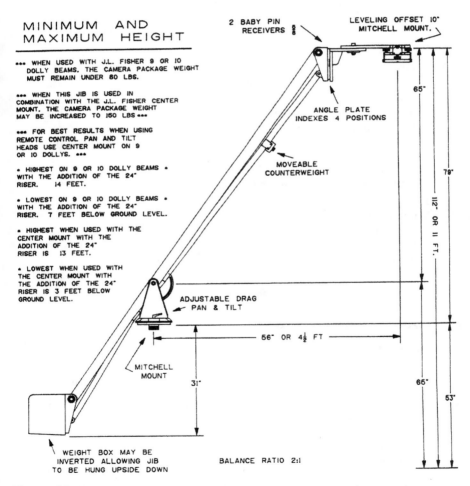

Figure 29a   Minimum and maximum height of the Fisher jib arm (model 22).

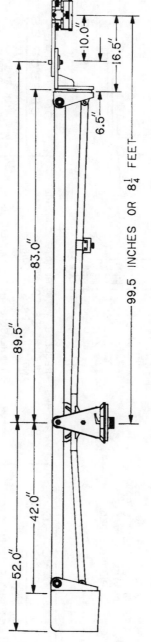

Figure 29b Features of the Fisher jib arm (model 22).

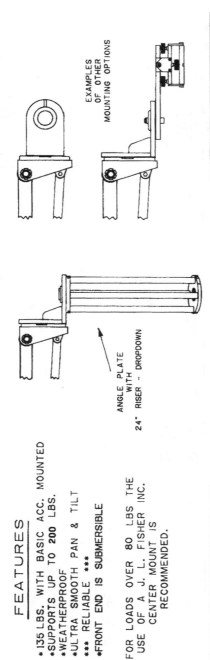

EXAMPLES
OF OTHER
MOUNTING OPTIONS

ANGLE PLATE
WITH
24" RISER - DROPDOWN

FEATURES

* 135 LBS. WITH BASIC ACC. MOUNTED
* SUPPORTS UP TO 200 LBS.
* WEATHERPROOF
* ULTRA SMOOTH PAN & TILT
* *** RELIABLE ***
* FRONT END IS SUBMERSIBLE

FOR LOADS OVER 80 LBS THE
USE OF A J. L. FISHER INC.
CENTER MOUNT IS
RECOMMENDED.

STANDARD ACCESSORIES

* LEVELING OFFSET 10°
* ANGLE PLATE
* DETACHABLE WEIGHT BOX
* 18 LARGE WEIGHTS 15 LBS. EA.
* 4 SMALL WEIGHTS 4 LBS. EA.
* PLATE WASHER HANDSCREW
  AND ALLEN WRENCH.
* RISER NUT

FOR BEST RESULTS WITH REMOTE CONTROL
PAN AND TILT HEADS DO NOT APPLY PAN
AND TILT DRAG ON JIB.

FOR SAFETY REASONS THIS EQUIPMENT IS
NOT EQUIPPED WITH A POSITIVE TILT
BRAKE. ONLY A DRAG MECHANISM.

NOT DESIGNED TO SUPPORT PERSONNEL

OPTIONAL ACCESSORIES

* BABY ANGLE PLATE
  USE WITH RISER
* 24" RISER - DROPDOWN
* 1-1/8 LIGHT PIN ADAPTER
* EXTENDED ANGLE PLATE
* 150MM CLAW BALL ADAPTER
* EXTRA WEIGHTS

Figure 29b *continued*

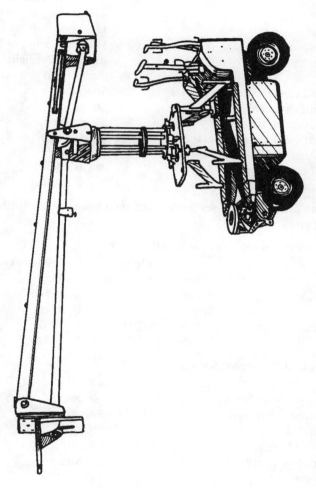

Figure 29c Fisher jib arm (model 22) shown on Fisher #10 dolly with center-mount kit.

Total weight of lead	324 lbs. (weights only)
Transportation of jib	Truck or van

V.I.P. Four-in-One Crane

Specifications

Platform height	13 ft., 22 ft. 4 in., or 28 ft. 8 in.
Platform lowest	−2 ft., −18 ft., or −20 ft.
Horizontal reach	13 ft. 4 in., 20 ft., or 27 ft. 6 in.
Crane's capacity	143 lbs., 275 lbs., or 550 lbs. (maximum weight of camera and head combined)
Dollies recommended to be used with	Supplied
Crane's attaching base	Supplied
Crane's receiving base	Mitchell mount
Heads that can be used on crane	Gear, remote, or fluid
Cameras that can be used on crane	Most
Weight of crane (empty)	385 lbs., 440 lbs., or 541 lbs.
Transportation of crane	Truck or van

NOTE: This crane can be used in several lengths and configurations, with or without personnel.

Egripment Four-in-One System Specifications

	Classic Dolly		Wide-Base Dolly	
Length	135 cm	4 ft. 6 in.	135 cm	5 ft. 6 in.
Width	98 cm	3 ft. 3 in.	125 cm	4 ft. 2 in.
Height	30 cm	1 ft.	43 cm	1 ft. 5 in.
Weight incl. Column	123 kg	270 lbs.	185 kg	407 lbs.
Column height	155 cm	5 ft. 2 in.	155 cm	5 ft. 2 in.

Egripment V.I.P. Specifications

Reach	400 cm	13 ft. 4 in.
Minimum platform height	−60 cm	−2 ft.
Maximum platform height	390 cm	13 ft.
Maximum load	250 kg	550 lbs.
Operational length	600 cm	20 ft.
Transportation length	252 cm	8 ft. 5 in.
Width	44 cm	1 ft. 5 in.
Height	72 cm	2 ft. 5 in.
Weight	175 kg	385 lbs.

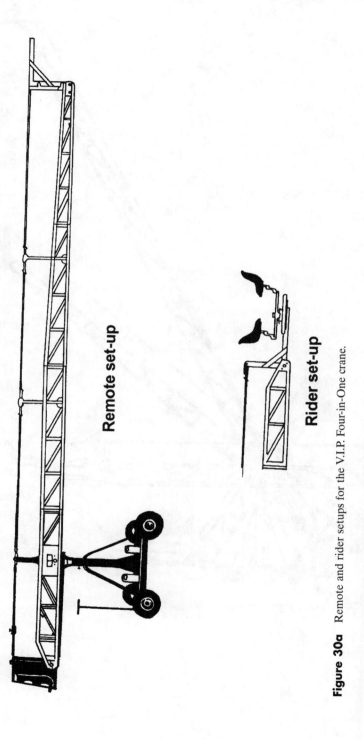

Remote set-up

Rider set-up

Figure 30a Remote and rider setups for the V.I.P. Four-in-One crane.

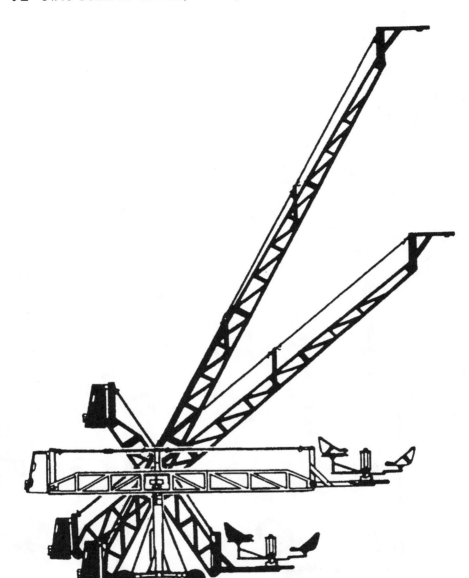

Figure 30b Some configurations for the V.I.P. Four-in-One crane.

Skyking/Skymote Cranes

Specifications

Platform height	26 ft. 8 in.
Platform lowest	−10 ft. 3 in.
Horizontal reach	26 ft. 8 in.
Crane's capacity	143 lbs. (maximum weight of camera and head combined)
Dollies recommended to be used with	Egriment wide-based dolly
Crane's attaching base (to dolly or crane)	Euro-style
Crane's receiving base	Euro-Ball
Heads that can be used on crane	Remote, gear, and fluid
Cameras that can be used on crane	Most
Weight of crane (empty)	713 lbs.
Transportation of crane	Large truck

NOTE: Remember, the heights given are maximum heights, but the crane can still be used in several shorter configurations. Check the manufacturer's specifications.

Egriment Skyking Specifications

		Wide-Base Dolly
Length	165 cm	5 ft. 6 in.
Width	125 cm	4 ft. 2 in.
Height	43 cm	1 ft. 5 in.
Weight incl. Column	185 kg	407 lbs.
Column height	155 cm	5 ft. 2 in.

Egriment Mini Skyking Specifications

Reach	400 cm	13 ft. 4 in.
Minimum platform height	−30 cm	−2 ft.
Maximum platform height	390 cm	13 ft.
Maximum load	250 kg	550 lbs.
Operational length	680 cm	22 ft. 8 in.
Transportation length	250 cm	8 ft. 5 in.
Width	44 cm	1 ft. 5 in.
Height	45 cm	1 ft. 6 in.
Weight	275 kg	605 lbs.

Egriment Skymote Specifications

Reach	600 cm	20 ft.
Minimum platform height	−560 cm	−18 ft. 8 in.
Maximum platform height	670 cm	22 ft. 4 in.
Maximum load	125 kg	275 lbs.
Operational length	800 cm	26 ft. 8 in.
Transportation length	230 cm	7 ft. 8 in.

Width	45 cm	1 ft. 6 in.
Height	54 cm	1 ft. 9 in.
Weight	200 kg	440 lbs.

Egripment Super Skymote Specifications

Reach	825 cm	27 ft. 6 in.
Minimum platform height	−600 cm	−20 ft.
Maximum platform height	860 cm	28 ft. 8 in.
Maximum load	65 kg	143 lbs.
Operational length	1,025 cm	34 ft. 2 in.
Transportation length	230 cm	7 ft. 8 in.
Width	45 cm	1 ft. 6 in.
Height	35 cm	1 ft. 2 in.
Weight	246 kg	541 lbs.

Egripment Skyking Specifications

Reach	645 cm	21 ft. 6 in.
Minimum platform height	−170 cm	−5 ft. 8 in.
Maximum platform height	650 cm	21 ft. 8 in.
Maximum load	250 kg	550 lbs.
Operational length	925 cm	30 ft. 10 in.
Transportation length	250 cm	8 ft. 4 in.
Width	44 cm	1 ft. 5 in.
Height	45 cm	1 ft. 6 in.
Weight	346 kg	761 lbs.

Egripment Skyking + Skymote Extension Specifications

Reach	800 cm	26 ft. 8 in.
Minimum platform height	−308 cm	−10 ft. 3 in.
Maximum platform height	800 cm	26 ft. 8 in.
Maximum load	65 kg	143 lbs.
Operational length	1,080 cm	36 ft. 4 in.
Transportation length	250 cm	8 ft. 4 in.
Width	44 cm	1 ft. 5 in.
Height	45 cm	1 ft. 6 in.
Weight	324 kg	713 lbs.

Super Jib

Specifications

Lens height	13 ft. 7 in.
Lens lowest	1 ft. 9 in.
Horizontal reach	4 ft.
Jib's capacity	331 lbs. (maximum weight of camera and head combined)

Dollies recommended to be used with	Panther
Jib's attaching base (to dolly or crane)	Boss or Euro Elemack-style receiver (female)
Jib's receiving base	Euro-Ball
Heads that can be used on jib	Fluid, gear, or remote
Camera that can be used on jib	Most
Weight of jib (empty)	340 lbs.
Transportation of jib	Small truck

NOTE: This jib *is* designed to support personnel.

Specifications for the Shotmaker Super Jib Arm

Maximum lens height		
from platform, using 12 in. riser	2.37 m	7 ft. $\frac{1}{2}$ in.
with high/low rig, using an adjustable riser	3.20 m	10 ft. 6 in.
Minimum lens height		
from platform	0.88 m	2 ft. 11 in.
with hi/low rig	0.53 m	1 ft. 9 in.
Arm reach		
from pivot point to camera lens	1.27 m	4 ft. 2 in.
from pivot point to counterweight rod	1.21 m	4 ft.
Minimum doorway clearance	1.29 m	4 ft. 3 in.
Dry weight (Super Panther and Super Jib)	154.22 kg	340 lbs.
Counterweight ratio	1/1.43	1/1.43

Accessories for the Shotmaker Super Jib Arm

- Standard ball adapter
- Offset ball adapter
- Mitchell adapter with four-way leveler
- Adapter converter, 150 mm (6 in.) to 100 mm (4 in.)
- Low-shot plate
- Connector pin
- Seat extension v/h: 10 cm (4 in.), 20 cm (8 in.), and 30 cm (12 in.)
- Running board platform
- Panther seat, circular
- Panther seat, contoured
- Bazooka riser column extensions: 10 cm (4 in.), 20 cm (8 in.), 30 cm (12 in.), 40 cm (16 in.), 50 cm (20 in.), and an adjustable riser from 39 cm (15$\frac{1}{2}$ in.) to 73 cm (29 in.)
- Lightweight jib with weight rod
- Low rig for lightweight jib
- Counterweight 15 kg (331 lbs.)
- Sidewinder outrigger, adjustable/rotatable
- Short outrigger, rotatable 40 cm (16 in.)
- U-Bangi

Figure 31 The Super Jib.

- Rotatable adapter
- Short steering rod
- Steering rod with drive control
- Steer-out extension
- Extra charger for one to two batteries
- Two-way charge cable
- Extension cable for handset
- Pneumatic wheels
- Case for lightweight jib with accessories
- Case for pneumatic wheels or studio wheels
- Case for U-Bangi and accessories
- Case for Panther accessories
- Case for Panther Dolly
- Cases for Super Jib
- Track sections: starter, 3 ft., 5 ft., 8 ft., 10 ft., 40-degree curve, and 90-degree curve

Xtend'R Jib/Arm (PDM MFG Co.)

Specifications

Lens height	14 ft.
Lens lowest	−3 ft. 4 in. (below ground level)
Vertical height	14 ft. (to camera mounting plate)
Horizontal reach	8 ft. 3 in.
Jib's capacity	100 lbs. (maximum weight of camera and head combined)
Dollies recommended to be used with	Fisher #10, Chapman Hybrid, or Hustler
Jib's attaching base	Mitchell mount (supplied with Xtend'R Jib)
Jib's receiving base	Mitchell mount
Heads that can be used on jib	Fluid, gear, and remote
Cameras that can be used on jib	Most
Weight of jib (empty)	225 lbs.
Shipping weight	1,170 lbs.
Transporation of jib	Truck or van

HIGHLIGHTS

1. Eliminates arc.
2. Moves in a straight line.
3. Collapsed size is 108 in. long, 25 in. wide, and 28 in. high.

SPECIFICATIONS

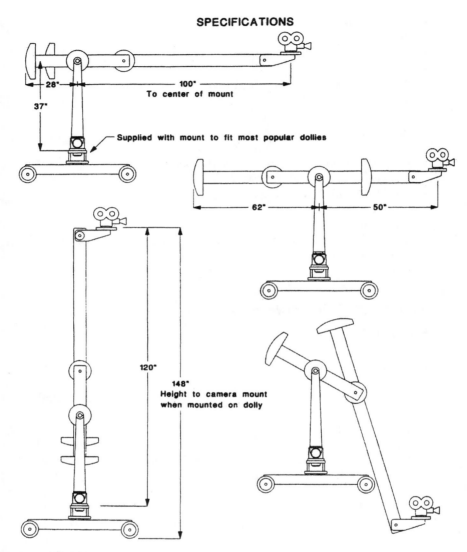

Figure 32a Xtend'R jib specifications.

Additional Specifications for the Xtend'R Jib/Arm

Travel

vertical	15 ft.
tilt range	over 180 degrees
horizontal reach	variable; from 1 ft. to 9 ft.

3 AXIS CAMERA BOOM FOR FILM & VIDEO
THE PROFESSIONAL VIEW NEEDS 3 AXIS FREEDOM

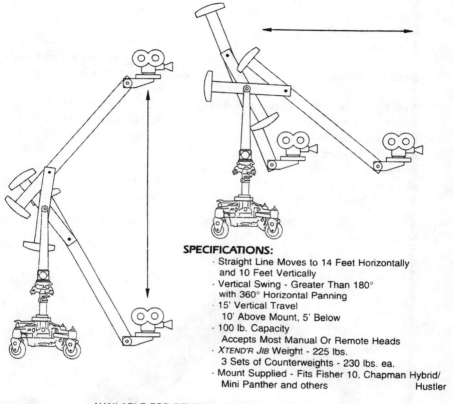

SPECIFICATIONS:
- Straight Line Moves to 14 Feet Horizontally and 10 Feet Vertically
- Vertical Swing - Greater Than 180° with 360° Horizontal Panning
- 15' Vertical Travel
  10' Above Mount, 5' Below
- 100 lb. Capacity
  Accepts Most Manual Or Remote Heads
- *XTEND'R JIB* Weight - 225 lbs.
  3 Sets of Counterweights - 230 lbs. ea.
- Mount Supplied - Fits Fisher 10, Chapman Hybrid/ Mini Panther and others   Hustler

AVAILABLE FOR RENTAL. LONG OR SHORT TERM

Figure 32b   More specifications for Xtend'R jib.

pan	360 degrees
Straight line move	
vertical	10 ft.
horizontal	14 ft.
Maximum height to camera mount	148 in. (on typical dolly)
Minimum height to camera mount	40 in. (below ground level; on typical dolly)

ZG Arm (Model 11-100, Ken Hill MFG)

Specifications

Lens height	14 ft.
Lens lowest	−6 ft.
Horizontal reach	11 ft.
Arm's capacity	100 lbs. (maximum weight of camera and head combined)
Dollies recommended to be used with	Fisher #10 (with a center mount)
Arm's attaching base (to dolly or crane)	K. Hill (supplied)
Arm's receiving base	K. Hill (supplied)
Heads that can be used on arm	Gear, remote, or fluid
Cameras that can be used on arm	Most
Weight of arm (empty)	175 lbs.
Shipping weight	650 lbs.
Transportation of arm	Small truck or cube van

NOTE: Training tape and demonstration reels are available. Call K. Hill Manufacturing.

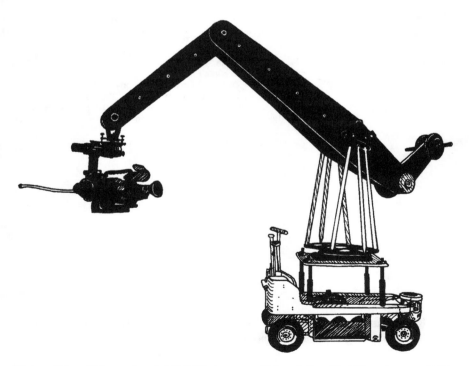

Figure 33a ZG arm (model 11-100) shown on Fisher dolly with ZG center-mount kit.

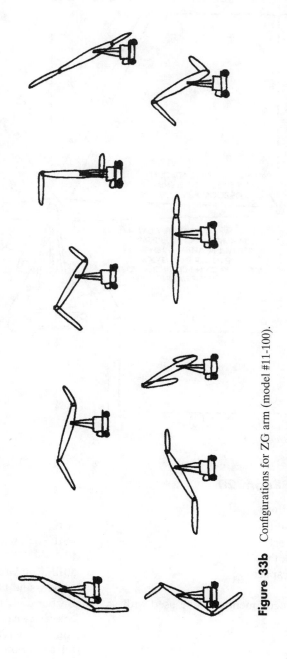

Figure 33b Configurations for ZG arm (model #11-100).

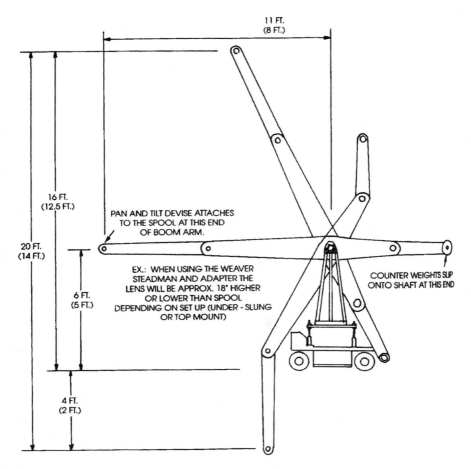

Figure 33b *continued*

Barber Boom 20

Specifications

Lens height	20 ft.
Lens lowest	−6 ft. (below ground level)
Horizontal reach	12 ft.
Boom's capacity	50 lbs. (maximum weight of camera and head combined)
Dollies recommended to be used with	Barber dolly (but a converter can be used to convert to a Mitchell base for center-mount dollies)
Boom's attaching base (to dolly or crane)	Supplied with Boom

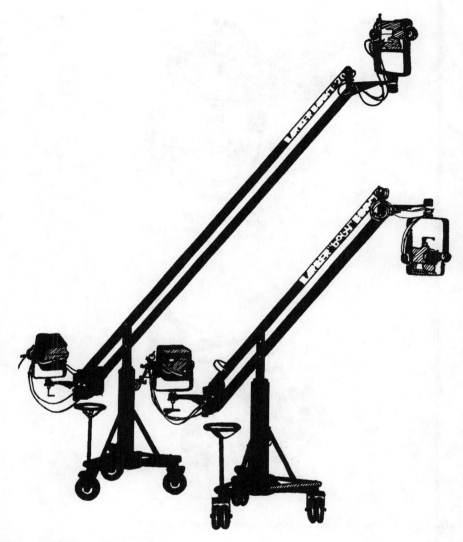

Figure 34a Barber Boom 20.

Boom's receiving base	Supplied with Boom
Heads that can be used on boom	Supplied with Boom
Cameras that can be used on boom	Most (no Imax, Vista Vision, or Mitchel Mark)
Weight of boom (empty)	120 lbs.
Transporation of boom	Small truck or van

Figure 34b Top-mounted Barber Boom head.

Figure 34c Bottom-mounted (underslung) Barber Boom head.

Additional Specifications for the Barber Boom 20

Maximum radius	12 ft.
Maximum turning diameter	24 ft.
Overall length	17 ft.
From fulcrum to monitor	5 ft.
Vertical span	20 ft.
Maximum height	16 ft.
Minimum height	4 ft. (below ground level)

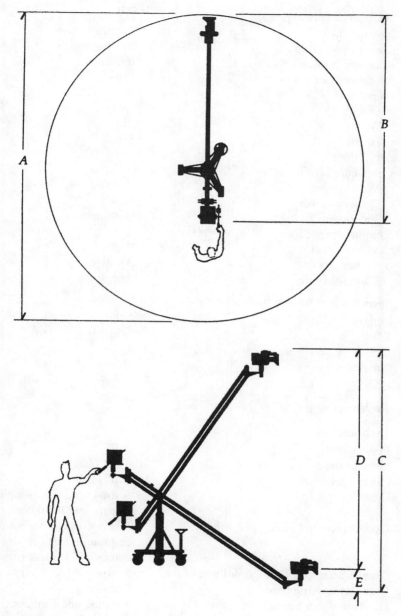

Figure 34d Specifications for Barber Boom.

Horizontal boom span	22 ft.
Boom radius	360 degrees
Camera pan radius	360 degree
Camera tilt radius	180 degree
Maximum camera load	45 lbs.
Dimensions	
Length	174 in.
Width	18 in.
Height	34 in.
Setup time	15 to 30 min.
Cable connections	
Video monitor	Built-in
Camera power	Built-in
Video power	Built-in
Remote connection	
Video monitor	Built-in
Camera focus	Accessory
Camera zoom	Accessory

Specifications for the Barber Dolly

Length	38 in.
Width	38 in.
Height	45 in.
Maximum weight	850 lbs.

Technocrane

Specifications

Lens height	20 ft. 2 in.
Lens lowest	−10 ft. 2 in.
Horizontal reach	20 ft. 1 in.
Crane's capacity	80 lbs. (maximum weight of camera and head combined)
Dollies recommended to be used with	Technocrane base, but may be mounted on certain cranes and camera cars
Crane's attaching base (to dolly or crane)	Euro-style
Crane's receiving base	Euro-Ball
Heads that can be used on crane	Technocrane Remote (supplied)
Cameras that can be used on crane	All production cameras and some Sfx cameras
Total weight of crane (maximum)	2,000 lbs.
Transportation of crane	Truck supplied by Technocrane

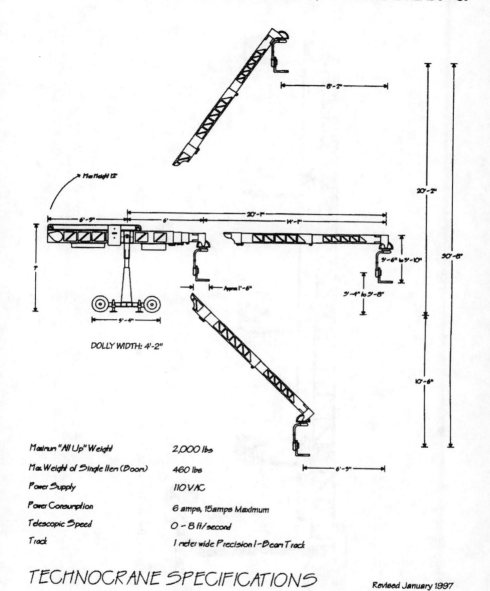

Maximum "All Up" Weight	2,000 lbs
Max Weight of Single Item (Boom)	460 lbs
Power Supply	110 VAC
Power Consumption	6 amps, 15amps Maximum
Telescopic Speed	0 – 8 ft/second
Track	1 meter wide Precision I-Beam Track

TECHNOCRANE SPECIFICATIONS   Revised January 1997

Figure 35a   Technocrane specifications.

HIGHLIGHTS

1. Technocrane can telescope during a shot, from a reach of 6 ft. to 20 ft., at up to 8 ft. per second.
2. The crane can be mounted on top of Technocrane's truck, allowing a higher reach.

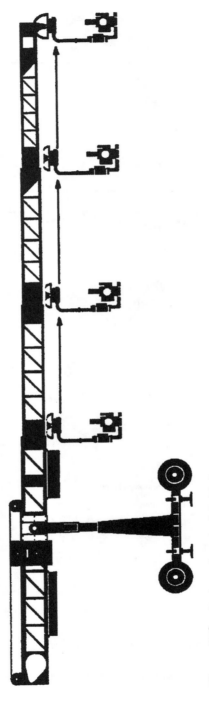

Figure 35b Horizontal reach of the Technocrane.

Additional Specifications for the Technocrane

Maximum "all up" weight	2,000 lbs.
Maximum weight of single item (boom)	410 lbs.
Power supply	110 VAC
Power consumption	4 amps, 15 amps maximum
Telescopic speed	0 to 8 ft./second
Track	1-meter-wide Precision I-Beam Track

Louma Crane

Specifications

Lens height	27 ft.
Lens lowest	−14 ft. 6 in. (below ground level)
Horizontal reach	4 ft. to 24 ft. 8 in. (in 1-ft. increments)
Crane's capacity	74 lbs. (maximum weight of camera)
Dolly	Supplied with Louma Crane

NOTE: Louma can also be used on the Titan and Super Nova cranes.

Crane's attaching base (to dolly or crane)	Mitchell mount
Crane's receiving base	Mitchell mount
Heads that can be used on crane	Remote or Vinten/Weaver/Steadman (supplied with Louma)
Cameras that can be used on jib	Most (anything up to 75 lbs.)
Weight of crane	1,694 lbs. (shipping weight including dolly)
Transportation of crane	Cube van (supplied by Louma)

NOTE: The Louma crane may also be used in shorter configurations, all the way down to 4 feet. See supplier's list for all the added equipment that comes with the package.

Louma Head Specifications

Maximum load	75 lbs.
Minimum dimensions through which head will pass	1 ft. 7 in. width, 2 ft. 5 in. height

NOTE: The head is controlled by wheels and is operated from a remote control console located up to 100 ft. away from the crane.

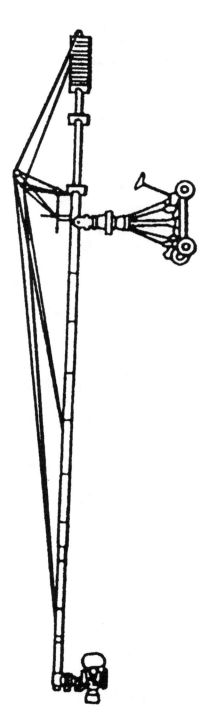

Figure 36 Louma crane.

Flying Dutchman—The Louma Third Axis Head Specification

Maximum camera weight	47 lbs.

Specifications for the Louma Arm

Minimum length of arm	4 ft.
Maximum length of arm	25 ft.
Maximum height from ground level	27 ft.
Maximum arm swing (60 degrees above to 65 degrees below horizontal)	42 ft.
Maximum length of arm without reinforcement cables	15 ft.

Specifications for the Louma Dolly

Minimum width of dolly (configured to pass through doorways)	28 in.
Overall dimensions in normal configurations	44 in. width by 48 in. length
Minimum height from ground to pivot	4 ft.
Maximum height from ground to pivot	8 ft.
Maximum weight of the Louma when configured as a 25-ft. arm (including dolly)	1,694 lbs.

Enlouva II Crane

Specifications

Lens height	24 ft.
Lens lowest	−11 ft.
Horizontal reach	19 ft. 5 in.
Crane's capacity	140 lbs. (maximum weight of camera and head combined)
Dollies recommended to be used with	Enlouva dolly, Shotmaker Mammoth (but will work on the Super Panther or the Pyramid base)
Crane's attaching base (to dolly or crane)	Elemack base
Crane's receiving base	Mitchell mount
Heads that can be used on crane	All remote
Cameras that can be used on crane	Most

Call manufacturers of crane if camera weight is in question.

Weight of crane (empty)	345 lbs.
Transportation of crane	Truck

HIGHLIGHTS

This crane can be broken down into shorter sections and still have perfect balance. (See manufacturer's instructions and specifications.)

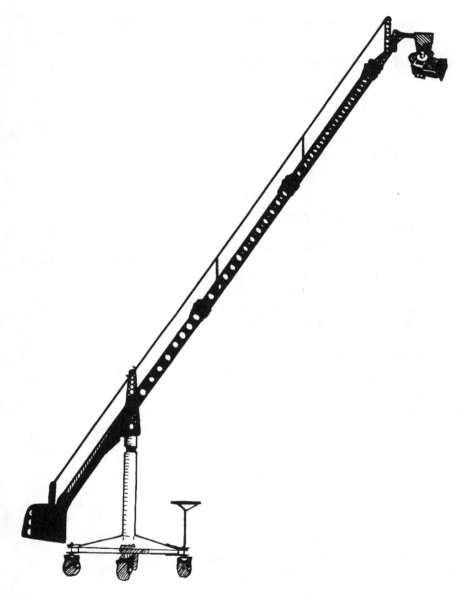

Figure 37   Enlouva II crane.

> **T.O.T.**
> Always move crane arm after releasing the brake. This is a safety check to ensure that the brake is fully off.

Additional Specifications for the Enlouva II Crane

Height	Up to 24 ft.
Arm reach	Up to 18 ft.
Assembly time	30 minutes
Operational weight	Less than 1,000 lbs. (including camera, remote head, and weights)

Enlouva IIIA Crane

Specifications

Lens height	25 ft.
Lens lowest	−15 ft.
Horizontal reach	7 ft. 3 in. to 22 ft. 3 in. (in 3-ft. increments)
Crane's capacity	140 lbs. (maximum weight of camera and head combined)
Dollies recommended to be used with	Enlouva dolly, Shotmaker Mammoth, the Pyramid base (when securely fastened down)
Crane's attaching base (to dolly or crane)	100 mm Elemack-style base
Crane's receiving base	Mitchell mount
Heads that can be used on crane	Most remote and fluid heads
Cameras that can be used on crane	Most

Call manufacturers of crane if camera weight is in question.

Weight of crane (empty)	455 lbs.
Transportation of crane	Pickup truck or van

HIGHLIGHTS

1. Assembly time: 15 minutes.
2. Crane has a four-way leveling head for pedestal, plus a two-way leveling for the spoon bill (receiver).
3. The crane can be used in six different lengths with any fluid head.

Additional Specifications for the Enlouva III Crane

Maximum lens height (with remove head standing)	23 ft. 6 in.

Figure 38a Positions of the Enlouva IIIA crane.

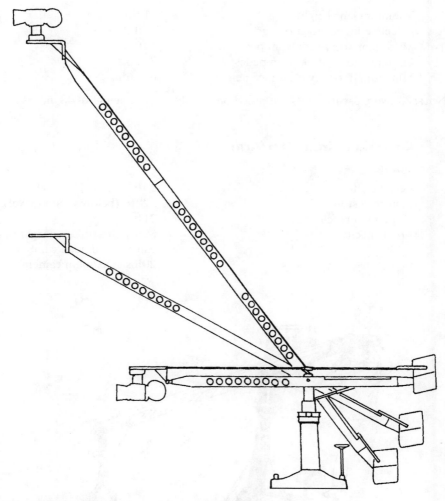

Figure 38b Positions of the Enlouva III crane.

Minimum lens height	–12 in.
Effective lift range at one go	35 ft. 6 in.
Maximum arm reach from pedestal	19 ft. 6 in.
Minimum arm reach from pedestal	7 ft. 6 in.
Minimum doorway clearance height	6 ft. 6 in.

NOTE: Above measurements are based on a dolly column height of 48 inches.

Cam-Mate Crane/Jib/Arm

Specifications

Lens height	25 ft.
Lens lowest	–20 ft. (below ground level)
Horizontal reach	21 ft.
Jib's capacity	80 lbs. (maximum weight of camera and head combined; 20 lbs. maximum camera weight)

Figure 39a   Cam-Mate on track.

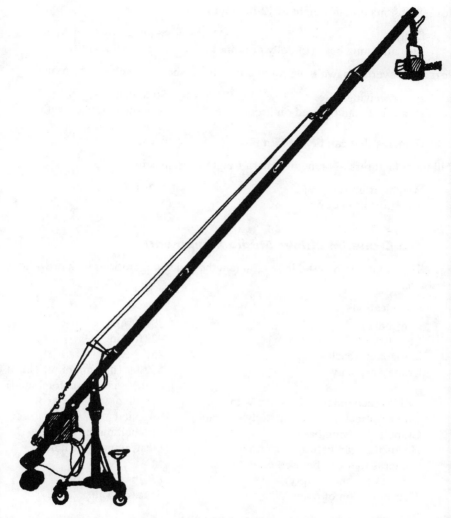

Figure 39b Cam-Mate—high angle.

NOTE: 80 lbs. maximum weight at 12-ft. length only

Dolly	Supplied by Cam-Mate
Jib's attaching base (to dolly or crane)	Comes with crane

NOTE: A converter is available to mount to the Fisher #10 with center mount.

Jib's receiving base	Slide plate
Heads that can be used on jib	Remote (supplied with crane arm)
Cameras that can be used on jib	Most

Call manufacturers of crane if camera weight is in question.

Weight of jib (empty)	85 lbs.
Transportation of jib	Small truck

The Crane (Mathews Studio Equipment)

This crane can be used in several lengths and configurations with or without personnel.

Specifications

Lens height	28 ft. 6 in.
Lens lowest	−22 ft. 4 in.
Horizontal reach	25 ft.
Crane's capacity	550 lbs. (maximum weight of camera and head combined)
Dollies recommended for use with	Supplied
Crane's attaching base (to dolly or crane)	Supplied
Crane's receiving base	Mitchell mount
Heads that can be used on crane	Gear, remote, or fluid
Cameras that can be used on crane	Most
Weight of crane (empty)	850 lbs.
Transportation of crane	Truck or van

NOTE: This crane *is* designed to support personnel!

HIGHLIGHTS

1. The Crane operates on wide ultralight tracks that can swingfold to 62 cm for doorway use. Rough-terrain wheels and studio wheels are available.
2. Terrain and track wheels are interchangeable without jacking. Wheels are steerable front and back for maneuvering into confined corners.
3. The Crane base can be used independently as a dolly on terrain wheels or track wheels.
4. Single-seat TV camera swivels. Rising columns and four-way levelers are available.

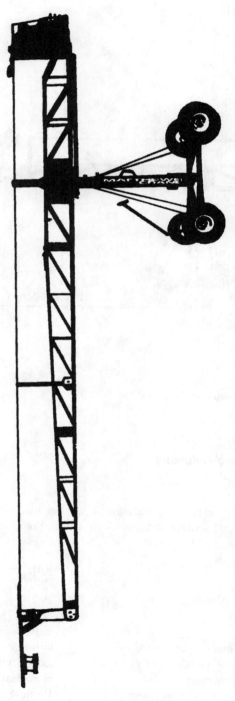

Figure 40a The Crane.

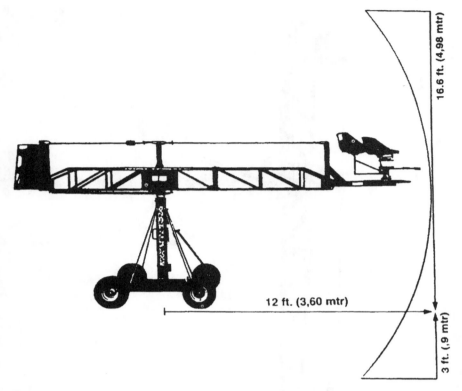

Figure 40b Specifications for The Crane.

Giraffe Crane (Filmair)

Specifications

NOTE: Remember, the heights given are maximum heights, but the crane can still be used in several shorter configurations. Check the manufacturer's specifications.

Platform height	30 ft.
Platform lowest	−20 ft.
Horizontal reach	25 ft.
Crane's capacity	175 lbs. (maximum weight of camera and head combined)
Dollies recommended to be used with	Giraffe wide-based dolly
Crane's attaching base (to dolly)	Euro-style
Crane's receiving base	Euro-Ball
Heads that can be used on crane	Remote, gear, and fluid

Figure 41a The Giraffe crane.

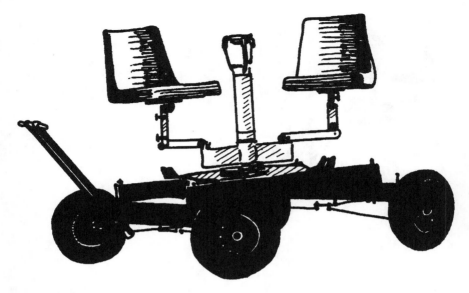

Figure 41b   The Giraffe crane base.

Cameras that can be used on crane	Most
Weight of crane (empty)	645 lbs.
Transportation of crane	Large truck

NOTE: This crane *is* designed to support personnel!

Additional Specifications for the Giraffe Crane

First Modular Extension

Height	6.1 m	20 ft.
Two crew and camera	220 kg	484 lbs.
Assembled weight	250 kg	550 lbs.

The Standard Crane

Height	5 m	16 ft.
Two crew and camera	250 kg	550 lbs.
Assembled weight	225 kg	494 lbs.

NOTE: The Standard Crane operates on 1-meter-wide tracks for extra stability.

Mini-Crane

Height	3.4 m	11 ft.
Two crew and camera	250 kg	550 lbs.
Assembled weight	170 kg	366 lbs.

NOTE: The Mini-Crane fits 62-cm-wide doorway tracks.

Second Modular Extension
Height	7.2 m	24 ft.
One crew and camera	160 kg	350 lbs.
Assembled weight	270 kg	592 lbs.

Cam Remote Extension
Height	9 m	30 ft.
Cam remote and camera	80 kg	175 lbs.
Assembled weight	290 kg	645 lbs.

Swiss Crane

Specifications

Lens height (maximum)	32 ft.
Lens lowest	−32 ft.
Horizontal reach (maximum)—six sections	9 ft. to 35 ft.
Crane's capacity	25 lbs. (camera weight); 155 lbs. (camera and head weight combined

NOTE: There is a camera weight restriction of approximately 100 lbs. at maximum length.

Dollies recommended to be used with	Swiss dolly
Crane's attaching base (to dolly or crane)	Swiss mount (supplied)
Crane's receiving base	Two-way leveling Mitchell mount (supplied by Swiss Company)
Heads that can be used on crane	Remote
Cameras that can be used on crane	Most
Weight of crane (empty)	490 lbs.
Transportation of crane	Truck or van

HIGHLIGHTS

1. Carbon fiber construction makes it lightweight and stiff.
    a. Its light weight makes it easy to transport and to assemble.
    b. Its stiffness means there is less boom whip and shake.
2. You can set up the crane and change length fast, without tools.
3. The crane can be assembled and operated by two people.

Additional Specifications for the Swiss Crane

Maximum height of center post	6 ft. 6 in.
Minimum height of center post	4 ft. 6 in.
Maximum arm clearance height	5 ft.
Maximum gross weight	1,710 lbs.
Dolly width	31½ in.
Center post to dolly edge	15 in.

Figure 42a The Swiss crane.

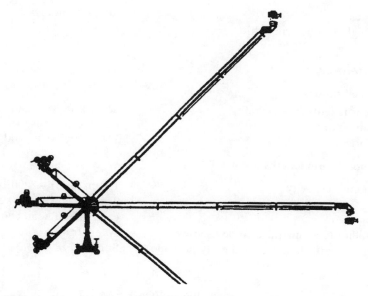

Figure 42b   Configurations of the Swiss crane.

Figure 42c   Boom span of the Swiss crane.

Track   24½ in. round track
Weight of one arm section   22 lbs.

Akela Jr.

Specifications

Lens heights (underslung)   32 ft., 39 ft., 46 ft., and 53 ft.
Lens lowest   Depends on base
Horizontal reach   32 ft., 39 ft., 46 ft., and 53 ft.

NOTE: Shorter arm lengths are possible.

Crane's capacity   150 lbs., 175 lbs., 200 lbs., and
                                            225 lbs. (maximum weight of
                                            camera and head combined)

Dollies recommended to be used with   Akela trailer
Crane's attaching base (to dolly or crane) Supplied

SPECIFICATIONS

ARM REACH	LENS HEIGHT UNDERSLUNG	OVERALL ARM LENGTH	MAX. NOSE LOAD (INCLUDES REMOTE HEAD & CAMERA PKG.)
32'	32'	41'	225 lbs.
39'	39'	48'	200 lbs.
46'	46'	55'	175 lbs.
53'	53'	62'	150 lbs.

Weight (w/chassis & weights) ...3000 lbs.   Pedestal to rear ....9'
Dolly Dimension ....6' x 6'   Steerable Dolly (Conventional) 1
Pedestal Height ....9'   Operator (provided) 1

*The Akela Jr. is lightweight and can be broken down into highly portable elements enabling assembly in the remotest of locations.

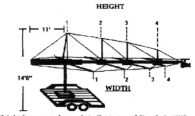

*Height from crane base w/o trailer to top of #1 pole is 13'6".
*Optimum working space required is 17' back from the Pedestal.

Figure 43b   Pole section dimensions for 32 ft. to 53 ft. in underslung position for Akela Jr. crane.

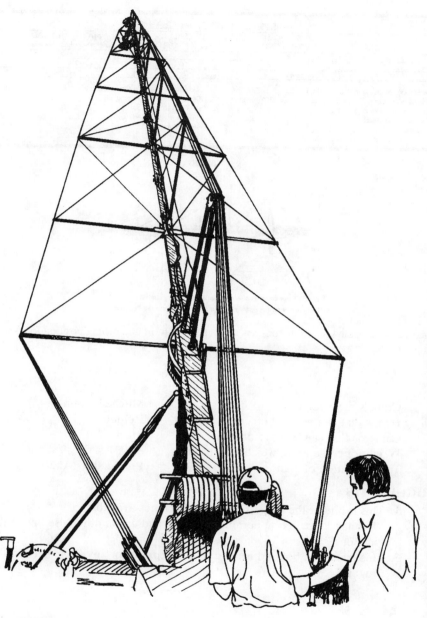

Figure 43a   The Akela crane.

SPECIFICATIONS (Akela Sr.)

ARM REACH	LENS HEIGHT UNDERSLUNG	OVERALL ARM LENGTH	MAX. NOSE LOAD (includes remote head & camera pkg.)
71'6"	68'	83'	200 lbs.
58'6"	55'	70'	250 lbs.
45'6"	44'	57'	300 lbs.

Weight (w/ Main Chassis & weights) .... 7000 lbs.	Weight (w/Portable Chassis & weights).............. 5000 lbs.
Chassis w/Steering .... 10'6" x 12'2"	Chassis without Steering .... 8' x 10'
Pedestal Pivot Point Height ....10'	Pedestal to Rear.. 12'
Overall Crane Height ....15'	Operator (Provided)... 2
....	Setup Time .... 3 hrs.
....	Strike Time .... 2 hrs.

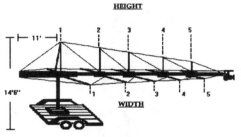

*Height from crane base w/o trailer to top of #1 pole is 13'6".
*Optimum working space required is 17' back from the Pedestal.

Figure 43c   Pole section dimensions for 44 ft. to 68 ft. in underslung position for Akela Sr. crane.

Crane's receiving base	Mitchell mount
Heads that can be used on crane	Remote
Cameras that can be used on crane	Most
Weight of crane (with weights on trailer)	3,000 lbs.
Transportation of crane	Provided by Akela

HIGHLIGHTS

1. This is one of the longest and highest cranes available.
2. Modular construction permits assembly and use in otherwise impossible locations.
3. This crane can be used instead of a helicopter for any shots between 6 in. and 53 ft.

Akela Sr.

Specifications

Lens heights (underslung)	44 ft., 55 ft., and 68 ft.
Lens lowest	Depends on base
Horizontal reach	45 ft. 6 in., 58 ft. 6 in., and 71 ft. 6 in.

SPECIFICATIONS

ARM REACH	LENS HEIGHT UNDERSLUNG	OVERALL ARM LENGTH	MAX. NOSE LOAD (INCLUDES REMOTE HEAD & CAMERA PKG.)
85'	79'	94'	100 lbs.

MAX. CAMERA WEIGHT............................45 lbs.

Weight (w/Main Chassis & weights) . . . . .8000lbs.
Chassis w/Steering . . . . .10'6" x 12'2"
Pedestal Pivot Point Height . . . . .10'
Overall Crane Height .15'

Weight (w/Portable Chassis & weights) . .6000lbs.
Chassis w/out Steering . . . . .8' x 10'
Pedestal to Rear . . . . .12'
Operator (provided) 2

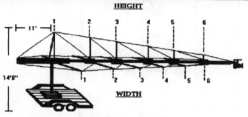

HEIGHT

WIDTH

*Height from crane base w/o trailer to top of #1 pole is 13'6".

*Optimum working space required is 17' back from the Pedestal.

Figure 43d Pole section dimensions for 79 ft. in underslung position for Akela Plus crane.

NOTE: Shorter arm lengths are possible.

Crane's capacity	200 lbs., 250 lbs., and 300 lbs.
Dollies recommended to be used with	Akela trailer
Crane's attaching base (to dolly or crane)	Supplied
Crane's receiving base	Mitchell mount
Heads that can be used on crane	Remote
Cameras that can be used on crane	Most
Weight of crane (with weights on trailer)	7,000 lbs.
Transportation of crane	Provided by Akela

HIGHLIGHTS

1. This is one of the longest and highest cranes available.
2. Modular construction permits assembly and use in otherwise impossible locations.
3. This crane can be used instead of a helicopter for any shots between 6 in. and 71 ft. 6 in.

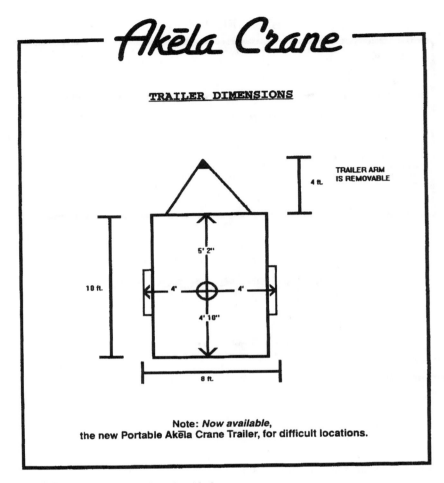

Figure 43e Trailer dimensions for Akela crane.

Motorized Cranes

The Chapman company is my top choice for motorized cranes. In my humble opinion, you will never find safer or better engineered cranes in the industry. Be safe, be smart, and call for a Chapman motorized crane. It's an Academy award winner.

NOTE: It is advised that the user of Chapman/Leonard equipment check with the manufacturer for the latest updates on *all* equipment. Leave nothing to chance. Be smart. Check first.

Super Nova

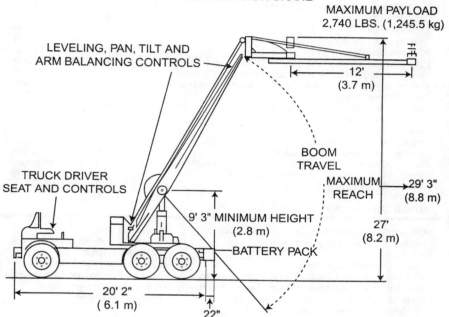

SUPER NOVA
STAGE AND LOCATION CRANE

MAXIMUM PAYLOAD
2,740 LBS. (1,245.5 kg)

LEVELING, PAN, TILT AND
ARM BALANCING CONTROLS

12'
(3.7 m)

BOOM
TRAVEL

MAXIMUM
REACH

29' 3"
(8.8 m)

TRUCK DRIVER
SEAT AND CONTROLS

9' 3" MINIMUM HEIGHT
(2.8 m)

27'
(8.2 m)

BATTERY PACK

20' 2"
(6.1 m)

22"

OVERALL CRANE WIDTH 7' 7 1/2" (2.3 m)
TRAVELING WEIGHT 27,500 LBS. (12,500 kg)
TRAVELING WEIGHT WITH BATTERY PACK 29,500 LBS. (13,409 kg)

MOBILE CRANE ACCESSORIES

4' Hydraulic Riser - (Mobile Crane & Western Dolly)
Telescoping Arm Adapter - Mobile Crane
Super Nova Sideboard - (Set of 2)
Mobile Crane Long Sliding Tow Bar
Steel Leveling Head - Mobile Crane
Vehicle Tow Dolly - Mobile Crane
12" Camera Riser (Steel) - Mobile Crane
Mobile Crane Ramp / Riser
6' Camera Extension - Mobile Crane
12' Camera Extension - Mobile Crane
10' Camera Riser - Mobile Crane
Super Casper Mobile Crane Extension

2 Camera Plate - Mobile Crane, Steel
2 Cam. Plate Setup Package - Mobile Crane, Steel
3' Drop Down - Mobile Crane
6' Drop Down - Mobile Crane
10' Drop Down - Mobile Crane
Nitrogen Bottle & Regulator - Mobile Crane
180° Remote Camera Platform - **Mobile Crane**
Lead Bucket Extension - Mobile Crane
360° Remote Camera Platform - **Mobile Crane**
Nose Platform - SteadiCam Platform
Titan Track - 20' Single Piece
Super Nova Battery Pack

Figure 44   Super Nova stage and location crane.

Lens Height (with 12" Riser, Turret and Camera)	27 ft.	8.2 m
Base Mount Height	23 ft. 6 in.	7.2 m
Reach beyond Chassis to Lens	17 ft. 3 in.	5.5 m
Reach beyond Chassis with Extension	29 ft. 3 in.	8.8 m
Vertical Travel of Boom above Ground	23 ft.	7 m
Vertical Travel of Boom below Ground	3 ft. 7 in.	1.1 m
Chassis Width	7 ft. 71/2 in.	2.3 m
Chassis Length	20 ft. 2 in.	6.1 m
Chassis Length w/ Battery Pack	22 ft.	6.7 m
Minimum Chassis Height	9 ft. 3 in.	2.8 m
Fully Extended Boom Length	30 ft. 11 in.	9.4 m
Maximum Length of Boom and Chassis w/ Battery Pack	39 ft. 2 in.	11.9 m
Clearance Height for Man and Camera with Arm Level and Post down	11 ft.	3.4 m
Crane Traveling Weight	27,500 lbs.	12,500 kg
Crane Traveling Weight with Battery Pack	29,500 lbs.	13,409 kg
Arm Balancing Ratio	2.5 : 1	
Tread	6 ft. 4 in.	1.9 m
Wheel Base (Outside Wheels)	13 ft. 10 1/2 in.	4.2 m
Ground Clearance with Arm Level (Post up)	8 ft. 5 in.	2.6 m
Maximum Speed on Level Ground with Battery Power (ft./sec.)	8 ft. 8 in./sec.	2.6 m/sec.
Minimum Turn Radius to Extremity of Chassis	23 ft. 3 in.	7 m
*Maximum Payload (with Bucket Extension)	2,740 lbs.	1,245.5 kg

OTHER SUPER NOVA FEATURES

- Remote Controlled Power Steering for Rear Wheels
- Heavy Duty Braking Applied to All 6 Wheels
- Pans 360°
- Electric Powered for Silence
- Smooth, Automatic Leveling in Less Than 10 Seconds
- Hand or Foot / Geared or Belt Driven Camera Turrets
- Qualified Driver Dispatched with Every Order
- Battery Pack System for Remote Power to Cameras
- Battery Pack System for Remote Lighting Power for up to 12k HMI's

- Cruises at 50 mph
- Gasoline Engine for Highway Travel
- Defies Most Terrain
- Crab Steering capabilities
- 6-Wheel Steering and 6-Wheel Drive
- Battery Powered Arm Brakes
- Push Button Balancing

*Payload Includes All Items (i.e. Man, Camera, Platform, Turret, Crane Arm, etc.) on Base Mount.

*It is advised that the user of Chapman/Leonard equipment check with the manufacturer for the latest updates on *all* equipment.

Figure 44 *continued*

Titan II

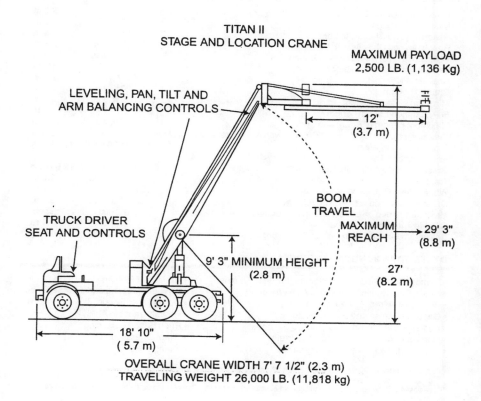

TITAN II
STAGE AND LOCATION CRANE

MAXIMUM PAYLOAD
2,500 LB. (1,136 Kg)

LEVELING, PAN, TILT AND
ARM BALANCING CONTROLS

12'
(3.7 m)

BOOM
TRAVEL

TRUCK DRIVER
SEAT AND CONTROLS

MAXIMUM
REACH

29' 3"
(8.8 m)

9' 3" MINIMUM HEIGHT
(2.8 m)

27'
(8.2 m)

18' 10"
(5.7 m)

OVERALL CRANE WIDTH 7' 7 1/2" (2.3 m)
TRAVELING WEIGHT 26,000 LB. (11,818 kg)

MOBILE CRANE ACCESSORIES

4' Hydraulic Riser - (Mobile Crane & Western Dolly)
Telescoping Arm Adapter - Mobile Crane
Super Nova Sideboard - (Set of 2)
Mobile Crane Long Sliding Tow Bar
Steel Leveling Head - Mobile Crane
12" Camera Riser (Steel) - Mobile Crane
Mobile Crane Ramp / Riser
6' Camera Extension - Mobile Crane
12' Camera Extension - Mobile Crane
10' Camera Riser - Mobile Crane
Super Casper Mobile Crane Extension

2 Camera Plate - Mobile Crane, Steel
2 Cam. Plate Setup Package - Mobile Crane, Steel
3' Drop Down - Mobile Crane
6' Drop Down - Mobile Crane
10' Drop Down - Mobile Crane
Nitrogen Bottle & Regulator - Mobile Crane
180° Remote Camera Platform - Mobile Crane
Lead Bucket Extension - Mobile Crane
360° Remote Camera Platform - Mobile Crane
Nose Platform - SteadiCam Platform
Titan Track - 20' Single Piece

Figure 45 Titan II stage and location crane.

SPECIFICATIONS

Lens Height (with 12" Riser, Turret and Camera)	27 ft.	8.2 m
Base Mount Height	23 ft. 6in.	7.2 m
Reach beyond Chassis to Lens	17 ft. 3 in.	5.5 m
Reach beyond Chassis with Extension	29 ft. 3 in.	8.8 m
Vertical Travel of Boom above Ground	23 ft.	7 m
Vertical Travel of Boom below Ground	3 ft. 7 in.	1.1 m
Chassis Width	7 ft. 71/2 in.	2.3 m
Chassis Length	20 ft. 2 in.	6.1 m
Minimum Chassis Height	9 ft. 3 in.	2.8 m
Fully Extended Boom Length	30 ft. 11 in.	9.4 m
Maximum Length of Boom and Chassis	37 ft. 4 in.	11.4 m
Clearance Height for Man and Camera with Arm Level and Post Down	11 ft.	3.4 m
Crane Traveling Weight	26,000 lbs.	11,818 kg
Arm Balancing Ratio	2.5 : 1	
Gross Weight with 600 lb. Nose Load	26,600 lbs.	12,091 kg
Tread	6 ft. 4 in.	1.9 m
Wheel Base (Outside Wheels)	13 ft. 10 1/2 in.	4.2 m
Ground Clearance with Arm Level (Post up)	8 ft. 5 in.	2.6 m
Maximum Speed on Level Ground with Battery Power (ft./sec.)	8.8 ft/sec.	2.6 m/sec.
Outside Turn Radius of Chassis	23 ft. 3 in.	7 m
*Maximum Payload (with Bucket Extension)	2,500 lbs.	1,136.3 kg

OTHER TITAN II / NOVA FEATURES

- Remote Controlled Power Steering for Rear Wheels
- Heavy Duty Braking Applied to All 6 Wheels
- Battery Powered Hydraulic Arm Brakes
- Gasoline Engine and Electric Motor
- Hydraulic Leveling in Less Than 10 Seconds
- Hand or Foot Operated Camera Turrets
- Qualified Driver Sent with Every Order

- Cruises at 50 mph
- 6-Wheel Steering and 6-Wheel Drive
- Defies Most Terrain
- Partial Crabbing Ability
- Push Button Balancing
- Silent Operation
- Swings 360°

*Payload Includes All Items (i.e. Man, Camera, Platform, Turret, Crane Arm, etc.) on Base Mount.

*It is advised that the user of Chapman/Leonard equipment check with the manufacturer for the latest updates on *all* equipment.

Figure 45 *continued*

Apollo

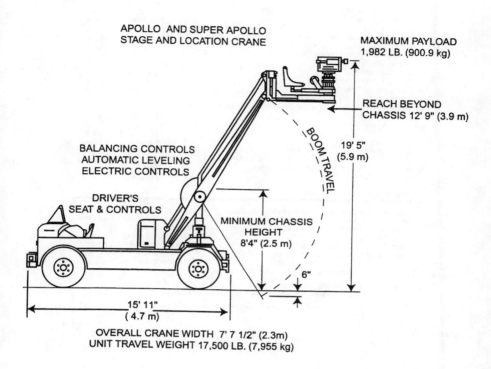

APOLLO AND SUPER APOLLO
STAGE AND LOCATION CRANE

MAXIMUM PAYLOAD
1,982 LB. (900.9 kg)

REACH BEYOND
CHASSIS 12' 9" (3.9 m)

BOOM TRAVEL

19' 5"
(5.9 m)

BALANCING CONTROLS
AUTOMATIC LEVELING
ELECTRIC CONTROLS

DRIVER'S
SEAT & CONTROLS

MINIMUM CHASSIS
HEIGHT
8'4" (2.5 m)

6"

15' 11"
(4.7 m)

OVERALL CRANE WIDTH 7' 7 1/2" (2.3m)
UNIT TRAVEL WEIGHT 17,500 LB. (7,955 kg)

MOBILE CRANE ACCESSORIES

4' Hydraulic Riser - (Mobile Crane & Western Dolly)
Telescoping Arm Adapter - Mobile Crane
Super Nova Sideboard - (Set of 2)
Mobile Crane Long Sliding Tow Bar
Steel Leveling Head - Mobile Crane
Vehicle Tow Dolly - Apollo Crane
12" Camera Riser (Steel) - Mobile Crane
Mobile Crane Ramp / Riser
6' Camera Extension - Mobile Crane
12' Camera Extension - Mobile Crane
10' Camera Riser - Mobile Crane

Super Casper Mobile Crane Extension
2 Camera Plate - Mobile Crane, Steel
2 Cam. Plate Setup Package - Mobile Crane, Steel
3' Drop Down - Mobile Crane
6' Drop Down - Mobile Crane
10' Drop Down - Mobile Crane
Nitrogen Bottle & Regulator - Mobile Crane
180° Remote Camera Platform - Mobile Crane
Lead Bucket Extension - Mobile Crane
360° Remote Camera Platform - Mobile Crane
Nose Platform - SteadiCam Platform

Figure 46 Apollo and Super Apollo stage and location crane.

SPECIFICATIONS

Lens Height (with 12 " Riser, Turret and Camera)	19 ft. 5 in.	5.9 m
Base Mount Height	15 ft. 11 in.	4.9 m
Reach beyond Chassis to Lens	12 ft. 9 in.	3.9 m
Reach beyond Chassis with Extension	18 ft. 9 in.	5.7 m
Vertical Travel of Boom above Ground	15 ft. 5 in.	4.7 m
Vertical Travel of Boom below Ground	10 1/2 in.	27 cm
Chassis Width	7 ft. 7 1/2 in.	2.3 m
Chassis Length	15 ft. 11 in.	4.7 m
Minimum Chassis Height	8 ft. 4 in.	2.5 m
Fully Extended Boom Length	23 ft.	7 m
Maximum Length of Boom and Chassis	29 ft. 4 in.	8.9 m
Clearance Height for Man and Camera w/ Arm Level and Post down	10 ft. 1 in.	3 m
Crane Traveling Weight	17,500 lbs.	7,955 kg
Arm Balancing Ratio	1.9 : 1	
Tread	6 ft. 4 in.	1.9 m
Wheel Base	10 ft. 6 1/2 in.	3.2 m
Ground Clearance w/ Arm Level (Post Up)	7 ft.	2.1 m
Maximum Speed on Level Ground with Battery Power (ft./sec.)	11.2 ft./ sec.	3.4 m/ sec
Minimum Turn Radius to Extremity of Chassis	21 ft. 2 in.	6.5 m
*Maximum Payload	1,982 lbs.	900.9 kg

OTHER APOLLO FEATURES

- Remote Controlled Power Steering for Rear Wheels
- Heavy Duty Braking Applied to All 4 Wheels
- Battery Powered Hydraulic Arm Brakes
- Gasoline Engine and Electric Motor
- Hydraulic Leveling in Less Than 5 Seconds
- Hand or Foot Operated Camera Turrets
- Qualified Driver Sent with Every Order
- Super Apollo Comes with a Built-In Generator to Recharge

- Cruises at 50 mph
- 4-Wheel Steering and 4-Wheel Drive
- Defies Most Terrain
- Partial Crabbing Ability
- Swings 360 Degrees
- Battery Powered Arm Brakes
- Push Button Balancing

 Batteries while in Remote Locations

*Payload Includes All Items (i.e. Man, Camera, Platform, Turret, Crane Arm, etc.) on Base Mount.

*It is advised that the user of Chapman/Leonard equipment check with the manufacturer for the latest updates on *all* equipment.

Figure 46 *continued*

Zeus

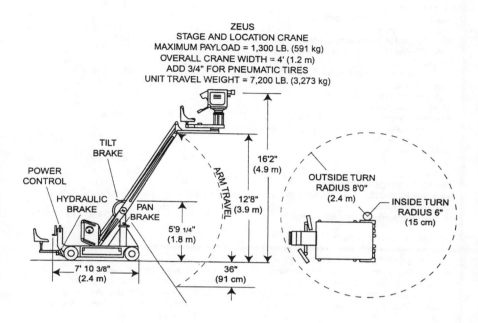

STAGE CRANE ACCESSORIES

Aluminum Leveling Head - Stage Crane
6" Camera Riser - Crane
12" Camera Riser - Crane
3' Camera Riser - Crane
3' Camera Extension - Stage Crane
8' Camera Extension (Remote Use - Stage Crane Only)
10' Camera Extension (Remote Use - Stage Crane Only)
3' Camera Drop Down - Crane
Bucket Seat
Kidney Seat
4" Seat Arm - Stage Crane
6" Seat Arm - Stage Crane
12" Seat Arm - Stage Crane
19" Seat Arm - Stage Crane
3" Seat Riser - Stage Crane
6" Seat Riser - Stage Crane
12" Seat Riser - Stage Crane
Film (Hand-Operated) Turret - Geared

Film (Hand-Operated) Turret - Belted
Electric, Video / Film Turret
TV (Foot-Operated) Turret
Free Head Turret
Offset Turret
Hydraulic Jack & Handle
Stage Crane Tires (2nd Set) - Pneumatic
Stage Crane Tires (2nd Set) - Solid
Stage Crane Track (10' Section)
¼ Lead Weight
½ Lead Weight
Lead Weight
Stage Crane Slide Weight (8 lbs.)
Stage Crane Slide Weight (16 lbs.)
Lead Bucket Extension
Zeus Sideboard
Circular Platform w/ Rails - 48"
Circular Platform w/ Rails - 72"
Crane Steadicam Platform Adapter Package

Figure 47 Zeus stage and location crane.

Lens Height (w/ 12 in. Riser)	16 ft. 2 in.	4.9 m
Base Mount Height	12 ft. 8 in.	3.9 m
Reach beyond Chassis to Lens	11 ft. 6 in.	3.5 m
*Maximum Payload	1,300 lbs.	591 kg
Vertical Travel of Boom above Ground	12 ft. 2 in.	3.7 m
Vertical Travel of Boom below Ground	3 ft.	91 cm
Chassis Width	4 ft.	1.2 m
Outside Dimensions w/ Pneumatic Tires	4 ft. 3/4 in.	1.2 m
Chassis Length	7 ft. 10 3/8 in.	2.4 m
Minimum Chassis Height	5 ft. 9 1/4 in.	1.8 m
Fully Extended Boom Length	18 ft. 6 in.	5.6 m
Maximum Length of Boom and Chassis	19 ft. 4 in.	5.9 m
Clearance Height for Man and Camera w/ Arm Level	8 ft. 6 in.	5 m
Crane Weight w/ Turret	4,800 lbs.	2,182 kg
Arm Balancing Ratio	2.25 : 1	
Tread	43 7/8 in.	1.1 m
Wheel Base	5 ft. 7 1/4 in.	1.7 m
Ground Clearance w/ Arm Level	55 in.	1.4 m
Maximum Speed on Level Ground Drop Down (to Crane Mount)	11.2 ft. / sec.	2.8 m / sec.
Outside Turn Radius	8 ft.	2.4 m
Normal Operating Weight Less Payload*	6, 150 lbs.	2,795.4 kg

OTHER ZEUS FEATURES

- Operates on 8 Tires (6 Front, 2 Rear)
- Friction Brakes for Pan and Tilt Movement
- On a Full Charge, Batteries Allow 24 Hours Use
- Charger Tapers off as Batteries Are Energized
- Battery Charge Pre-Set for either 110v or 220v
- Selection of Turrets, Risers, Extensions and Aluminum Track
- Electric Powered for Smooth, Silent Operation in Forward and Reverse Modes

- Rocker Suspension
- Turnaround Front Wheels
- All Steel Construction
- Solid or Pneumatic Tires Available
- Hydraulic Chassis and Parking Brake
- 360 Degree Arm Swing

*Payload Includes All Items (i.e. Man, Camera, Platform, Turret, Crane Arm, etc.) on Base Mount.

*It is advised that the user of Chapman/Leonard equipment check with the manufacturer for the latest updates on *all* equipment.

Figure 47 *continued*

Electra II/Nike

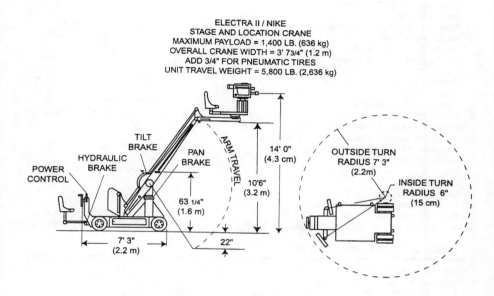

STAGE CRANE ACCESSORIES

Aluminum Leveling Head - Stage Crane
6" Camera Riser - Crane
12" Camera Riser - Crane
3' Camera Riser - Crane
3' Camera Extension - Stage Crane
8' Camera Extension (Remote Use - Stage Crane Only)
10' Camera Extension (Remote Use - Stage Crane Only)
3' Camera Drop Down - Crane
Bucket Seat
Kidney Seat
4" Seat Arm - Stage Crane
6" Seat Arm - Stage Crane
12" Seat Arm - Stage Crane
19" Seat Arm - Stage Crane
3" Seat Riser - Stage Crane
6" Seat Riser - Stage Crane
12" Seat Riser - Stage Crane
Film (Hand-Operated) Turret - Geared

Film (Hand-Operated) Turret - Belted
Electric, Video / Film Turret
TV (Foot-Operated) Turret
Free Head Turret
Offset Turret
Hydraulic Jack & Handle
Stage Crane Tires (2nd Set) - Pneumatic
Stage Crane Tires (2nd Set) - Solid
Stage Crane Track (10' Section)
¼ Lead Weight
½ Lead Weight
Lead Weight
Stage Crane Slide Weight (8 lbs.)
Stage Crane Slide Weight (16 lbs.)
Lead Bucket Extension
Zeus Sideboard
Circular Platform w/ Rails - 48"
Circular Platform w/ Rails - 72"
Crane Steadicam Platform Adapter Package

Figure 48   Electra II/Nike stage and location crane.

SPECIFICATIONS

Lens Height (with 12 in. Riser)	14 ft.	4.3 m
Base Mount Height	10 ft. 6 in.	3.2 m
Reach beyond Chassis to Lens	9 ft. 6 in.	2.9 m
*Maximum Payload	1,400 lbs.	636 kg
Vertical Travel of Boom above Ground	10 ft.	3 m
Vertical Travel of Boom below Ground	2 ft.	60 cm
Chassis Width	3 ft. 8 in.	1.1 m
Outside dimensions w/ Pneumatic Tires	3 ft. 9 1/2 in.	1.2 m
Chassis Length	7 ft. 3 in.	2.2 m
Minimum Chassis Height	5 ft. 3 1/2 in.	1.6 m
Fully Extended Boom Length	15 ft. 9 in.	4.8 m
Maximum Length of Boom and Chassis	16 ft. 9 in.	5.1 m
Clearance Height for Man and Camera w/ Arm Level	8 ft.	2.4 m
Crane Weight w/Turret	4,000 lbs.	1,818 kg
Arm Balancing Ratio	2 : 1	
Tread	39 7/8 in.	1 m
Wheel Base	5 ft. 1/2 in.	1.5 m
Ground Clearance w/ Arm Level	4 ft. 1 in.	1.2 m
Maximum Speed on Level Ground	9.8 ft. / sec.	2.5 m / sec.
Outside Turn Radius	6 ft. 3 in.	1.9 m
Normal Operating Weight Less Payload ˙	5,200 lbs.	2,364 kg

OTHER ELECTRA II / NIKE FEATURES

- Operates on 6 Tires (4 Front, 2 Rear)
- Solid or Pneumatic Tires Available
- On a Full Charge, Batteries Allow 24 Hours Use
- Charger Tapers off as Batteries Are Energized
- Battery Charge Pre-Set for either 110v or 220v
- Friction Brakes for Pan and Tilt Movement
- Selection of Turrets, Risers, Extensions and Aluminum Track
- Electric Powered for Smooth, Silent Operation in Forward / Reverse Modes

- Rocker Suspension
- Turnaround Front Wheels
- All Steel Construction
- Hydraulic Chassis / Parking Brake
- 360 Degree Arm Swing

*Payload Includes All Items (i.e. Man, Camera, Platform, Turret, Crane Arm, etc.) on Base Mount.

*It is advised that the user of Chapman/Leonard equipment check with the manufacturer for the latest updates on *all* equipment.

Figure 48 *continued*

ATB II Sport Package

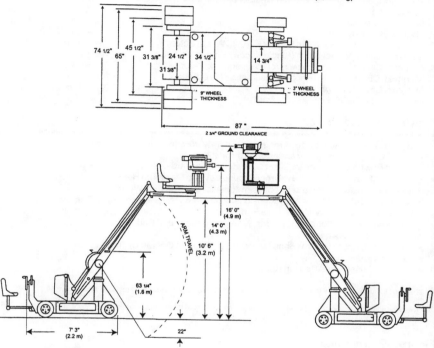

ATB ACCESSORIES

CS / ATB 7" Riser
ATB Knobby Pneumatic Tires - (Set of 6)
ATB Solid Tires - (Set of 6)
ATB Sand Pneumatic Tires - (Set of 6)
ATB Golf Pneumatic Tires - (Set of 6)
ATB Stage Pneumatic Tires - (Set of 6)
ATB Front Mounted Low Deck
Sport ATB Dual Platform Setup
Aluminum Leveling Head - Stage Crane
6" Camera Riser - Crane
12" Camera Riser - Crane
Bucket Seat
Kidney Seat
4" Seat Arm - Stage Crane
6" Seat Arm - Stage Crane
12" Seat Arm - Stage Crane
19" Seat Arm - Stage Crane

3" Seat Riser - Stage Crane
6" Seat Riser - Stage Crane
12" Seat Riser - Stage Crane
Film (Hand-Operated) Turret - Geared
Film (Hand-Operated) Turret - Belted
TV (Foot-Operated) Turret
Free Head Turret
Offset Turret
Stage Crane Tires (2nd Set) - Pneumatic
Stage Crane Tires (2nd Set) - Solid
Stage Crane Track (10' Section)
¼ Lead Weight
½ Lead Weight
Lead Weight
Stage Crane Slide Weight (8 lbs.)
Stage Crane Slide Weight (16 lbs.)
Circular Platform w/ Rails - 48"
Crane Steadicam Platform Adapter Package

Figure 49 ATB II sport package.

SPECIFICATIONS

Lens Height (Turret)	14 ft.	4.3 m
Lens Height (Platform)	16 ft.	4.9 m
Base Mount Height	10 ft. 6 in.	3.2 m
*Maximum Payload (Turret)	600 lbs.	273 kg
*Maximum Payload for Front of the Arm (Platform)	600 lbs.	273 kg
*Maximum Payload for Back of the Arm (Platform)	600 lbs.	273 kg
Maximum Horizontal Reach (to Lens without Extension)	9 ft. 6 in.	2.9 m
Chassis Length	7 ft. 3 in.	2.2 m
Maximum Chassis Width	6 ft. 2 1/2 in.	1.9 m
Minimum Chassis Width	34 1/2 in.	88 cm
Center to Center Wheel Width for Track (Solid Wheel Setup)	31 3/8 in.	80 cm
Center to Center Wheel Width (Single Knobby Pneumatic Setup)	45 1/2 in.	1.2 m
Center to Center Width (Double Knobby Pneumatic Setup)	65 in.	1.7 m
Maximum Chassis Width (Knobby Pneumatic Wheel Setup)	6 ft. 2 1/2 in.	1.9 m
Minimum Chassis Height	5 ft. 3 1/4 in.	1.6 m
Normal Operating Weight Less Payload*	5,200 lbs.	2,364 kg

OTHER ATB II FEATURES

• **Remote Actuator to Control Arm Independently** from the Camera Platform or Crane Operator Seat
• Built-In Charging System Operates on 110v or 220v
• Electric Powered for Smooth, Silent Operation in Forward and Reverse Modes
• Up to 12' of Vertical Boom Travel from Ground Level to Maximum Height
• Tires Come in Your Choice of Knobby, Pneumatic or Solid Track Wheels
• Selection of Turrets, Risers and Extensions, Aluminum Track Available upon Request
• 36 volt System Will Give Exceptional Performance and Acceleration along Sport Sidelines
• Comes with 48" Platform, Sideboards, Monitor Platform and Padding
• 360 Degree Arm Swing
• Versatility for Use with Film (Hand Operated) or TV (Foot Operated) Turrets
• Rocker Suspension
• Hydraulic Chassis and Parking Brake

*Payload Includes All Items (i.e. Man, Camera, Platform, Turret, Crane Arm, etc.) on Base Mount.

*It is advised that the user of Chapman/Leonard equipment check with the manufacturer for the latest updates on *all* equipment.

Figure 49 *continued*

Olympian

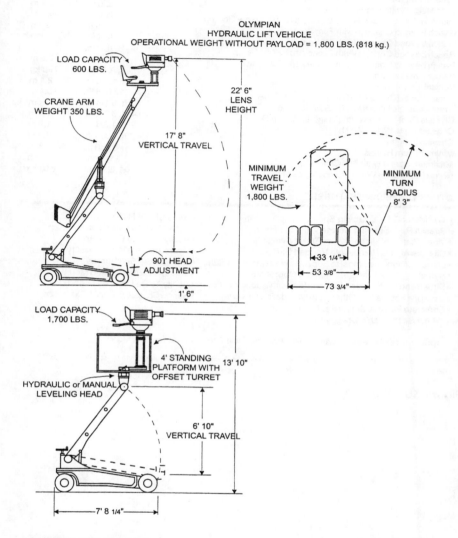

Figure 50 Olympian hydraulic lift vehicle.

OLYMPIAN ACCESSORIES
6" Mitchell Riser
Olympian Hydraulic Leveling Head
Olympian Track (10' Section)
Olympian 2' Camera Riser
Circular Platform w/ Rails - 48"
Circular Platform w/ Rails - 72"
Olympian Platform Monitor Bracket

6' Adjustable (Olympian) Crane Arm
6' (Olympian) Crane Arm
Olympian Balloon Tires - (Set of 8)
Olympian Solid Tires - (Set of 6)
Olympian Long Sideboard
Olympian Short Sideboard
Olympian II Camera Offset Plate
10' Fiberglass Ramp - Rated for 3,000 lbs.

Lens Height (with Standard Film, TV, or Platform Setup)	13 ft. 10 in.	4.2 m
Lens Height (with Crane Arm Setup)	22 ft. 6 in.	6.9 m
Minimum Lens Height (with Crane Arm Setup, below Ground Level)	1 ft. 6 in.	46 cm
Reach beyond Chassis (with Film Setup)	9 ft.	23 cm
Reach beyond Chassis (with TV Setup)	1 ft. 4 in.	41 cm
Reach beyond Chassis (with Crane Arm (Film) Setup)	10 ft. 9 in.	3.3 m
Reach beyond Chassis (with Crane Arm (TV) Setup)	8 ft. 7 in.	2.6 m
*Maximum Payload	1,700 lbs.	798 kg
Vertical Travel (Standard Setup)	6 ft. 10 in.	2.1 m
Boom Travel (Crane Arm Setup)	17 ft. 8 in.	5.4 m
Chassis Single Wheel Width (Standard Setup Only)	2 ft. 9 1/4 in.	85 cm
Chassis Dual Wheel Width (Standard Setup Only)	4 ft. 5 3/8 in.	1.4 m
Chassis Triple Wheel Width	6 ft. 1 3/4 in.	1.9 m
Chassis Length	7 ft. 8 1/4 in.	2.3 m
Minimum Turn Radius	8 ft. 3 in.	2.5 m
Maximum Speed (with Full Charge)	18 mph	30 kph
Normal Operating Weight Less Payload*	1,800 lbs.	818 kg

OTHER OLYMPIAN FEATURES

- Two Motor Drive Enabling Speeds up to 18 mph
- Special Rear Steering Design with 20:1 Ratio
- Video Platform, Video or Film Turret Available
- Chassis Allows Removable Padded Barrier
- Large Balloon Tires (4psi to 30psi), for Movement in Sand
- Hydraulic Lift for Smooth, One-Man Operation
- Streamline Profile Does Not Interfere with Audience View
- Great for Football (or Other Sports) Sideline Coverage
- Complete Football Safety Package (Includes: Padding, Wheel Skirts, Cable Draggers)

- Rigid Single Beam Lift
- Flexibility in Camera Operator Setup
- Ability to Carry Crane Arm
- Hydraulic Leveling Accessory
- Detachable Sideboards
- Variable Camera Head Mount
- Ability To Be Used on or off Track
- Narrow Chassis w/ Variable Tire Widths

*Payload Includes All Items (i.e. Man, Camera, Platform, Turret, Crane Arm, etc.) on Base Mount.

*It is advised that the user of Chapman/Leonard equipment check with the manufacturer for the latest updates on *all* equipment.

Figure 50 *continued*

Olympian II Hydraulic Lift Vehicle

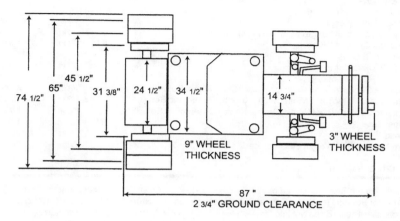

OLYMPIAN II HYDRAULIC LIFT VEHICLE
MAXIMUM RATED PAYLOAD = 1,800 LBS. (818 kg)
OPERATING WEIGHT = 3,300 LBS. (1,500 kg)

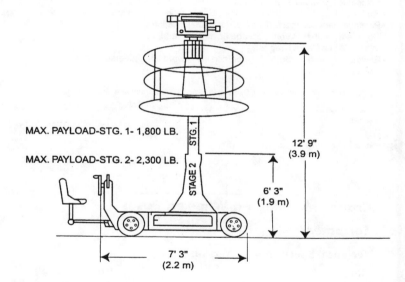

OLYMPIAN II ACCESSORIES
6" Mitchell Riser
Olympian 2' Camera Riser
Olympian Platform Monitor Bracket
Olympian II Camera Offset Plate
ATB Knobby Pneumatic Tires - (Set of 6)
Bucket Seat
Kidney Seat

Figure 51 Olympian II hydraulic lift vehicle.

SPECIFICATIONS

Maximum Camera Mount Height	12 ft. 9 in.	3.9 m
Minimum Camera Mount Height	6 ft. 3 in.	1.9 m
*Maximum Payload - Stage 1	2,300 lbs.	1,045.4 kg
*Maximum Payload - Stage 2	1,800 lbs.	818.1 kg
Vertical Travel	6 ft. 6 in.	2 m
Minimum Ground Clearance	2 3/4 in.	7 cm
Chassis Deck Height	16 in.	41 cm
Maximum Chassis Length without Seat or Platform	7 ft. 3 in.	2.2 m
Maximum Chassis Width	6 ft. 2 1/2 in.	1.9 m
Minimum Chassis Width	34 1/2 in.	88 cm
Platform Diameter	72 in.	1.8 m
Platform Rail Height	3 ft. 1 in.	94 cm
Center to Center Wheel Width for Track (Solid Wheel Setup)	31 3/8 in.	80 cm
Center to Center Wheel Width (Single Knobby Pneumatic Setup)	45 1/2 in.	1.2 m
Center to Center Wheel Width (Double Knobby Pneumatic Setup)	65 in.	1.7 m
Wheel Base	5 ft. 1 1/2 in.	1.6 m
Speed	13 ft./sec.	4 m/sec.
Normal Operating Weight Less Payload*	3,300 lbs.	1,500 kg

OTHER OLYMPIAN II FEATURES

- Drive System Enables Speed of 13 ft./sec.
- Great for Football (or Other Sports) Sideline Coverage
- Streamline Profile Does Not Interfere with Audience View
- Relocated Hydraulic System Gives Driver Better Access
- Platform Mounts on Column for Easy Transportation
- Package Reduces to 2 ft. 10 1/2 in. for Transportation
- Complete Football Safety Package (Includes: Padding, Wheel Skirts, Cable Draggers)
- Electric Powered for Smooth Operation in Forward and Reverse Modes
- Over 6' of Vertical Camera Travel
- Built-In Battery Charger (110v/220v)
- Wraparound Platform Rail (38 in.)
- Silent Operation for Sound Stages
- Hydraulic Chassis and Parking Brake

*Payload Includes All Items (i.e. Man, Camera, Platform, Turret, Crane Arm, etc.) on Base Mount.

*It is advised that the user of Chapman/Leonard equipment check with the manufacturer for the latest updates on *all* equipment.

Figure 51 *continued*

Cranes Mounted on Wheeled Bases

Egripment

Technical Specifications, Version 1

Range	9 ft. to 14 ft. 9 in.
Maximum platform height	275 cm/9 ft.
Lift range	275 cm/9 ft.
Maximum play load capacity	220 kg/484 lbs.
Weight including dolly	149 kg/327 lbs.

Technical Specifications, Version 2

Maximum platform height	350 cm/11 ft. 6 in.
Lift range	425 cm/14 ft.

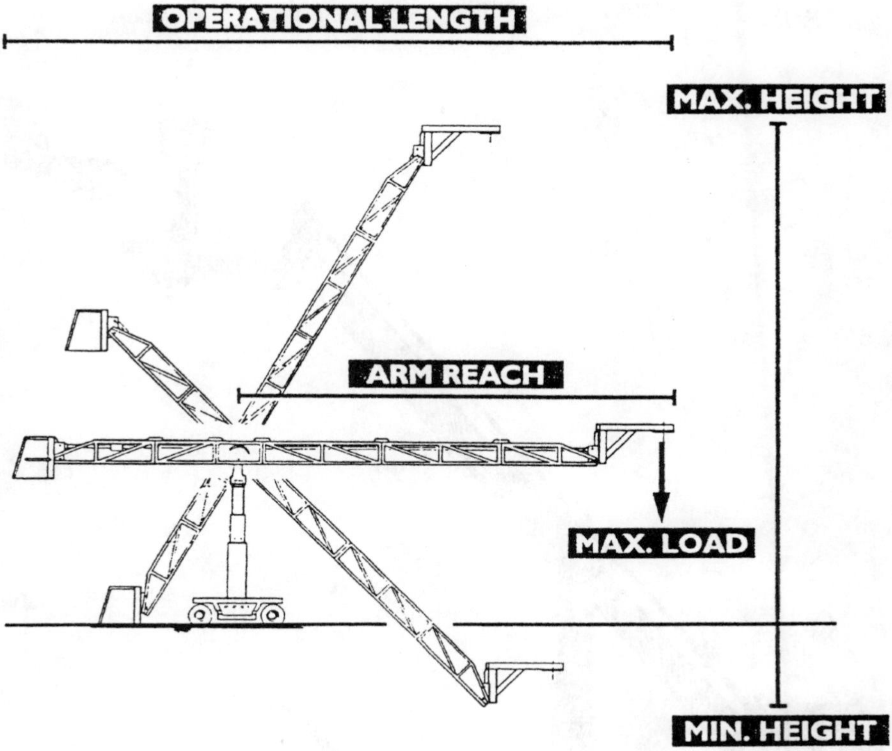

Figure 52 Egripment.

Maximum play load capacity	130 kg/286 lbs.
Weight including dolly	165 kg/343 lbs.

Technical Specifications, Version 3

Maximum platform height	367 cm/12 ft.
Lift range	442 cm/14 ft. 6 in.
Maximum play load capacity	80 kg/176 lbs.
Weight including dolly	144 kg/316 lbs.

Technical Specifications, Version 4

Maximum platform height	450 cm/14 ft. 9 in.
Lift range	600 cm/19 ft. 8 in.
Maximum play load capacity	60 kg/132 lbs.
Weight including dolly	154 kg/338 lbs.

Felix

Figure 53   Felix.

Piccolo

Specifications

Range	9 ft. 5 in. to 15 ft. 4 in.
Operational length	460 cm/15 ft. 4 in.
Arm reach	282 cm/9 ft. 5 in.
Maximum platform height	260 cm/8 ft. 8 in.
Minimum platform height	10 cm/4 in.
Maximum load	250 kg/550 lbs.

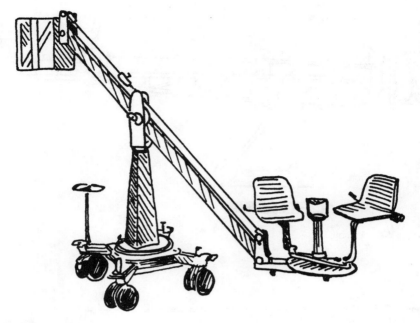

Figure 54   Felix.

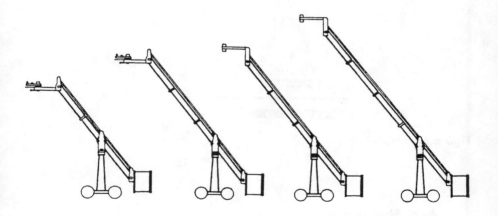

FELIX

Figure 55   Felix dolly versions 1, 2, 3, and 4.

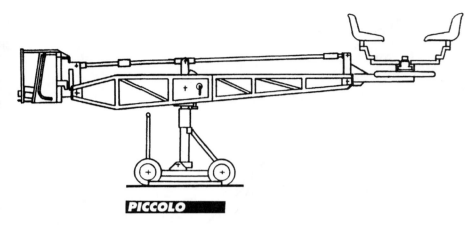

Figure 56 Piccolo.

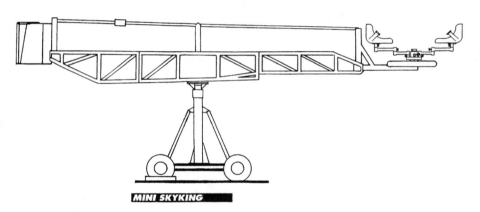

Figure 57 Mini Skyking.

Mini Skyking

Specifications

Range	11 ft. 6 in. to 22 ft. 8 in.
Operational length	680 cm/22 ft. 8 in.
Arm reach	344 cm/11 ft. 6 in.
Maximum platform height	390 cm/13 ft.
Minimum platform height	30 cm/−1 ft.
Maximum load	250 kg/550 lbs.

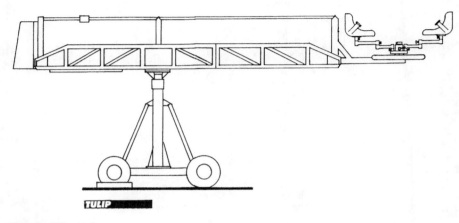

Figure 58 Tulip.

Tulip

Specifications

Range	12 ft. 1 in. to 20 ft.
Operational length	600 cm/20 ft.
Arm reach	363 cm/12 ft. 1 in.
Maximum platform height	390 cm/13 ft.
Minimum platform height	−60 cm/−2 ft.
Maximum load	250 kg/550 lbs.

T.O.T.
Always use A/C plywood or A/D plywood for dolly track.

Super Maxi-Jib

Specifications

Range	15 ft. 4 in. to 21 ft. 4 in.
Operational length	640 cm/21 ft. 4 in.
Arm reach	460 cm/15 ft. 4 in.
Maximum platform height	455 cm/15 ft. 2 in.
Minimum platform height	160 cm/−5 ft. 4 in.
Maximum load	35 kg/77 lbs.

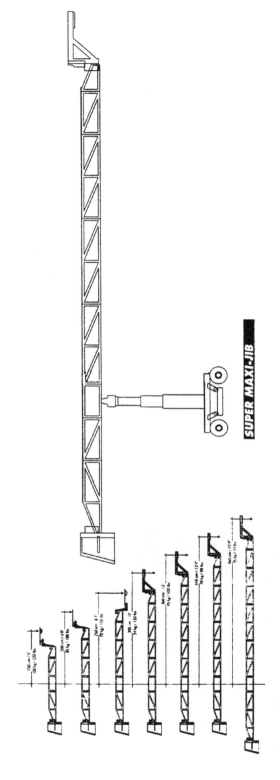

Figure 59 Super Maxi-Jib.

Piccolo and Extension

Specifications

Range	15 ft. to 20 ft. 10 in.
Operational length	625 cm/20 ft. 10 in.
Arm reach	450 cm/15 ft.
Maximum platform height	420 cm/14 ft.
Minimum platform height	−100 cm/−3 ft. 4 in.
Maximum load	65 kg/145 lbs.

Super Technocrane

Specifications

Range	to 30 ft.
Power	240 volt A/C 4,563 Hz
Power consumption	13 amps max
Maximum "all up weight"	1,150 kg/2,530 lbs.
Maximum weight of single item (boom)	250 kg/550 lbs.
Weight of individual counterweight	14 kg/31 lbs.

Remote Head

Maximum tilt	unlimited
Maximum pan	unlimited
Controls	gear head or joy stick
Control cables	25–50 m/82–164 ft.

Super Skyking/Super Skymote

Specifications

Range	27 ft. 10 in. to 34 ft. 5 in.
Operational length	1,036 cm/34 ft. 5 in.
Arm reach	834 cm/27 ft. 10 in.
Maximum platform height	860 cm/28 ft. 8 in.
Minimum platform height	350 cm/11 ft. 8 in.
Maximum load	65 kg/145 lbs.

Phoenix

Technical Specifications, Version 1

Range	9 ft. to 34 ft.
Maximum platform height	2.9 m/9 ft. 6 in.
Lift range	2.60 m/8 ft. 6 in.
Maximum play load capacity	250 kg/550 lbs.
Counterweight at maximum payload	151 kg/332 lbs.
Total weight	460 kg/1,012 lbs.

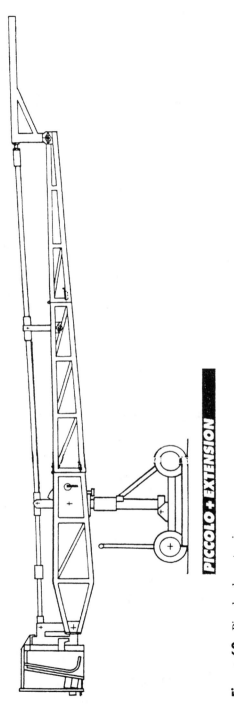

Figure 60 Piccolo plus extension.

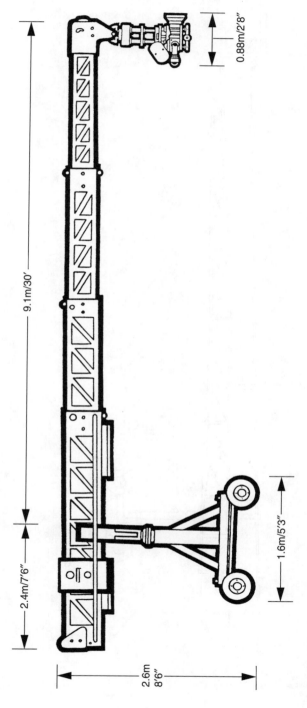

Figure 61 Super Technocrane.

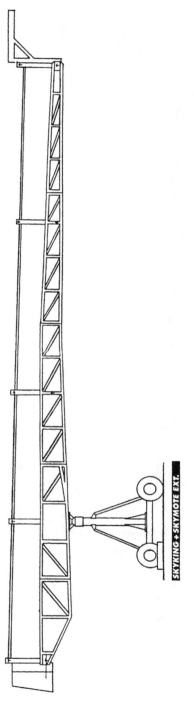

Figure 62 Skyking and Skymote extension.

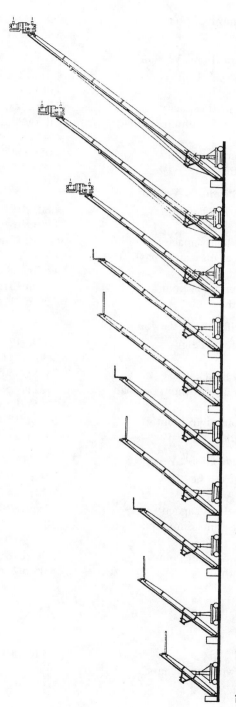

Figure 63 Phoenix.

Arm length from pivot point	2.90 m/9 ft. 6 in.
Total arm length	5.45 m/17 ft. 10 in.

Technical Specifications, Version 2

Maximum platform height	4.0 m/13 ft.
Lift range	4.90 m/16 ft.
Maximum play load capacity	250 kg/550 lbs.
Counterweight at maximum payload	410 kg/902 lbs.
Total weight	494 kg/1,086 lbs.
Arm length from pivot point	4.35 m/14 ft. 4 in.
Total arm length	6.90 m/22 ft. 8 in.

Technical Specifications, Version 3

Maximum platform height	4.80 m/16 ft.
Lift range	4.90 m/16 ft.
Maximum play load capacity	85 kg/187 lbs.
Counterweight at maximum payload	130 kg/286 lbs.
Total weight	479 kg/1,053 lbs.
Arm length from pivot point	3.95 m/13 ft.
Total arm length	6.50 m/21 ft. 5 in.

Technical Specifications, Version 4

Maximum platform height	5.15 m/17 ft.
Lift range	7.30 m/24 ft.
Maximum play load capacity	250 kg/550 lbs.
Counterweight at maximum payload	713 kg/1,568 lbs.
Total weight	526 kg/1,157 lbs.
Arm length from pivot point	5.90 m/19 ft. 5 in.
Total arm length	8.45 m/27 ft. 9 in.

Technical Specifications, Version 5

Maximum platform height	5.90 m/19 ft. 4 in.
Lift range	7.30 m/24 ft.
Maximum play load capacity	85 kg/187 lbs.
Counterweight at maximum payload	302 kg/664 lbs.
Total weight	509 kg/1,119 lbs.
Arm length from pivot point	5.50 m/18 ft. 1 in.
Total arm length	8.05 m/26 ft. 6 in.

Strada

Specifications

Range	45 to 85 ft.
85-ft. weight (with main chassis and weights)	8,000 lbs.

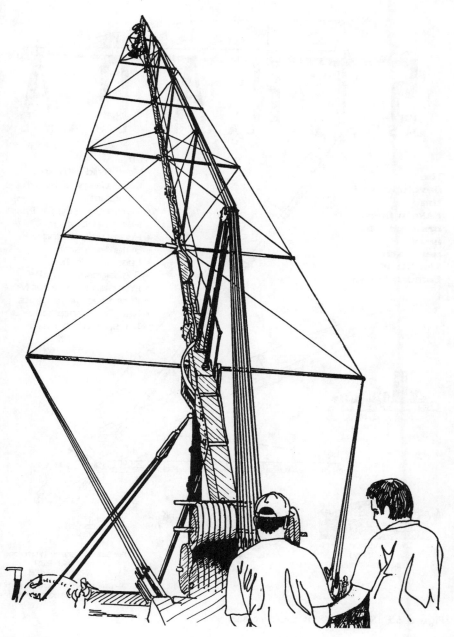

Figure 64 The Strada crane.

The Developers of the *Akela Crane bring you the next generation... the Strada Camera Crane

- More Rigid with New Cable Design & New Tube Structure
- Motorized Dolly for Easier Placement
- Hydraulic Steering
- 3 Tier Pedestal
- Less Set Up Time
- 3 Additional Lengths
- Precision Handle for More Controlled Movements
- New Self Contained Transportation Trailer

STRADA NY
(914) 773-6555
Fax (914) 747-4740

AUSTRALIA
The Grip Shop
61-2-9564-0059
Fax 61-2-9564-0083

STRADA LA
Toll Free (877) 632-8444
Fax (541) 549-4226

For Sales & Leasing Information
(541) 549-4229
Fax (541) 549-422

E-mail: info@stradacranes.com
web site: www.stradacranes.com

*Akela Trademark owned by Camera Platforms International

Figure 65 Strada 45–85 ft. camera crane.

72-ft. weight (with main chassis and weights)	7,500 lbs.
Main chassis with steering	7 ft. 6 in. by 10 ft. 6 in.
Pedestal to rear	12 ft.
Minimum operating space from pedestal placement	15 ft.
85-ft. weight (with portable chassis and weights)	6,000 lbs.
72-ft. weight (with portable chassis and weights)	5,500 lbs.
Portable chassis	7 ft. 6 in. by 8 ft. 6 in.

Reach	Lens Underslung	Overall Arm Length	Max. Nose Load
85 ft.	78 ft.	97 ft.	100 lbs.
79 ft.	73 ft.	91 ft.	125 lbs.
72 ft.	68 ft.	84 ft.	200 lbs
65 ft.	62 ft.	77 ft.	225 lbs
58 ft.	55 ft.	70 ft.	250 lbs
52 ft.	48 ft.	64 ft.	275 lbs
45 ft.	42 ft.	57 ft.	300 lbs

Jibs

Mini-Jib Liberty

Specifications

Operational length	70 cm/5 ft. 8 in.
Arm reach	100 cm/3 ft. 14 in.
Maximum platform height	175 cm/5 ft. 10 in.
Minimum platform height	25 cm/10 ft.
Maximum load	45 kg/99 lbs.

Mini-Jib Classic

Specifications

Operational length	5 ft. 8 in.
Arm reach	3 ft. 14 in.
Maximum platform height	75 cm/5 ft. 10 in.
Minimun platform height	5 cm/10 in.
Maximum load	5 kg/99 lbs.

Mini-Jib Long

Specifications

Operational length	260 cm/8 ft. 8 in.
Arm reach	165 cm/5 ft. 6 in.

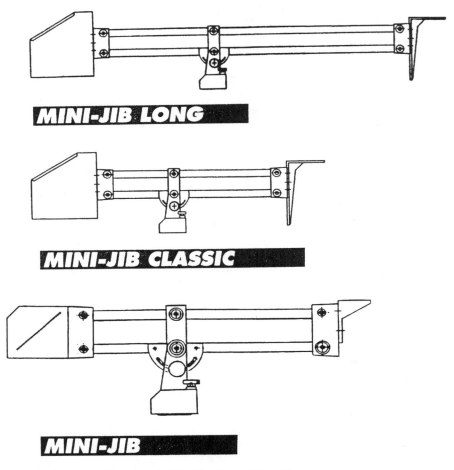

Figure 66 Mini-Jib long, Mini-Jib Classic, and Mini-Jib.

Maximum platform height   210 cm/7 ft.
Minimum platform height   0 cm/0 in.
Maximum load   45 kgs/99 lbs.

Euro-Jib

Specifications
Lens height   About 4 ft.
Lens lowest   1 ft. 6 in.
Horizontal reach   77 lbs.

Figure 67   Euro-Jib.

Jib capacity	(max camera and head combined weight)
Dollies used on EuroJib Base (recommended)	All
Jibs attaching base (to dolly or crane)	Supplied
Jibs receiving base	Euro-Ball
Heads usable on jibs	Fluid
Cameras used on Jib	Most

Call manufacturer of jib if camera weight is in question.

Weight of jib (empty)	35 lbs.
Transportation of jib	Trunk or van

T.O.T.

Feel of each dolly:

- Turn knob a few times to get the feel of the hydraulics of each dollies lifting beam (arm).

EZ FX Jib

*It is advised that the user of Chapman/Leonard equipment check with the manufacturer for the latest updates on *all* equipment.

Figure 68 EZ FX Jib.

J.F.C. CROSSARMS

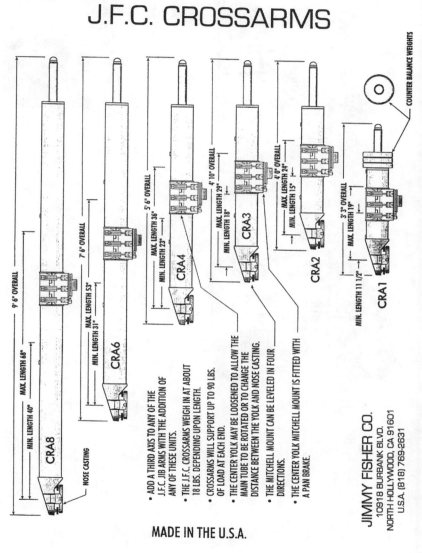

JF Crossarm

- ADD A THIRD AXIS TO ANY OF THE J.F.C. JIB ARMS WITH THE ADDITION OF ANY OF THESE UNITS.
- THE J.F.C. CROSSARMS WEIGH IN AT ABOUT 18 LBS. DEPENDING UPON LENGTH.
- CROSSARMS WILL SUPPORT UP TO 90 LBS. OF LOAD AT EACH END.
- THE CENTER YOLK MAY BE LOOSENED TO ALLOW THE MAIN TUBE TO BE ROTATED OR TO CHANGE THE DISTANCE BETWEEN THE YOLK AND NOSE CASTING.
- THE MITCHELL MOUNT CAN BE LEVELED IN FOUR DIRECTIONS.
- THE CENTER YOLK MITCHELL MOUNT IS FITTED WITH A PAN BRAKE.

MADE IN THE U.S.A.

JIMMY FISHER CO.
1091B BURBANK BLVD.
NORTH HOLLYWOOD, CA 91601
U.S.A. (818) 769-2631

Figure 69 JF Crossarm.

COUNTER BALANCE WEIGHTS

CRA8 — 9' 6" OVERALL, MAX. LENGTH 68", MIN. LENGTH 40"

CRA6 — 7' 6" OVERALL, MAX. LENGTH 53", MIN. LENGTH 31"

CRA4 — 5' 6" OVERALL, MAX. LENGTH 36", MIN. LENGTH 23"

CRA3 — 4' 10" OVERALL, MAX. LENGTH 29", MIN. LENGTH 18"

CRA2 — 4' 0" OVERALL, MAX. LENGTH 24", MIN. LENGTH 15"

CRA1 — 3' 3" OVERALL, MAX. LENGTH 19", MIN. LENGTH 11 1/2"

NOSE CASTING

Figure 70   JF Crossarm.

Lenny Mini

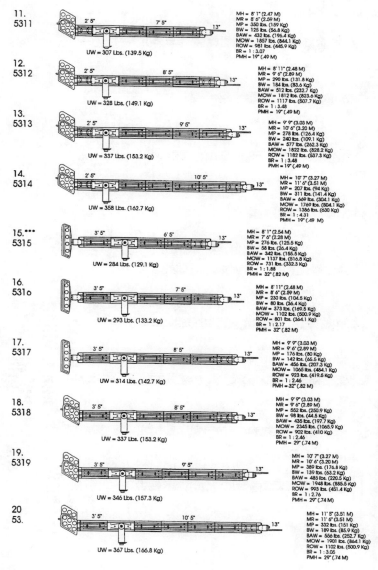

Figure 71 Lenny Mini.

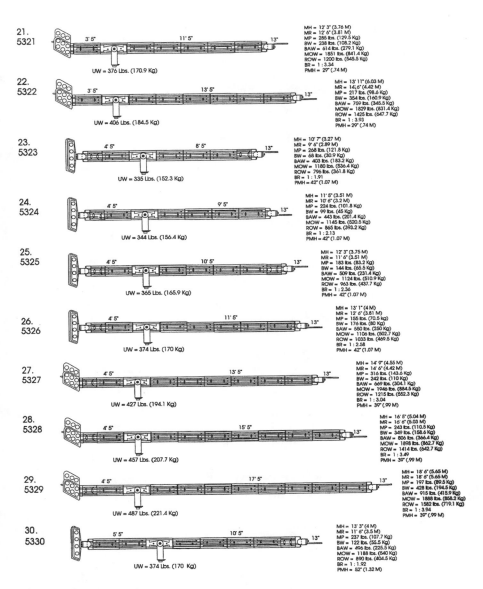

21.
5321

UW = 376 Lbs. (170.9 Kg)

MH = 12' 3" (3.76 M)
MR = 12' 6" (3.81 M)
MP = 285 lbs. (129.5 Kg)
BW = 238 lbs. (108.2 Kg)
BAW = 614 lbs. (279.1 Kg)
MOW = 1851 lbs. (841.4 Kg)
ROW = 1200 lbs. (545.5 Kg)
BR = 1 : 3.34
PMH = 29" (.74 M)

22.
5322

UW = 406 Lbs. (184.5 Kg)

MH = 13' 11" (6.03 M)
MR = 14;6" (4.42 M)
MP = 217 lbs. (98.6 Kg)
BW = 354 lbs. (160.9 Kg)
BAW = 759 lbs. (345.5 Kg)
MOW = 1829 lbs. (831.4 Kg)
ROW = 1425 lbs. (647.7 Kg)
BR = 1 : 3.93
PMH = 29" (.74 M)

23.
5323

UW = 335 Lbs. (152.3 Kg)

MH = 10' 7" (3.27 M)
MR = 9' 6" (2.89 M)
MP = 268 lbs. (121.8 Kg)
BW = 68 lbs. (30.9 Kg)
BAW = 403 lbs. (183.2 Kg)
MOW = 1180 lbs. (536.4 Kg)
ROW = 796 lbs. (361.8 Kg)
BR = 1 : 1.91
PMH = 42" (1.07 M)

24.
5324

UW = 344 Lbs. (156.4 Kg)

MH = 11' 5" (3.51 M)
MR = 10' 6" (3.2 M)
MP = 224 lbs. (101.8 Kg)
BW = 99 lbs. (45 Kg)
BAW = 443 lbs. (201.4 Kg)
MOW = 1145 lbs. (520.5 Kg)
ROW = 865 lbs. (393.2 Kg)
BR = 1 : 2.13
PMH = 42" (1.07 M)

25.
5325

UW = 365 Lbs. (165.9 Kg)

MH = 12' 3" (3.75 M)
MR = 11' 6" (3.51 M)
MP = 183 lbs. (83.2 Kg)
BW = 144 lbs. (65.5 Kg)
BAW = 509 lbs. (231.4 Kg)
MOW = 1124 lbs. (510.9 Kg)
ROW = 963 lbs. (437.7 Kg)
BR = 1 : 2.36
PMH = 42" (1.07 M)

26.
5326

UW = 374 Lbs. (170 Kg)

MH = 13' 1" (4 M)
MR = 12' 6" (3.81 M)
MP = 155 lbs. (70.5 Kg)
BW = 176 lbs. (80 Kg)
BAW = 550 lbs. (250 Kg)
MOW = 1106 lbs. (502.7 Kg)
ROW = 1033 lbs. (469.5 Kg)
BR = 1 : 2.58
PMH = 42" (1.07 M)

27.
5327

UW = 427 Lbs. (194.1 Kg)

MH = 14' 9" (4.55 M)
MR = 14' 6" (4.42 M)
MP = 316 lbs. (143.6 Kg)
BW = 242 lbs. (110 Kg)
BAW = 669 lbs. (304.1 Kg)
MOW = 1946 lbs. (884.5 Kg)
ROW = 1215 lbs. (552.3 Kg)
BR = 1 : 3.04
PMH = 39" (.99 M)

28.
5328

UW = 457 Lbs. (207.7 Kg)

MH = 16' 5" (5.04 M)
MR = 16' 6" (5.03 M)
MP = 243 lbs. (110.5 Kg)
BW = 349 lbs. (158.6 Kg)
BAW = 806 lbs. (366.4 Kg)
MOW = 1898 lbs. (862.7 Kg)
ROW = 1414 lbs. (642.7 Kg)
BR = 1 : 3.49
PMH = 39" (.99 M)

29.
5329

UW = 487 Lbs. (221.4 Kg)

MH = 18' 6" (5.65 M)
MR = 18' 6" (5.65 M)
MP = 197 lbs. (89.5 Kg)
BW = 428 lbs. (194.5 Kg)
BAW = 915 lbs. (415.9 Kg)
MOW = 1888 lbs. (858.2 Kg)
ROW = 1582 lbs. (719.1 Kg)
BR = 1 : 3.94
PMH = 39" (.99 M)

30.
5330

UW = 374 Lbs. (170 Kg)

MH = 13' 3" (4 M)
MR = 11' 6" (3.5 M)
MP = 237 lbs. (107.7 Kg)
BW = 122 lbs. (55.5 Kg)
BAW = 496 lbs. (225.5 Kg)
MOW = 1188 lbs. (540 Kg)
ROW = 890 lbs. (404.5 Kg)
BR = 1 : 1.92
PMH = 52" (1.32 M)

Figure 71 *continued*

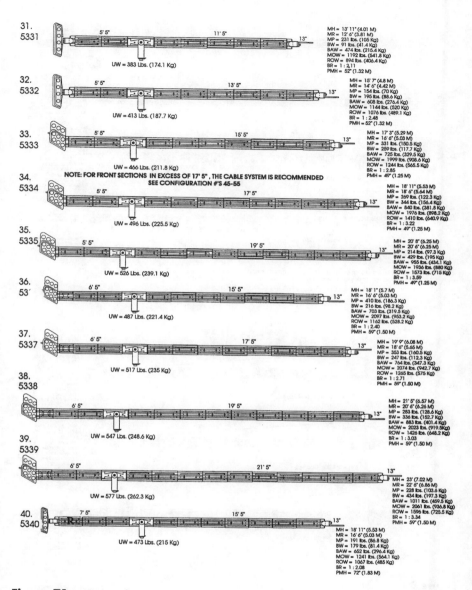

31.
5331

5' 5" 11' 5" 13"

UW = 383 Lbs. (174.1 Kg)

MH = 13' 11" (4.01 M)
MR = 12' 6" (3.81 M)
MP = 231 lbs. (105 Kg)
BW = 91 lbs. (41.4 Kg)
BAW = 474 lbs. (215.4 Kg)
MOW = 1192 lbs. (541.8 Kg)
ROW = 894 lbs. (406.4 Kg)
BR = 1 : 2.11
PMH = 52" (1.32 M)

32.
5332

5' 5" 13' 5" 13"

UW = 413 Lbs. (187.7 Kg)

MH = 15' 7" (4.8 M)
MR = 14' 6" (4.42 M)
MP = 154 lbs. (70 Kg)
BW = 195 lbs. (88.6 Kg)
BAW = 608 lbs. (276.4 Kg)
MOW = 1144 lbs. (520 Kg)
ROW = 1076 lbs. (489.1 Kg)
BR = 1 : 2.48
PMH = 52" (1.32 M)

33.
5333

5' 5" 15' 5" 13"

UW = 466 Lbs. (211.8 Kg)

MH = 17' 3" (5.29 M)
MR = 16' 6" (5.03 M)
MP = 331 lbs. (150.5 Kg)
BW = 259 lbs. (117.7 Kg)
BAW = 725 lbs. (329.5 Kg)
MOW = 1999 lbs. (908.6 Kg)
ROW = 1244 lbs. (565.5 Kg)
BR = 1 : 2.85
PMH = 49" (1.25 M)

34.
5334

NOTE: FOR FRONT SECTIONS IN EXCESS OF 17' 5", THE CABLE SYSTEM IS RECOMMENDED
SEE CONFIGURATION #'S 45-55

5' 5" 17' 5" 13"

UW = 496 Lbs. (225.5 Kg)

MH = 18' 11" (5.53 M)
MR = 18' 6" (5.64 M)
MP = 269 lbs. (122.3 Kg)
BW = 344 lbs. (156.4 Kg)
BAW = 840 lbs. (381.8 Kg)
MOW = 1976 lbs. (898.2 Kg)
ROW = 1410 lbs. (640.9 Kg)
BR = 1 : 3.22
PMH = 49" (1.25 M)

35.
5335

5' 5" 19' 5" 13"

UW = 526 Lbs. (239.1 Kg)

MH = 20' 8" (6.25 M)
MR = 20' 6" (6.25 M)
MP = 214 lbs. (97.3 Kg)
BW = 429 lbs. (195 Kg)
BAW = 955 lbs. (434.1 Kg)
MOW = 1936 lbs. (880 Kg)
ROW = 1573 lbs. (715 Kg)
BR = 1 : 3.59
PMH = 49" (1.25 M)

36.
53'

6' 5" 15' 5" 13"

UW = 487 Lbs. (221.4 Kg)

MH = 18' 1" (5.7 M)
MR = 16' 6" (5.03 M)
MP = 410 lbs. (186.3 Kg)
BW = 216 lbs. (98.2 Kg)
BAW = 703 lbs. (319.5 Kg)
MOW = 2097 lbs. (953.2 Kg)
ROW = 1162 lbs. (528.2 Kg)
BR = 1 : 2.40
PMH = 59" (1.50 M)

37.
5337

6' 5" 17' 5" 13"

UW = 517 Lbs. (235 Kg)

MH = 19' 9" (6.08 M)
MR = 18' 6" (5.65 M)
MP = 353 lbs. (160.5 Kg)
BW = 247 lbs. (112.3 Kg)
BAW = 764 lbs. (347.3 Kg)
MOW = 2074 lbs. (942.7 Kg)
ROW = 1265 lbs. (575 Kg)
BR = 1 : 2.71
PMH = 59" (1.50 M)

38.
5338

6' 5" 19' 5" 13"

UW = 547 Lbs. (248.6 Kg)

MH = 21' 5" (6.57 M)
MR = 20' 6" (6.26 M)
MP = 283 lbs. (128.6 Kg)
BW = 336 lbs. (152.7 Kg)
BAW = 883 lbs. (401.4 Kg)
MOW = 2023 lbs. (919.9 Kg)
ROW = 1426 lbs. (648.2 Kg)
BR = 1 : 3.03
PMH = 59" (1.50 M)

39.
5339

6' 5" 21' 5" 13"

UW = 577 Lbs. (262.3 Kg)

MH = 23' (7.02 M)
MR = 22' 6" (6.86 M)
MP = 228 lbs. (103.6 Kg)
BW = 434 lbs. (197.3 Kg)
BAW = 1011 lbs. (459.5 Kg)
MOW = 2061 lbs. (936.8 Kg)
ROW = 1596 lbs. (725.5 Kg)
BR = 1 : 3.34
PMH = 59" (1.50 M)

40.
5340

7' 5" 15' 5" 13"

UW = 473 Lbs. (215 Kg)

MH = 18' 11" (5.53 M)
MR = 16' 6" (5.03 M)
MP = 191 lbs. (86.8 Kg)
BW = 179 lbs. (81.4 Kg)
BAW = 652 lbs. (296.4 Kg)
MOW = 1241 lbs. (564.1 Kg)
ROW = 1067 lbs. (485 Kg)
BR = 1 : 2.08
PMH = 72" (1.83 M)

Figure 71 *continued*

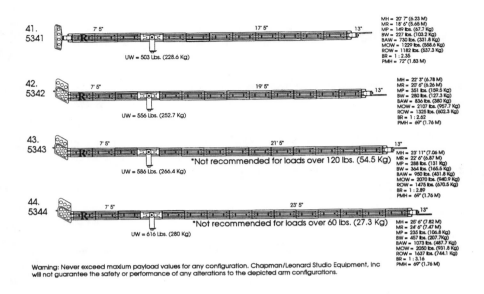

41.
5341

7' 5"   17' 5"   13"

UW = 503 Lbs. (228.6 Kg)

MH = 20' 7" (6.23 M)
MR = 18' 6" (5.65 M)
MP = 149 lbs. (67.7 Kg)
BW = 227 lbs. (103.2 Kg)
BAW = 730 lbs. (331.8 Kg)
MOW = 1229 lbs. (558.6 Kg)
ROW = 1182 lbs. (537.3 Kg)
BR = 1 : 2.35
PMH = 72" (1.83 M)

42.
5342

7' 5"   19' 5"   13"

UW = 556 Lbs. (252.7 Kg)

MH = 22' 3" (6.78 M)
MR = 20' 6" (6.26 M)
MP = 351 lbs. (159.5 Kg)
BW = 280 lbs. (127.3 Kg)
BAW = 836 lbs. (380 Kg)
MOW = 2107 lbs. (957.7 Kg)
ROW = 1325 lbs. (602.3 Kg)
BR = 1 : 2.62
PMH = 69" (1.76 M)

43.
5343

7' 5"   21' 5"   13"

*Not recommended for loads over 120 lbs. (54.5 Kg)

UW = 586 Lbs. (266.4 Kg)

MH = 23' 11" (7.06 M)
MR = 22' 6" (6.87 M)
MP = 288 lbs. (131 Kg)
BW = 364 lbs. (165.5 Kg)
BAW = 950 lbs. (431.8 Kg)
MOW = 2070 lbs. (940.9 Kg)
ROW = 1475 lbs. (670.5 Kg)
BR = 1 : 2.89
PMH = 69" (1.76 M)

44.
5344

7' 5"   23' 5"   13"

*Not recommended for loads over 60 lbs. (27.3 Kg)

UW = 616 Lbs. (280 Kg)

MH = 25' 6" (7.82 M)
MR = 24' 6" (7.47 M)
MP = 235 lbs. (106.8 Kg)
BW = 457 lbs. (207.7Kg)
BAW = 1073 lbs. (487.7 Kg)
MOW = 2050 lbs. (931.8 Kg)
ROW = 1637 lbs. (744.1 Kg)
BR = 1 : 3.16
PMH = 69" (1.76 M)

Warning: Never exceed maxium payload values for any configuration. Chapman/Leonard Studio Equipment, Inc
will not guarantee the safety or performance of any alterations to the depicted arm configurations.

CABLE SYSTEM

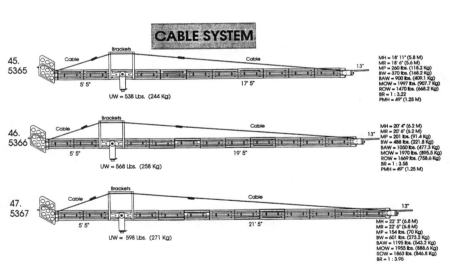

45.
5365

Cable   Brackets   Cable   13"

5' 5"   17' 5"

UW = 538 Lbs. (244 Kg)

MH = 18' 11" (5.8 M)
MR = 18' 6" (5.6 M)
MP = 260 lbs. (118.2 Kg)
BW = 370 lbs. (168.2 Kg)
BAW = 900 lbs. (409.1 Kg)
MOW = 1997 lbs. (907.7 Kg)
ROW = 1470 lbs. (668.2 Kg)
BR = 1 : 3.22
PMH = 49" (1.25 M)

46.
5366

Cable   Brackets   Cable   13"

5' 5"   19' 5"

UW = 568 Lbs. (258 Kg)

MH = 20' 4" (6.2 M)
MR = 20' 6" (6.2 M)
MP = 201 lbs. (91.4 Kg)
BW = 488 lbs. (221.8 Kg)
BAW = 1050 lbs. (477.3 Kg)
MOW = 1970 lbs. (895.5 Kg)
ROW = 1669 lbs. (758.6 Kg)
BR = 1 : 3.58
PMH = 49" (1.25 M)

47.
5367

Cable   Brackets   Cable   13"

5' 5"   21' 5"

UW = 598 Lbs. (271 Kg)

MH = 22' 3" (6.8 M)
MR = 22' 6" (6.8 M)
MP = 154 lbs. (70 Kg)
BW = 601 lbs. (273.2 Kg)
BAW = 1195 lbs. (543.2 Kg)
MOW = 1955 lbs. (888.6 Kg)
ROW = 1863 lbs. (846.8 Kg)
BR = 1 : 3.95

Figure 71 *continued*

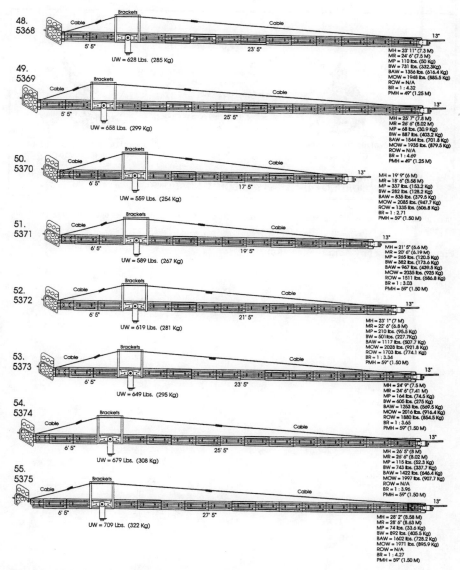

48.
5368

UW = 628 Lbs. (285 Kg)

MH = 23' 11" (7.3 M)
MR = 24' 6" (7.5 M)
MP = 110 lbs. (50 Kg)
BW = 731 lbs. (332.3Kg)
BAW = 1356 lbs. (616.4 Kg)
MOW = 1948 lbs. (885.5 Kg)
ROW = N/A
BR = 1 : 4.32
PMH = 49" (1.25 M)

49.
5369

UW = 658 Lbs. (299 Kg)

MH = 25' 7" (7.8 M)
MR = 26' 6" (8.02 M)
MP = 68 lbs. (30.9 Kg)
BW = 887 lbs. (403.2 Kg)
BAW = 1544 lbs. (701.8 Kg)
MOW = 1935 lbs. (879.5 Kg)
ROW = N/A
BR = 1 : 4.69
PMH = 49" (1.25 M)

50.
5370

UW = 559 Lbs. (254 Kg)

MH = 19' 9" (6 M)
MR = 18' 6" (5.58 M)
MP = 337 lbs. (153.2 Kg)
BW = 282 lbs. (128.2 Kg)
BAW = 836 lbs. (379.5 Kg)
MOW = 2085 lbs. (947.7 Kg)
ROW = 1335 lbs. (606.8 Kg)
BR = 1 : 2.71
PMH = 59" (1.50 M)

51.
5371

UW = 589 Lbs. (267 Kg)

MH = 21' 5" (6.6 M)
MR = 20' 6" (6.19 M)
MP = 265 lbs. (120.5 Kg)
BW = 382 lbs. (173.6 Kg)
BAW = 967 lbs. (439.5 Kg)
MOW = 2035 lbs. (925 Kg)
ROW = 1511 lbs. (686.8 Kg)
BR = 1 : 3.03
PMH = 59" (1.50 M)

52.
5372

UW = 619 Lbs. (281 Kg)

MH = 23' 1" (7 M)
MR = 22' 6" (6.8 M)
MP = 210 lbs. (95.5 Kg)
BW = 501lbs. (227.7Kg)
BAW = 1117 lbs. (507.7 Kg)
MOW = 2028 lbs. (921.8 Kg)
ROW = 1703 lbs. (774.1 Kg)
BR = 1 : 3.34
PMH = 59" (1.50 M)

53.
5373

UW = 649 Lbs. (295 Kg)

MH = 24' 9" (7.5 M)
MR = 24' 6" (7.41 M)
MP = 164 lbs. (74.5 Kg)
BW = 605 lbs. (275 Kg)
BAW = 1253 lbs. (569.5 Kg)
MOW = 2016 lbs. (916.4 Kg)
ROW = 1880 lbs. (854.5 Kg)
BR = 1 : 3.65
PMH = 59" (1.50 M)

54.
5374

UW = 679 Lbs. (308 Kg)

MH = 26' 5" (8 M)
MR = 26' 6" (8.02 M)
MP = 115 lbs. (52.3 Kg)
BW = 743 lbs. (337.7 Kg)
BAW = 1422 lbs. (646.4 Kg)
MOW = 1997 lbs. (907.7 Kg)
ROW = N/A
BR = 1 : 3.96
PMH = 59" (1.50 M)

55.
5375

UW = 709 Lbs. (322 Kg)

MH = 28' 2" (8.58 M)
MR = 28' 5" (8.63 M)
MP = 74 lbs. (33.6 Kg)
BW = 892 lbs. (405.5 Kg)
BAW = 1602 lbs. (728.2 Kg)
MOW = 1971 lbs. (895.9 Kg)
ROW = N/A
BR = 1 : 4.27
PMH = 59" (1.50 M)

*It is advised that the user of Chapman/Leonard equipment check with the manufacturer for the latest updates on *all* equipment.

Figure 71 *continued*

KEEP THE CRANE ARM BALANCED AT ALL TIMES. AVOID SUDDEN DISEMBARKING OF PERSONNEL OR REMOVING OF EQUIPMENT

The Lenny Arm rear section combination should be configurated so that the bucket touches the ground before the Lenny Arm vertical travel limits are obtained.

Bucket reaches ground
(RECOMMENDED)

Bucket does not reach ground
(NOT RECOMMENDED)

WARNING: DO NOT EXCEED THE LISTED POST MOUNT HEIGHTS (PMH) VALUES TO AVOID INVALIDATING OUR SAFETY RECOMMENDATIONS.

*It is advised that the user of Chapman/Leonard equipment check with the manufacturer for the latest updates on *all* equipment.

Figure 72 Lenny Arm rear section.

LENNY MINI IS FOR REMOTE USE ONLY
The Lenny Mini can be mounted on these Chapman/Leonard products:

Super Peewee®
(With High Post Kit)
MAXIMUM PAYLOAD =
1,100 Lbs. (500 Kg)
Operating Weight of unit =
386 Lbs. (175 Kg)
Min. Carrying Wt. of unit =
280 Lbs. (127 Kg)

Hybrid
(With High Post Kit)
MAXIMUM PAYLOAD =
1900 Lbs. (863 Kg)
Operating Weight of unit =
501 Lbs. (227 Kg)
Min. Carrying Wt. of unit =
396 Lbs. (180 Kg)

Hy Hy®
(With 7.5" riser)
MAXIMUM PAYLOAD =
2900 Lbs. (1318 Kg)
Operating Weight of unit =
325 Lbs. (148 Kg)
Minimum Carrying Weight
of unit = 260 Lbs. (118 Kg)

Olympian
MAXIMUM PAYLOAD =
1700 Lbs. (795 Kg)
Weight of unit =
1790 Lbs. (813 Kg)

Pedolly®
Chassis
(with Center Post Insert)
MAXIMUM PAYLOAD =
1,100 Lbs. (500 Kg)
Weight of unit =
248 Lbs. (112 Kg)
Minimum carrying weight:.
179 Lbs. (81.4 Kg)

ATB Base
(7.5" riser optional)
MAXIMUM PAYLOAD =
5,500 Lbs. (2,500 Kg)
Weight of unit =
2339 Lbs. (1,063 Kg)

CS Base
(With 7.5" riser)
MAXIMUM PAYLOAD =
5,500 Lbs. (2,500 Kg)
Operating Weight of unit =
771 Lbs. (350 Kg)
Min. Carrying Wt. of unit =
302 Lbs. (137 Kg)

Camera Car Mount
(7.5" riser optional)
MAXIMUM PAYLOAD =
3300 Lbs. (1519 Kg)
Weight of unit =
515 Lbs. (237 Kg)

For Apollo
22' 8"
(6.9 M)

For Super Nova
30' 8"
(9.3 M)

Mobile Crane
For SUPER NOVA/APOLLO With Platform and 2 Ft. riser: MAXIMUM
PAYLOAD = 2,700 Lbs. (1,227 Kg).Platform at 1/2 circle weighs 285
Lbs. (131 Kg). Platform at full circle weighs 412 Lbs. (189 Kg). These
weights, depending on application, are deducted from Maximum
Payload. Subtract 8 Ft. (2.4 M) for Apollo height.

The maximum height for the LENNY MINI is calculated by using the bearings at both ends of the arm as points of reference. Assuming that the arm is at its maximum angle of elevation (56°) and that the arm touches the ground, the maximum height is calculated by multiplying the arm length by sin56° (.829). The forward bearing height is approximately the same as the camera lens height when the camera is underslung. Additional height can be achieved by the use of risers or by overslinging.

The maximum payloads and operational weights for the LENNY MINI have been calculated using a CAMERA PLATE (7 Lbs.) and NOSE SEGMENT (18 Lbs.). Please consider these facts while deciding which configuration is to be chosen for a given task.

To calculate specific operational weight for any given configuration, please use the following formula:

Specific Operational Weight	=	BAW (Balanced arm weight, no payload.)	+	payload (camera weight, risers, etc.)	+	payload x balance ratio (Weight in bucket required to balance the given payload.)

SPECIFIC OPERATIONAL HEIGHT ON ELEVATED PLATFORMS =

PLATFORM MOUNT HEIGHT (Ground to mount)	+	FORWARD LENGTH OF ARM x .829 (Center post to fwd. bearing)	+	1.1 Ft. (.35 M) (Center post bearing to mount)

Actual Height (H) = MH - (PMH x BR - Actual Mount Height x BR)

Chapman/Leonard Studio Equipment, Inc.

WEST COAST:
12950 RAYMER STREET
N HOLLYWOOD, CA. 91605
(888) 88 DOLLY or (888) 883-6559
FAX: (888) 50 CRANE or(888) 502-7623

TIME SAVING CAMERA CRANES, DOLLIES, REMOTE ARMS, BASES & PEDESTALS

EAST COAST:
9460 DELEGATES DRIVE
ORLANDO, FL. 32837
(888) 33 STAGE or (888) 337-8243
FAX: (407) 855-1653

*It is advised that the user of Chapman/Leonard equipment check with the manufacturer for the latest updates on *all* equipment.

Figure 73 Lenny Mini.

Lenny Arm Plus

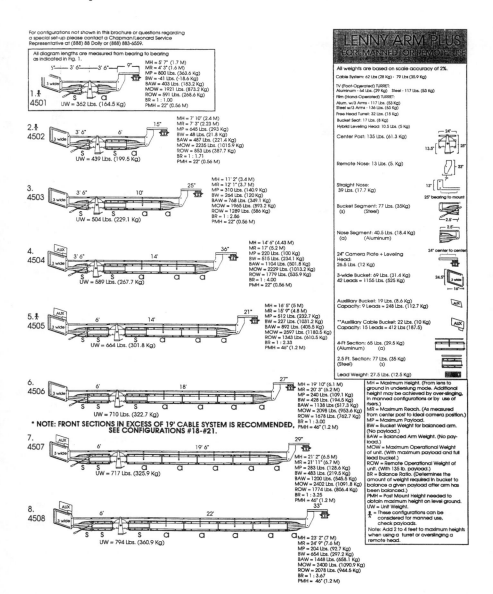

For configurations not shown in this brochure or questions regarding a special set-up please contact a Chapman/Leonard Service Representative at (888) 88 Dolly or (888) 883-6559.

All diagram lengths are measured from bearing to bearing as indicated in Fig. 1.

1.
4501
MH = 5' 7" (1.7 M)
MR = 4' 3" (1.6 M)
MP = 800 Lbs. (363.6 Kg)
BW = -41 Lbs. (-18.6 Kg)
BAW = 403 Lbs. (183.2 Kg)
MOW = 1921 Lbs. (873.2 Kg)
ROW = 591 Lbs. (268.6 Kg)
BR = 1 : 1.00
PMH = 22" (0.56 M)
UW = 362 Lbs. (164.5 Kg)

2.
4502
MH = 7' 10" (2.4 M)
MR = 7' 3" (2.23 M)
MP = 645 Lbs. (293 Kg)
BW = 48 Lbs. (21.8 Kg)
BAW = 487 Lbs. (221.4 Kg)
MOW = 2235 Lbs. (1015.9 Kg)
ROW = 853 Lbs. (387.7 Kg)
BR = 1 : 1.71
PMH = 22" (0.56 M)
UW = 439 Lbs. (199.5 Kg)

3.
4503
MH = 11' 2" (3.4 M)
MR = 12' 1" (3.7 M)
MP = 310 Lbs. (140.9 Kg)
BW = 264 Lbs. (120 Kg)
BAW = 768 Lbs. (349.1 Kg)
MOW = 1965 Lbs. (893.2 Kg)
ROW = 1289 Lbs. (586 Kg)
BR = 1 : 2.86
PMH = 22" (0.56 M)
UW = 504 Lbs. (229.1 Kg)

4.
4504
MH = 14' 6" (4.43 M)
MR = 17' (5.2 M)
MP = 220 Lbs. (100 Kg)
BW = 515 Lbs. (234.1 Kg)
BAW = 1104 Lbs. (501.8 Kg)
MOW = 2229 Lbs. (1013.2 Kg)
ROW = 1779 Lbs. (535.9 Kg)
BR = 1 : 4.00
PMH = 22" (0.56 M)
UW = 589 Lbs. (267.7 Kg)

5.
4505
MH = 16' 5" (5 M)
MR = 15' 9" (4.8 M)
MP = 512 Lbs. (232.7 Kg)
BW = 227 Lbs. (1031.2 Kg)
BAW = 892 Lbs. (405.5 Kg)
MOW = 2597 Lbs. (1180.5 Kg)
ROW = 1343 Lbs. (610.5 Kg)
BR = 1 : 2.33
PMH = 46" (1.2 M)
UW = 664 Lbs. (301.8 Kg)

6.
4506
MH = 19' 10" (6.1 M)
MR = 20' (6.2 M)
MP = 240 Lbs. (109.1 Kg)
BW = 428 Lbs. (194.5 Kg)
BAW = 1138 Lbs. (517.3 Kg)
MOW = 2098 Lbs. (953.6 Kg)
ROW = 1678 Lbs. (762.7 Kg)
BR = 1 : 3.00
PMH = 46" (1.2 M)
UW = 710 Lbs. (322.7 Kg)

* NOTE: FRONT SECTIONS IN EXCESS OF 19' CABLE SYSTEM IS RECOMMENDED, SEE CONFIGURATIONS #18-#21.

7.
4507
MH = 21' 2" (6.5 M)
MR = 21' 11" (6.7 M)
MP = 283 Lbs. (128.6 Kg)
BW = 483 Lbs. (219.5 Kg)
BAW = 1200 Lbs. (545.5 Kg)
MOW = 2402 Lbs. (1091.8 Kg)
ROW = 1774 Lbs. (806.4 Kg)
BR = 1 : 3.25
PMH = 46" (1.2 M)
UW = 717 Lbs. (325.9 Kg)

8.
4508
MH = 23' 2" (7 M)
MR = 24' 9" (7.6 M)
MP = 204 Lbs. (92.7 Kg)
BW = 654 Lbs. (297.2 Kg)
BAW = 1448 Lbs. (658.1 Kg)
MOW = 2400 Lbs. (1090.9 Kg)
ROW = 2078 Lbs. (944.5 Kg)
BR = 1 : 3.67
PMH = 46" (1.2 M)
UW = 794 Lbs. (360.9 Kg)

LENNY ARM PLUS
FOR MANNED OR REMOTE USE

All weights are based on scale accuracy of 2%.

Cable System: 62 Lbs (28 Kg) - 79 Lbs (35.9 Kg)

TV (Foot-Operated) TURRET:
Aluminum - 64 Lbs. (29 Kg) Steel - 117 Lbs. (53 Kg)

Film (Hand-Operated) TURRET:
Alum. w/3 Arms - 117 Lbs. (53 Kg)
Steel w/3 Arms - 136 Lbs. (53 Kg)

Free Head Turret: 32 Lbs. (15 Kg)
Bucket Seat: 17 Lbs. (8 Kg)
Hybrid Leveling Head: 10.5 Lbs. (5 Kg)

Center Post: 135 Lbs. (61.3 Kg)

Remote Nose: 13 Lbs. (5. Kg)

Straight Nose:
39 Lbs. (17.7 Kg)

Bucket Segment: 77 Lbs. (35Kg)
(s)   (Steel)

Nose Segment: 40.5 Lbs. (18.4 Kg)
(a)   (Aluminum)

24" Camera Plate + Leveling Head:
26.5 Lbs. (12 Kg)

3-wide Bucket: 69 Lbs. (31.4 Kg)
42 Leads = 1155 Lbs. (525 Kg)

Auxiliary Bucket: 19 Lbs. (8.6 Kg)
Capacity: 9 Leads = 248 Lbs. (112.7 Kg)

**Auxiliary Cable Bucket: 22 Lbs. (10 Kg)
Capacity: 15 Leads = 412 Lbs (187.5)

4-Ft Section: 65 Lbs. (29.5 Kg)
(Aluminum)   (a)

2.5 Ft. Section: 77 Lbs. (35 Kg)
(Steel)   (s)

Lead Weight: 27.5 Lbs (12.5 Kg)

MH = Maximum Height. (From lens to ground in undersling mode. Additional height may be achieved by over-slinging in manned configurations or by use of risers.)
MR = Maximum Reach. (As measured from center post to ideal camera position.)
MP = Maximum Payload.
BW = Bucket Weight for balanced arm. (No payload.)
BAW = Balanced Arm Weight. (No payload.)
MOW = Maximum Operational Weight of unit. (With maximum payload and full lead bucket.)
ROW = Remote Operational Weight of unit. (With 135 lb. payload.)
BR = Balance Ratio. (Determines the amount of weight required in bucket to balance a given payload after arm has been balanced.)
PMH = Post Mount Height needed to obtain maximum height on level ground.
UW = Unit Weight.
⚥ = These configurations can be considered for manned use, check payloads.
Note: Add 2 to 4 feet to maximum heights when using a turret or oversinging a remote head.

Figure 74 Lenny Arm Plus.

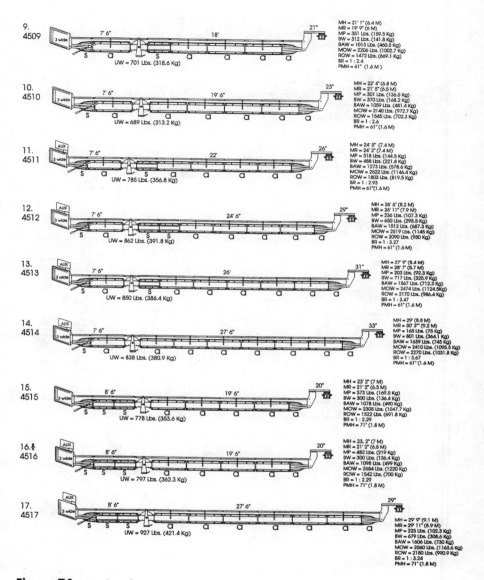

Figure 74 *continued*

CABLE SYSTEM

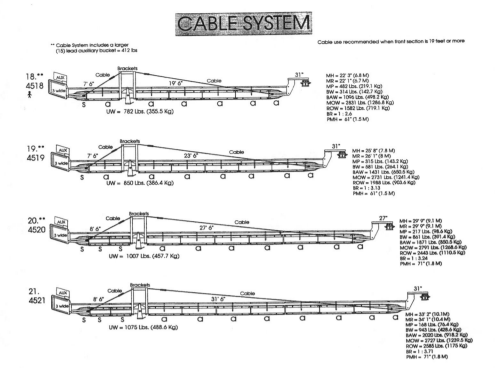

** Cable System includes a larger
(15) lead auxiliary bucket = 412 lbs

Cable use recommended when front section is 19 feet or more

18.**
4518

MH = 22' 3" (6.8 M)
MR = 22' 1" (6.7 M)
MP = 482 Lbs. (219.1 Kg)
BW = 314 Lbs. (142.7 Kg)
BAW = 1096 Lbs. (498.2 Kg)
MOW = 2831 Lbs. (1286.8 Kg)
ROW = 1582 Lbs. (719.1 Kg)
BR = 1 : 2.6
PMH = 61" (1.5 M)

UW = 782 Lbs. (355.5 Kg)

19.**
4519

MH = 25' 8" (7.8 M)
MR = 26' 1" (8 M)
MP = 315 Lbs. (143.2 Kg)
BW = 581 Lbs. (264.1 Kg)
BAW = 1431 Lbs. (650.5 Kg)
MOW = 2731 Lbs. (1241.4 Kg)
ROW = 1988 Lbs. (903.6 Kg)
BR = 1 : 3.13
PMH = 61" (1.5 M)

UW = 850 Lbs. (386.4 Kg)

20.**
4520

MH = 29' 9" (9.1 M)
MR = 29' 9" (9.1 M)
MP = 217 Lbs. (98.6 Kg)
BW = 861 Lbs. (391.4 Kg)
BAW = 1871 Lbs. (850.5 Kg)
MOW = 2791 Lbs. (1268.6 Kg)
ROW = 2443 Lbs. (1110.5 Kg)
BR = 1 : 3.24
PMH = 71" (1.8 M)

UW = 1007 Lbs. (457.7 Kg)

21.
4521

MH = 33' 2" (10.1M)
MR = 34' 1" (10.4 M)
MP = 168 Lbs. (76.4 Kg)
BW = 943 Lbs. (428.6 Kg)
BAW = 2020 Lbs. (918.2 Kg)
MOW = 2727 Lbs. (1239.5 Kg)
ROW = 2585 Lbs. (1175 Kg)
BR = 1 : 3.71
PMH = 71" (1.8 M)

UW = 1075 Lbs. (488.6 Kg)

Keep the crane arm balanced at all times. Avoid sudden disembarking of personnel or equipment disassembly.

The Lenny Arm rear section combination should be configurated so that the bucket touches the ground before the Lenny Arm vertical travel limits are obtained.

Bucket reaches ground.
(RECOMMENDED)

Bucket does not reach ground.
(NOT RECOMMENDED)

WARNING: DO NOT EXCEED THE LISTED POST MOUNT HEIGHTS (PMH) VALUES TO AVOID INVALIDATING OUR SAFETY RECOMMENDATIONS.

Figure 74 *continued*

The Lenny Arm Plus can be mounted on these Chapman/Leonard products:

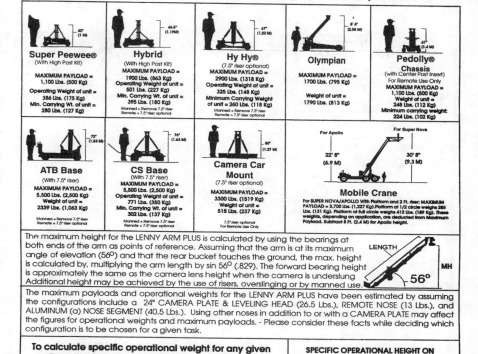

Super Peewee®
(With High Post Kit)

MAXIMUM PAYLOAD = 1,100 Lbs. (500 Kg)

Operating Weight of unit = 386 Lbs. (175 Kg)
Min. Carrying Wt. of unit = 280 Lbs. (127 Kg)

Hybrid
(With High Post Kit)

MAXIMUM PAYLOAD = 1900 Lbs. (863 Kg)
Operating Weight of unit = 501 Lbs. (227 Kg)
Min. Carrying Wt. of unit = 395 Lbs. (180 Kg)
Manned = Remove 7.5" riser
Remote = 7.5" riser optional

Hy Hy®
(7.5" riser optional)

MAXIMUM PAYLOAD = 2900 Lbs. (1318 Kg)
Operating Weight of unit = 325 Lbs. (148 Kg)
Minimum Carrying Weight of unit = 260 Lbs. (118 Kg)
Manned = Remove 7.5" riser
Remote = 7.5" riser optional

Olympian

MAXIMUM PAYLOAD = 1700 Lbs. (795 Kg)

Weight of unit = 1790 Lbs. (813 Kg)

Pedolly®
Chassis
(with Center Post Insert)
For Remote Use Only
MAXIMUM PAYLOAD = 1,100 Lbs. (500 Kg)
Weight of unit = 248 Lbs. (112 Kg)
Minimum carrying weight: 224 Lbs. (102 Kg)

ATB Base
(With 7.5" riser)

MAXIMUM PAYLOAD = 5,500 Lbs. (2,500 Kg)
Weight of unit = 2339 Lbs. (1,063 Kg)
Manned = Remove 7.5" riser
Remote = 7.5" riser optional

CS Base
(With 7.5" riser)

MAXIMUM PAYLOAD = 5,500 Lbs. (2,500 Kg)
Operating Weight of unit = 771 Lbs. (350 Kg)
Min. Carrying Wt. of unit = 302 Lbs. (137 Kg)
Manned = Remove 7.5" riser
Remote = 7.5" riser optional

Camera Car Mount
(7.5" riser optional)

MAXIMUM PAYLOAD = 3300 Lbs. (1519 Kg)
Weight of unit = 515 Lbs. (237 Kg)

7.5" riser optional
For Remote Use Only

For Apollo
22' 6" (6.9 M)

For Super Nova
30' 8" (9.3 M)

Mobile Crane

For SUPER NOVA/APOLLO With Platform and 2 Ft. riser: MAXIMUM PAYLOAD = 2,700 Lbs. (1,227 Kg).Platform at 1/2 circle weighs 286 Lbs. (131 Kg). Platform at full circle weighs 412 Lbs. (189 Kg). These weights, depending on application, are deducted from Maximum Payload. Subtract 8 Ft. (2.4 M) for Apollo height.

The maximum height for the LENNY ARM PLUS is calculated by using the bearings at both ends of the arm as points of reference. Assuming that the arm is at its maximum angle of elevation (56°) and that the rear bucket touches the ground, the max. height is calculated by, multiplying the arm length by sin 56° (.829). The forward bearing height is approximately the same as the camera lens height when the camera is underslung Additional height may be achieved by the use of risers, overslinging or by manned use.

LENGTH / MH / 56°

The maximum payloads and operational weights for the LENNY ARM PLUS have been estimated by assuming the configurations include a 24" CAMERA PLATE & LEVELING HEAD (26.5 Lbs.), REMOTE NOSE (13 Lbs.), and ALUMINUM (a) NOSE SEGMENT (40.5 Lbs.). Using other noses in addition to or with a CAMERA PLATE may affect the figures for operational weights and maximum payloads. - Please consider these facts while deciding which configuration is to be chosen for a given task.

To calculate specific operational weight for any given configuration, please use the following formula:

SPECIFIC OPERATIONAL HEIGHT ON ELEVATED PLATFORMS =

Specific Operational Weight	BAW + (Balanced arm weight, no payload.)	payload + (camera weight, risers, etc.)	payload x balance ratio (Weight in bucket required to balance the given payload.)	

PLATFORM MOUNT HEIGHT (Ground to mount)	+ FORWARD LENGTH OF ARM x .829 (Center post to fwd. bearing)	+ 1.1 Ft. (.35 M) (Center post bearing to mount)	

Actual Height (H) = MH - (PMH x BR - Actual Mount Height x BR)

Chapman/Leonard Studio Equipment, Inc.

WEST COAST:
12950 RAYMER STREET
N HOLLYWOOD, CA. 91605
(888) 88 DOLLY or (888) 883-6559
FAX: (888) 50 CRANE or(888) 502-7623

TIME SAVING CAMERA CRANES, DOLLIES, REMOTE ARMS, BASES & PEDESTALS

EAST COAST:
9460 DELEGATES DRIVE
ORLANDO, FL. 32837
(888) 33 STAGE or (888) 337-8243
FAX: (407) 855-1653

*It is advised that the user of Chapman/Leonard equipment check with the manufacturer for the latest updates on *all* equipment.

Figure 74   *continued*

Lenny Arm II

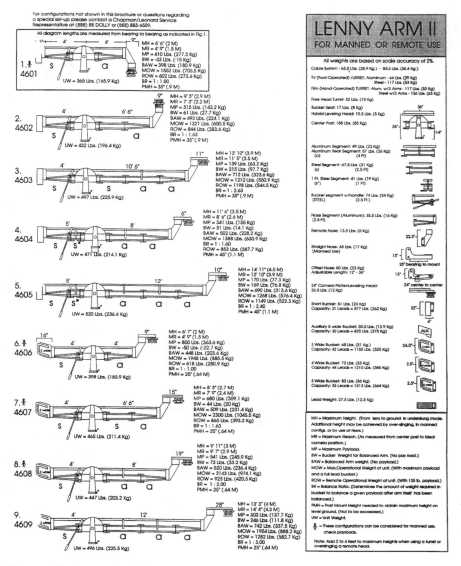

Figure 75 Lenny Arm II.

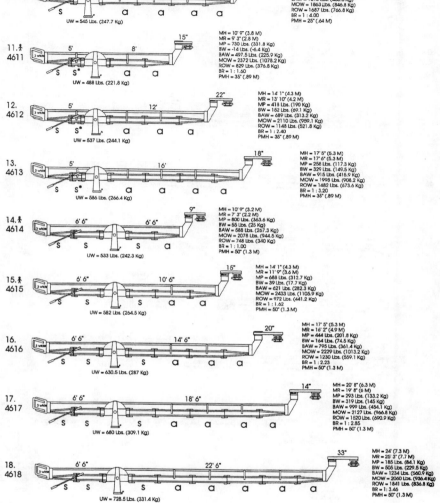

10.
4610

MH = 16' 7" (5 M)
MR = 19' 2" (5.8 M)
MP = 170 Lbs. (77.3 Kg)
BW = 468 Lbs. (212.7 Kg)
BAW = 1013 Lbs. (460.5 Kg)
MOW = 1863 Lbs. (846.8 Kg)
ROW = 1687 Lbs. (766.8 Kg)
BR = 1 : 4.00
PMH = 25" (.64 M)

4' 16' 38"
UW = 545 Lbs. (247.7 Kg)

11.
4611

MH = 10' 9" (3.8 M)
MR = 9' 3" (2.8 M)
MP = 730 Lbs. (331.8 Kg)
BW = -14 Lbs. (-6.4 Kg)
BAW = 497.5 Lbs. (225.9 Kg)
MOW = 2372 Lbs. (1078.2 Kg)
ROW = 829 Lbs. (376.8 Kg)
BR = 1 : 1.60
PMH = 35" (.89 M)

5' 8' 15"
UW = 488 Lbs. (221.8 Kg)

12.
4612

MH = 14' 1" (4.3 M)
MR = 13' 10" (4.2 M)
MP = 418 Lbs. (190 Kg)
BW = 152 Lbs. (69.1 Kg)
BAW = 689 Lbs. (313.2 Kg)
MOW = 2110 Lbs. (959.1 Kg)
ROW = 1148 Lbs. (521.8 Kg)
BR = 1 : 2.40
PMH = 35" (.89 M)

5' 12' 22"
UW = 537 Lbs. (244.1 Kg)

13.
4613

MH = 17' 5" (5.3 M)
MR = 17' 6" (5.3 M)
MP = 258 Lbs. (117.3 Kg)
BW = 329 Lbs. (149.5 Kg)
BAW = 915 Lbs. (415.9 Kg)
MOW = 1998 Lbs. (908.2 Kg)
ROW = 1482 Lbs. (673.6 Kg)
BR = 1 : 3.20
PMH = 35" (.89 M)

5' 16' 18"
UW = 586 Lbs. (266.4 Kg)

14.
4614

MH = 10' 9" (3.2 M)
MR = 7' 3" (2.2 M)
MP = 800 Lbs. (363.6 Kg)
BW = 55 Lbs. (25 Kg)
BAW = 588 Lbs. (267.3 Kg)
MOW = 2078 Lbs. (944.5 Kg)
ROW = 748 Lbs. (340 Kg)
BR = 1 : 1.00
PMH = 50" (1.3 M)

6' 6" 6' 6" 9"
UW = 533 Lbs. (242.3 Kg)

15.
4615

MH = 14' 1" (4.3 M)
MR = 11' 9" (3.6 M)
MP = 688 Lbs. (312.7 Kg)
BW = 39 Lbs. (17.7 Kg)
BAW = 2433 Lbs. (282.3 Kg)
MOW = 2433 Lbs. (1105.9 Kg)
ROW = 972 Lbs. (441.2 Kg)
BR = 1 : 1.62
PMH = 50" (1.3 M)

6' 6" 10' 6" 15"
UW = 582 Lbs. (264.5 Kg)

16.
4616

MH = 17' 5" (5.3 M)
MR = 16' 2" (4.9 M)
MP = 444 Lbs. (201.8 Kg)
BW = 164 Lbs. (74.5 Kg)
BAW = 795 Lbs. (361.4 Kg)
MOW = 2229 Lbs. (1013.2 Kg)
ROW = 1230 Lbs. (559.1 Kg)
BR = 1 : 2.23
PMH = 50" (1.3 M)

6' 6" 14' 6" 20"
UW = 630.5 Lbs. (287 Kg)

17.
4617

MH = 20' 8" (6.3 M)
MR = 19' 8" (6 M)
MP = 293 Lbs. (133.2 Kg)
BW = 319 Lbs. (145 Kg)
BAW = 999 Lbs. (454.1 Kg)
MOW = 2127 Lbs. (966.8 Kg)
ROW = 1520 Lbs. (690.9 Kg)
BR = 1 : 2.85
PMH = 50" (1.3 M)

6' 6" 18' 6" 14"
UW = 680 Lbs. (309.1 Kg)

18.
4618

MH = 24' (7.3 M)
MR = 25' 3" (7.7 M)
MP = 185 Lbs. (84.1 Kg)
BW = 505 Lbs. (229.5 Kg)
BAW = 1234 Lbs. (560.9 Kg)
MOW = 2060 Lbs. (936.4 Kg)
ROW = 1841 Lbs. (836.8 Kg)
BR = 1 : 3.46
PMH = 50" (1.3 M)

6' 6" 22' 6" 33"
UW = 728.5 Lbs. (331.4 Kg)

Figure 75 *continued*

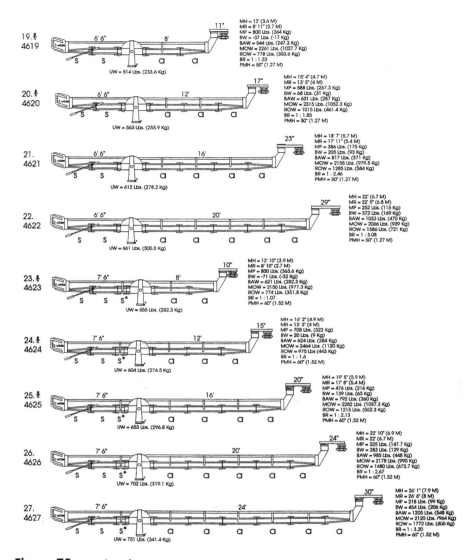

19. ♣
4619

6' 6"   8'   11"

MH = 12' (3.6 M)
MR = 8' 11" (2.7 M)
MP = 800 Lbs. (364 Kg)
BW = -37 Lbs. (-17 Kg)
BAW = 544 Lbs. (247.3 Kg)
MOW = 2261 Lbs. (1027.7 Kg)
ROW = 778 Lbs. (353.6 Kg)
BR = 1 : 1.23
PMH = 50" (1.27 M)

S   S   a   a
UW = 514 Lbs. (233.6 Kg)

20. ♣
4620

6' 6"   12'   17"

MH = 15' 4" (4.7 M)
MR = 13' 5" (4 M)
MP = 588 Lbs. (267.3 Kg)
BW = 68 Lbs. (31 Kg)
BAW = 631 Lbs. (287 Kg)
MOW = 2315 Lbs. (1052.3 Kg)
ROW = 1015 Lbs. (461.4 Kg)
BR = 1 : 1.85
PMH = 50" (1.27 M)

S   S   a   a   a
UW = 563 Lbs. (255.9 Kg)

21.
4621

6' 6"   16'   23"

MH = 18' 7" (5.7 M)
MR = 17' 11" (5.4 M)
MP = 205 Lbs. (93 Kg)
BW = 205 Lbs. (93 Kg)
BAW = 817 Lbs. (371 Kg)
MOW = 2155 Lbs. (979.5 Kg)
ROW = 1285 Lbs. (584 Kg)
BR = 1 : 2.46
PMH = 50" (1.27 M)

S   S   a   a   a   a
UW = 612 Lbs. (278.2 Kg)

22.
4622

6' 6"   20'   29"

MH = 22' (6.7 M)
MR = 22' 5" (6.8 M)
MP = 252 Lbs. (115 Kg)
BW = 372 Lbs. (169 Kg)
BAW = 1033 Lbs. (470 Kg)
MOW = 2066 Lbs. (939 Kg)
ROW = 1586 Lbs. (721 Kg)
BR = 1 : 3.08
PMH = 50" (1.27 M)

S   S   a   a   a   a   a
UW = 661 Lbs. (300.5 Kg)

23. ♣
4623

7' 6"   8'   10"

MH = 12' 10" (3.9 M)
MR = 8' 10" (2.7 M)
MP = -71 Lbs. (363.6 Kg)
BW = -71 Lbs. (-32 Kg)
BAW = 621 Lbs. (282.3 Kg)
MOW = 2150 Lbs. (977.3 Kg)
ROW = 774 Lbs. (351.8 Kg)
BR = 1 : 1.07
PMH = 60" (1.52 M)

S   S   S*   a   a
UW = 555 Lbs. (252.3 Kg)

24. ♣
4624

7' 6"   12'   15"

MH = 16' 2" (4.9 M)
MR = 13' 3" (4 M)
MP = 708 Lbs. (322 Kg)
BW = 20 Lbs. (9 Kg)
BAW = 624 Lbs. (284 Kg)
MOW = 2464 Lbs. (1120 Kg)
ROW = 975 Lbs. (443 Kg)
BR = 1 : 1.6
PMH = 60" (1.52 M)

S   S   S*   a   a   a
UW = 604 Lbs. (274.5 Kg)

25. ♣
4625

7' 6"   16'   20"

MH = 19' 5" (5.9 M)
MR = 17' 8" (5.4 M)
MP = 476 Lbs. (216 Kg)
BW = 139 Lbs. (63 Kg)
BAW = 792 Lbs. (360 Kg)
MOW = 2282 Lbs. (1037.3 Kg)
ROW = 1215 Lbs. (552.3 Kg)
BR = 1 : 2.13
PMH = 60" (1.52 M)

S   S   S*   a   a   a
UW = 653 Lbs. (296.8 Kg)

26.
4626

7' 6"   20'   24"

MH = 22' 10" (6.9 M)
MR = 22' (6.7 M)
MP = 325 Lbs. (147.7 Kg)
BW = 283 Lbs. (129 Kg)
BAW = 985 Lbs. (448 Kg)
MOW = 2178 Lbs. (990 Kg)
ROW = 1480 Lbs. (672.7 Kg)
BR = 1 : 2.67
PMH = 60" (1.52 M)

S   S   S*   a   a   a   a
UW = 702 Lbs. (319.1 Kg)

27.
4627

7' 6"   24'   30"

MH = 26' 1" (7.9 M)
MR = 26' 6" (8 M)
MP = 218 Lbs. (99 Kg)
BW = 454 Lbs. (206 Kg)
BAW = 1205 Lbs. (548 Kg)
MOW = 2120 Lbs. (964 Kg)
ROW = 1772 Lbs. (805 Kg)
BR = 1 : 3.20
PMH = 60" (1.52 M)

S   S   S*   a   a   a   a   a
UW = 751 Lbs. (341.4 Kg)

Figure 75   *continued*

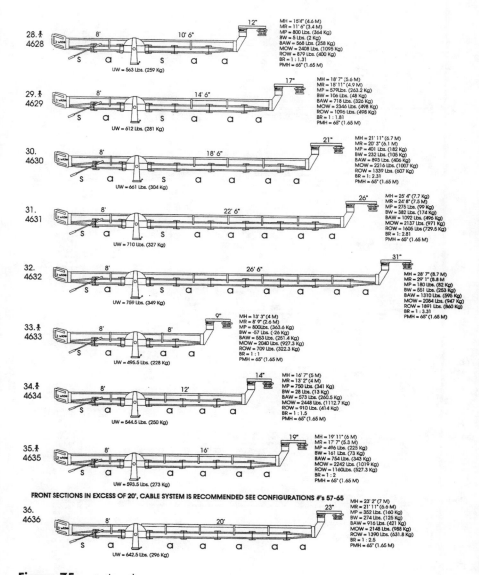

28. 🯅
4628

12"
MH = 15'4" (4.6 M)
MR = 11' 6" (3.4 M)
MP = 800 Lbs. (364 Kg)
BW = 5 Lbs. (2 Kg)
BAW = 568 Lbs. (258 Kg)
MOW = 2408 Lbs. (1095 Kg)
ROW = 879 Lbs. (400 Kg)
BR = 1 : 1.31
PMH = 65" (1.65 M)
UW = 563 Lbs. (259 Kg)

29. 🯅
4629

17"
MH = 18' 7" (5.6 M)
MR = 15' 11" (4.9 M)
MP = 579Lbs. (263.2 Kg)
BW = 106 Lbs. (48 Kg)
BAW = 718 Lbs. (326 Kg)
MOW = 2346 Lbs. (498 Kg)
ROW = 1096 Lbs. (498 Kg)
BR = 1 : 1.81
PMH = 65" (1.65 M)
UW = 612 Lbs. (281 Kg)

30.
4630

21"
MH = 21' 11" (6.7 M)
MR = 20' 3" (6.1 M)
MP = 401 Lbs. (182 Kg)
BW = 232 Lbs. (105 Kg)
BAW = 893 Lbs. (406 Kg)
MOW = 2216 Lbs. (1007 Kg)
ROW = 1339 Lbs. (607 Kg)
BR = 1: 2.31
PMH = 65" (1.65 M)
UW = 661 Lbs. (304 Kg)

31.
4631

26"
MH = 25' 4" (7.7 Kg)
MR = 24' 8" (7.5 M)
MP = 275 Lbs (99 Kg)
BW = 382 Lbs. (174 Kg)
BAW = 1092 Lbs. (496 Kg)
MOW = 2137 Lbs. (971 Kg)
ROW = 1605 lbs (729.5 Kg)
BR = 1: 2.81
PMH = 65" (1.65 M)
UW = 710 Lbs. (327 Kg)

32.
4632

31"
MH = 28' 7" (8.7 M)
MR = 29' 1" (8.8 M)
MP = 180 Lbs. (82 Kg)
BW = 551 Lbs. (253 Kg)
BAW = 1310 Lbs. (595 Kg)
MOW = 2084 Lbs. (947 Kg)
ROW = 1891 Lbs. (860 Kg)
BR = 1 : 3.31
PMH = 65" (1.65 M)
UW = 759 Lbs. (349 Kg)

33. 🯅
4633

9"
MH = 13' 3" (4 M)
MR = 8' 9" (2.6 M)
MP = 800Lbs. (363.6 Kg)
BW = -57 Lbs. (-26 Kg)
BAW = 553 Lbs. (251.4 Kg)
MOW = 2040 Lbs. (927.3 Kg)
ROW = 709 Lbs. (322.3 Kg)
BR = 1 : 1
PMH = 65" (1.65 M)
UW = 495.5 Lbs. (228 Kg)

34. 🯅
4634

14"
MH = 16' 7" (5 M)
MR = 13' 2" (4 M)
MP = 750 Lbs. (341 Kg)
BW = 28 Lbs. (13 Kg)
BAW = 573 Lbs. (260.5 Kg)
MOW = 2448 Lbs. (1112.7 Kg)
ROW = 910 Lbs. (414 Kg)
BR = 1 : 1.5
PMH = 65" (1.65 M)
UW = 544.5 Lbs. (250 Kg)

35. 🯅
4635

19"
MH = 19' 11" (6 M)
MR = 17' 7" (5.3 M)
MP = 496 Lbs. (225 Kg)
BW = 161 Lbs. (73 Kg)
BAW = 754 Lbs. (343 Kg)
MOW = 2242 Lbs. (1019 Kg)
ROW = 1160Lbs. (527.3 Kg)
BR = 1 : 2
PMH = 65" (1.65 M)
UW = 593.5 Lbs. (273 Kg)

FRONT SECTIONS IN EXCESS OF 20', CABLE SYSTEM IS RECOMMENDED SEE CONFIGURATIONS #'s 57-65

36.
4636

23"
MH = 23' 2" (7 M)
MR = 21' 11" (6.6 M)
MP = 352 Lbs. (160 Kg)
BW = 274 Lbs. (125 Kg)
BAW = 916 Lbs. (421 Kg)
MOW = 2148 Lbs. (988 Kg)
ROW = 1390 Lbs. (631.8 Kg)
BR = 1 : 2.5
PMH = 65" (1.65 M)
UW = 642.5 Lbs. (296 Kg)

Figure 75 *continued*

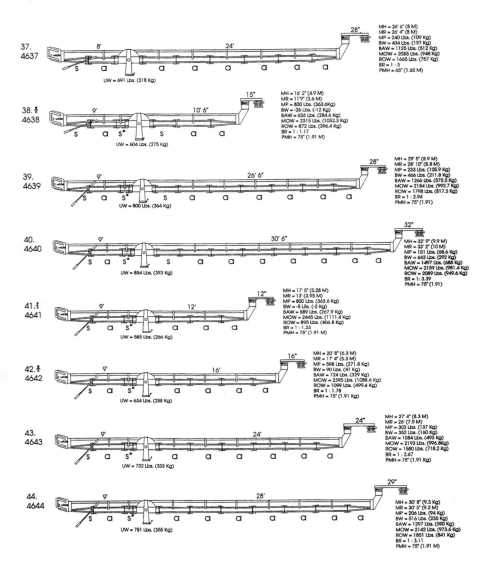

37.
4637

MH = 26' 6" (8 M)
MR = 26' 4" (8 M)
MP = 240 Lbs. (109 Kg)
BW = 434 Lbs. (197 Kg)
BAW = 1125 Lbs. (512 Kg)
MOW = 2085 Lbs. (948 Kg)
ROW = 1665 Lbs. (757 Kg)
BR = 1 : 3
PMH = 65" (1.65 M)

UW = 691 Lbs. (318 Kg)

38. 🏃
4638

MH = 16' 2" (4.9 M)
MR = 11'9" (3.6 M)
MP = 800 Lbs. (363.6Kg)
BW = -26 Lbs. (-12 Kg)
BAW = 626 Lbs. (284.6 Kg)
MOW = 2315 Lbs. (1052.3 Kg)
ROW = 872 Lbs. (396.4 Kg)
BR = 1 : 1.17
PMH = 75" (1.91 M)

UW = 604 Lbs. (275 Kg)

39.
4639

MH = 29' 5" (8.9 M)
MR = 28' 10" (8.8 M)
MP = 233 Lbs. (105.9 Kg)
BW = 466 Lbs. (211.8 Kg)
BAW = 1266 Lbs. (575.5 Kg)
MOW = 2184 Lbs. (992.7 Kg)
ROW = 1798 Lbs. (817.3 Kg)
BR = 1 : 2.94
PMH = 75" (1.91)

UW = 800 Lbs. (364 Kg)

40.
4640

MH = 32' 9" (9.9 M)
MR = 33' 2" (10 M)
MP = 151 Lbs. (68.6 Kg)
BW = 643 Lbs. (292 Kg)
BAW = 1497 Lbs. (688 Kg)
MOW = 2159 Lbs. (981.4 Kg)
ROW = 2089 Lbs. (949.6 Kg)
BR = 1 : 3.39
PMH = 75" (1.91)

UW = 854 Lbs. (393 Kg)

41. 🏃
4641

MH = 17' 5" (5.28 M)
MR = 13' (3.95 M)
MP = 800 Lbs. (363.6 Kg)
BW = -5 Lbs. (-2 Kg)
BAW = 589 Lbs. (267.9 Kg)
MOW = 2445 Lbs. (1111.4 Kg)
ROW = 895 Lbs. (406.8 Kg)
BR = 1 : 1.33
PMH = 75" (1.91 M)

UW = 585 Lbs. (266 Kg)

42. 🏃
4642

MH = 20' 8" (6.3 M)
MR = 17' 4" (5.3 M)
MP = 598 Lbs. (271.8 Kg)
BW = 90 Lbs. (41 Kg)
BAW = 724 Lbs. (329 Kg)
MOW = 2395 Lbs. (1088.6 Kg)
ROW = 1099 Lbs. (499.6 Kg)
BR = 1 : 1.78
PMH = 75" (1.91 M)

UW = 634 Lbs. (288 Kg)

43.
4643

MH = 27' 4" (8.3 M)
MR = 26' (7.9 M)
MP = 302 Lbs. (137 Kg)
BW = 352 Lbs. (160 Kg)
BAW = 1084 Lbs. (493 Kg)
MOW = 2193 Lbs. (996.8Kg)
ROW = 1580 Lbs. (718.2 Kg)
BR = 1 : 2.67
PMH = 75" (1.91 Kg)

UW = 732 Lbs. (333 Kg)

44.
4644

MH = 30' 8" (9.3 Kg)
MR = 30' 5" (9.2 M)
MP = 206 Lbs. (94 Kg)
BW = 516 Lbs. (235 Kg)
BAW = 1297 Lbs. (590 Kg)
MOW = 2142 Lbs. (973.6 Kg)
ROW = 1851 Lbs. (841 Kg)
BR = 1 : 3.11
PMH = 75" (1.91 M)

UW = 781 Lbs. (355 Kg)

Figure 75 *continued*

Four-wide bucket configurations:

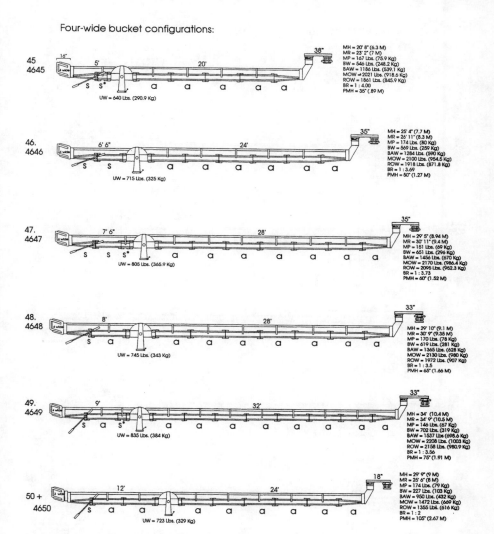

Figure 75 *continued*

Five-wide bucket configurations:

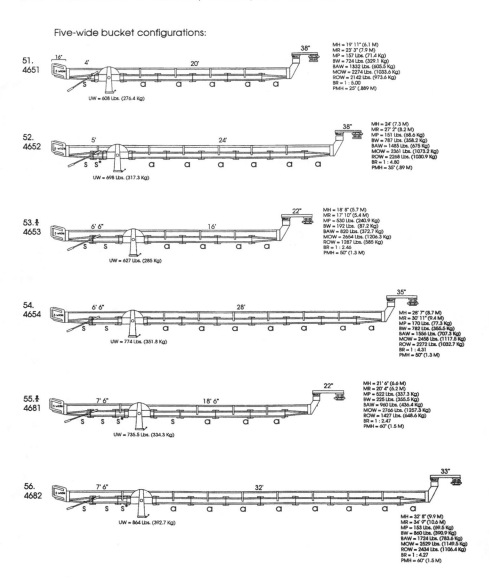

51.
4651

UW = 608 Lbs. (276.4 Kg)

MH = 19' 11" (6.1 M)
MR = 23' 3" (7.9 M)
MP = 157 Lbs. (71.4 Kg)
BW = 724 Lbs. (329.1 Kg)
BAW = 1332 Lbs. (605.5 Kg)
MOW = 2274 Lbs. (1033.6 Kg)
ROW = 2142 Lbs. (973.6 Kg)
BR = 1 : 5.00
PMH = 25" (.889 M)

52.
4652

UW = 698 Lbs. (317.3 Kg)

MH = 24' (7.3 M)
MR = 27' 2" (8.2 M)
MP = 151 Lbs. (68.6 Kg)
BW = 787 Lbs. (358.2 Kg)
BAW = 1485 Lbs. (675 Kg)
MOW = 2361 Lbs. (1073.2 Kg)
ROW = 2268 Lbs. (1030.9 Kg)
BR = 1 : 4.80
PMH = 35" (.89 M)

53.
4653

UW = 627 Lbs. (285 Kg)

MH = 18' 8" (5.7 M)
MR = 17' 10" (5.4 M)
MP = 530 Lbs. (240.9 Kg)
BW = 192 Lbs. (87.2 Kg)
BAW = 820 Lbs. (372.7 Kg)
MOW = 2654 Lbs. (1206.3 Kg)
ROW = 1287 Lbs. (585 Kg)
BR = 1 : 2.46
PMH = 50" (1.3 M)

54.
4654

UW = 774 Lbs. (351.8 Kg)

MH = 28' 7" (8.7 M)
MR = 30' 11" (9.4 M)
MP = 170 Lbs. (77.3 Kg)
BW = 782 Lbs. (355.5 Kg)
BAW = 1556 Lbs. (707.3 Kg)
MOW = 2458 Lbs. (1117.5 Kg)
ROW = 2272 Lbs. (1032.7 Kg)
BR = 1 : 4.31
PMH = 50" (1.3 M)

55.
4681

UW = 735.5 Lbs. (334.3 Kg)

MH = 21' 6" (6.6 M)
MR = 20' 4" (6.2 M)
MP = 522 Lbs. (337.3 Kg)
BW = 225 Lbs. (355.5 Kg)
BAW = 960 Lbs. (436.4 Kg)
MOW = 2766 Lbs. (1257.3 Kg)
ROW = 1427 Lbs. (648.6 Kg)
BR = 1 : 2.47
PMH = 60" (1.5 M)

56.
4682

UW = 864 Lbs. (392.7 Kg)

MH = 32' 8" (9.9 M)
MR = 34' 9" (10.6 M)
MP = 153 Lbs. (69.5 Kg)
BW = 860 Lbs. (390.9 Kg)
BAW = 1724 Lbs. (783.6 Kg)
MOW = 2529 Lbs. (1149.5 Kg)
ROW = 2434 Lbs. (1106.4 Kg)
BR = 1 : 4.27
PMH = 60" (1.5 M)

Figure 75 *continued*

CABLE SYSTEM

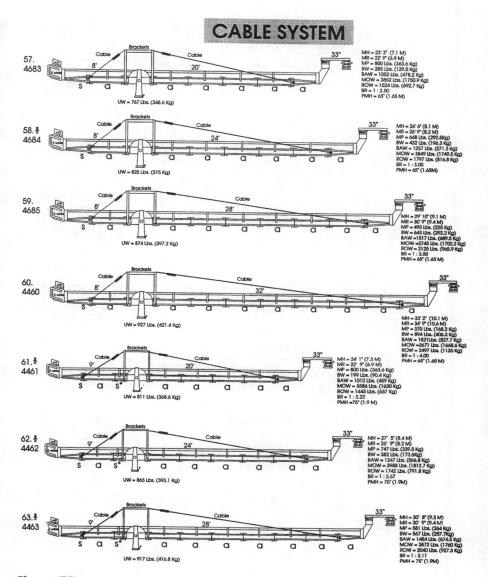

57.
4683

MH = 23' 3" (7.1 M)
MR = 22' 9" (6.9 M)
MP = 800 Lbs. (363.6 Kg)
BW = 285 Lbs. (129.5 Kg)
BAW = 1052 Lbs. (478.2 Kg)
MOW = 3852 Lbs. (1750.9 Kg)
ROW = 1524 Lbs. (692.7 Kg)
BR = 1 : 2.50
PMH = 65" (1.65 M)

UW = 767 Lbs. (348.6 Kg)

58.
4684

MH = 26' 6" (8.1 M)
MR = 26' 9" (8.2 M)
MP = 648 Lbs. (292.5Kg)
BW = 432 Lbs. (196.3 Kg)
BAW = 1257 Lbs. (571.3 Kg)
MOW = 3849 Lbs. (1749.5 Kg)
ROW = 1797 Lbs. (816.8 Kg)
BR = 1 : 3.00
PMH = 65" (1.65M)

UW = 825 Lbs. (375 Kg)

59.
4685

MH = 29' 10" (9.1 M)
MR = 30' 9" (9.4 M)
MP = 495 Lbs. (225 Kg)
BW = 643 Lbs. (292.2 Kg)
BAW =1517 Lbs. (689.5 Kg)
MOW =3745 Lbs. (1702.2 Kg)
ROW = 2125 Lbs. (965.9 Kg)
BR = 1 : 3.50
PMH = 65" (1.65 M)

UW = 874 Lbs. (397.2 Kg)

60.
4460

MH = 33' 2" (10.1 M)
MR = 34' 9" (10.6 M)
MP = 370 Lbs. (168.2 Kg)
BW = 894 Lbs. (406.3 Kg)
BAW = 1821Lbs. (827.7 Kg)
MOW =3671 Lbs. (1668.6 Kg)
ROW = 2497 Lbs. (1135 Kg)
BR = 1 : 4.00
PMH = 65" (1.65 M)

UW = 927 Lbs. (421.4 Kg)

61.
4461

MH = 24' 1" (7.3 M)
MR = 22' 9" (6.9 M)
MP = 800 Lbs. (363.6 Kg)
BW = 199 Lbs. (90.4 Kg)
BAW = 1010 Lbs. (459 Kg)
MOW = 3586 Lbs. (1630 Kg)
ROW = 1445 Lbs. (657 Kg)
BR = 1 : 2.22
PMH = 75" (1.9 M)

UW = 811 Lbs. (368.6 Kg)

62.
4462

MH = 27' 5" (8.4 M)
MR = 26' 9" (8.2 M)
MP = 747 Lbs. (339.5 Kg)
BW = 382 Lbs. (173.6Kg)
BAW = 1247 Lbs. (566.8 Kg)
MOW = 3988 Lbs. (1812.7 Kg)
ROW = 1742 Lbs. (791.8 Kg)
BR = 1 : 2.67
PMH = 75" (1.9M)

UW = 865 Lbs. (393.1 Kg)

63.
4463

MH = 30' 8" (9.3 M)
MR = 30' 9" (9.4 M)
MP = 581 Lbs. (264 Kg)
BW = 567 Lbs. (257.7Kg)
BAW = 1484 Lbs. (674.5 Kg)
MOW = 3872 Lbs. (1760 Kg)
ROW = 2040 Lbs. (927.3 Kg)
BR = 1 : 3.11
PMH = 75" (1.9M)

UW = 917 Lbs. (416.8 Kg)

Figure 75 *continued*

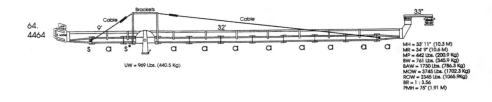

64.
4464

UW = 969 Lbs. (440.5 Kg)

MH = 33' 11" (10.3 M)
MR = 34' 9" (10.6 M)
MP = 442 Lbs. (200.9 Kg)
BW = 761 Lbs. (345.9 Kg)
BAW = 1730 Lbs. (786.3 Kg)
MOW = 3745 Lbs. (1702.3 Kg)
ROW = 2345 Lbs. (1066.9Kg)
BR = 1 : 3.56
PMH = 75' (1.91 M)

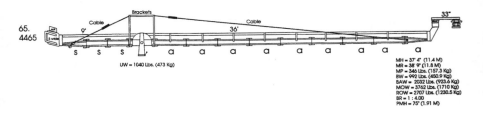

65.
4465

UW = 1040 Lbs. (473 Kg)

MH = 37' 4" (11.4 M)
MR = 38' 9" (11.8 M)
MP = 346 Lbs. (157.3 Kg)
BW = 992 Lbs. (450.9 Kg)
BAW = 2032 Lbs. (923.6 Kg)
MOW = 3762 Lbs. (1710 Kg)
ROW = 2707 Lbs. (1230.5 Kg)
BR = 1 : 4.00
PMH = 75' (1.91 M)

An additional increase in payload may be obtained by substituting the 3 wide bucket with a 4 wide bucket using this formula:
60 divided by Balance Ratio = payload increase.

An additional increase in payload may also be obtained by substituting the 3 wide bucket with a 5 wide bucket using this formula:
373 divided by BR = payload increase.

The auxilliary 5 wide bucket may be used with maximum 9 ft. back and maximum 36 ft. front in conjunction with cable system.

Bucket reaches ground.
(RECOMMENDED)

The Lenny Arm rear section combination should be configurated so that the bucket touches the ground before the Lenny Arm vertical travel limits are obtained.

Bucket does not reach ground.
(NOT RECOMMENDED)

WARNING: DO NOT EXCEED THE LISTED POST MOUNT HEIGHTS (PMH) VALUES TO AVOID INVALIDATING OUR SAFETY RECOMMENDATIONS.

---

*It is advised that the user of Chapman/Leonard equipment check with the manufacturer for the latest updates on *all* equipment.

Figure 75 *continued*

Lenny Arm II Plus

Lenny Arm II Plus® Assembly Configurations

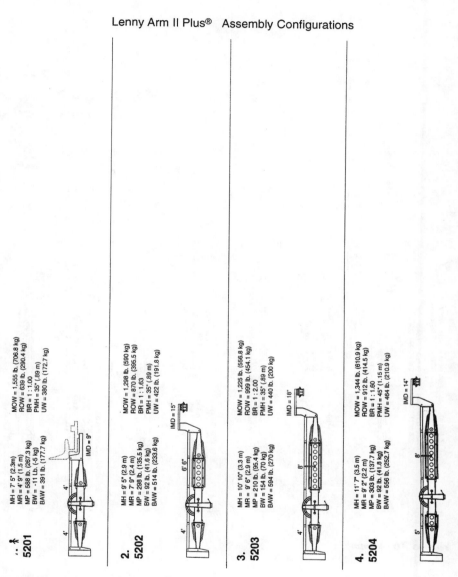

1.
5201

MH = 7' 5" (2.3m)
MR = 4' 9" (1.5 m)
MP = 588 lb. (267.3 kg)
BW = -11 Lb. (-5 kg)
BAW = 391 lb. (177.7 kg)

MOW = 1,555 lb. (706.8 kg)
ROW = 639 lb. (290.4 kg)
BR = 1 : 1.00.
PMH = 35" (.89 m)
UW = 380 lb. (172.7 kg)

IMD = 9'

2.
5202

MH = 9' 5" (2.9 m)
MR = 7' 9" (2.4 m)
MP = 298 lb. (135.5 kg)
BW = 92 lb. (41.6 kg)
BAW = 514 lb. (233.6 kg)

MOW = 1,298 lb. (590 kg)
ROW = 870 lb. (395.5 kg)
BR = 1 : 1.63
PMH = 35" (.89 m)
UW = 422 lb. (191.8 kg)

IMD = 15"

3.
5203

MH = 10' 10" (3.3 m)
MR = 9' 6" (2.9 m)
MP = 210 lb. (95.4 kg)
BW = 154 lb. (70 kg)
BAW = 594 lb. (270 kg)

MOW = 1,225 lb. (556.8 kg)
ROW = 999 lb. (454.1 kg)
BR = 1 : 2.00
PMH = 35" (.89 m)
UW = 440 lb. (200 kg)

IMD = 18"

4.
5204

MH = 11' 7" (3.5 m)
MR = 9' 2" (2.2 m)
MP = 303 lb. (137.7 kg)
BW = 92 lb. (41.8 kg)
BAW = 556 lb. (252.7 kg)

MOW = 1,344 lb. (610.9 kg)
ROW = 912 lb. (414.5 kg)
BR = 1 : 1.60
PMH = 45" (1.15 m)
UW = 464 lb. (210.9 kg)

IMD = 14"

Figure 76 Lenny Arm II Plus.

Lenny Arm II Plus® Assembly Configurations

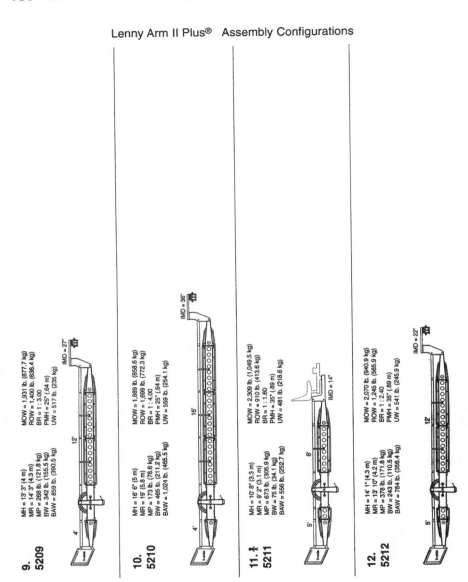

9.
5209

MH = 13' 3" (4 m)
MR = 14' 3" (4.3 m)
MP = 268 lb. (121.8 kg)
BW = 342 lb. (155.5 kg)
BAW = 859 lb. (390.5 kg)

MOW = 1,931 lb. (877.7 kg)
ROW = 1,400 lb. (636.4 kg)
BR = 1 : 3.00
PMH = 25" (.64 m)
UW = 517 lb. (235 kg)

IMD = 27"

10.
5210

MH = 16' 6" (5 m)
MR = 19' (5.8 m)
MP = 173 lb. (78.6 kg)
BW = 465 lb. (211.2 kg)
BAW = 1,024 lb. (465.5 kg)

MOW = 1,889 lb. (858.6 kg)
ROW = 1,699 lb. (772.3 kg)
BR = 1 : 4.00
PMH = 25" (.64 m)
UW = 559 lb. (254.1 kg)

IMD = 35"

11.
5211

MH = 10' 8" (3.3 m)
MR = 9' 2" (3.1 m)
MP = 673 lb. (34.1 kg)
BW = 75 lb. (34.1 kg)
BAW = 556 lb. (252.7 kg)

MOW = 2,309 lb. (1,049.5 kg)
ROW = 910 lb. (413.6 kg)
BR = 1 : 1.60
PMH = 35" (.89 m)
UW = 481 lb. (218.6 kg)

IMD = 14"

12.
5212

MH = 14' 1" (4.3 m)
MR = 13' 10" (4.2 m)
MP = 378 lb. (171.8 kg)
BW = 243 lb. (110.5 kg)
BAW = 784 lb. (356.4 kg)

MOW = 2,070 lb. (940.9 kg)
ROW = 1,245 lb. (565.9 kg)
BR = 1 : 2.40
PMH = 35" (.89 m)
UW = 541 lb. (245.9 kg)

IMD = 22"

Figure 76 *continued*

Lenny Arm II Plus® Assembly Configurations

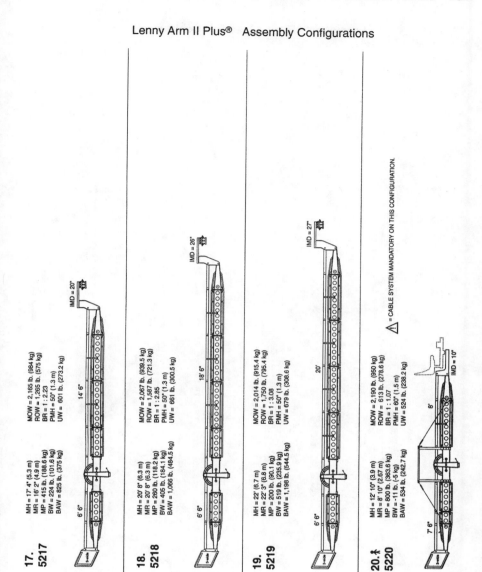

Figure 76 *continued*

Lenny Arm II Plus® Assembly Configurations

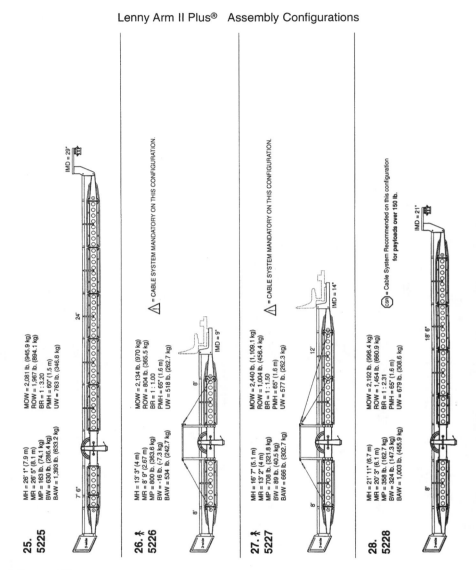

25.
5225

MH = 26' 1" (7.9 m)
MR = 26' 5" (8.1 m)
MP = 163 lb. (74.1 kg)
BW = 630 lb. (286.4 kg)
BAW = 1,393 lb. (633.2 kg)

MOW = 2,081 lb. (945.9 kg)
ROW = 1,967 lb. (894.1 kg)
BR = 1 : 3.20
PMH = 60" (1.5 m)
UW = 763 lb. (346.8 kg)

IMD = 29"

24'

7' 6"

26.
5226

MH = 13' 3" (4 m)
MR = 8' 9" (2.67 m)
MP = 800 lb. (363.6 kg)
BW = -16 lb. (-7.3 kg)
BAW = 534 lb. (242.7 kg)

MOW = 2,134 lb. (970 kg)
ROW = 804 lb. (365.5 kg)
BR = 1 : 1.00
PMH = 65" (1.6 m)
UW = 518 lb. (262.7 kg)

⚠ = CABLE SYSTEM MANDATORY ON THIS CONFIGURATION.

IMD = 9"

8'

8'

27.
5227

MH = 16' 7" (5.1 m)
MR = 13' 2" (4 m)
MP = 708 lb. (321.8 kg)
BW = 89 lb. (40.5 kg)
BAW = 666 lb. (302.7 kg)

MOW = 2,440 lb. (1,109.1 kg)
ROW = 1,004 lb. (456.4 kg)
BR = 1 : 1.50
PMH = 65" (1.6 m)
UW = 577 lb. (262.3 kg)

⚠ = CABLE SYSTEM MANDATORY ON THIS CONFIGURATION.

IMD = 14"

12'

8'

28.
5228

MH = 21' 11" (6.7 m)
MR = 20' 3" (6.1 m)
MP = 358 lb. (162.7 kg)
BW = 324 lb. (147.3 kg)
BAW = 1,003 lb. (455.9 kg)

MOW = 2,192 lb. (996.4 kg)
ROW = 1,454 lb. (660.9 kg)
BR = 1 : 2.31
PMH = 65" (1.6 m)
UW = 679 lb. (308.6 kg)

CSR = Cable System Recommended on this configuration for payloads over 150 lb.

IMD = 21"

18' 6"

8'

Figure 76 *continued*

Lenny Arm II Plus® Assembly Configurations

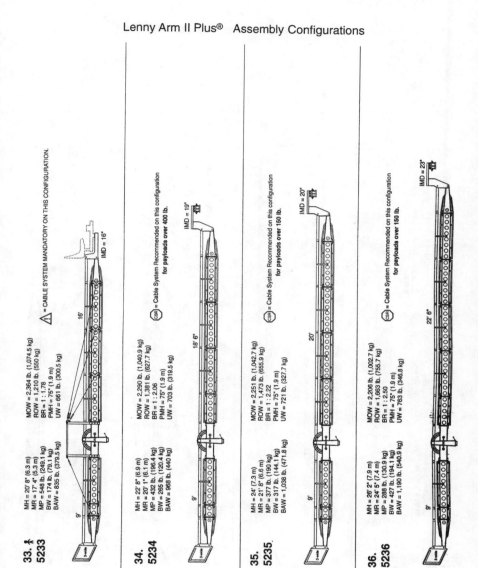

33. 5233

MH = 20' 8" (6.3 m)
MR = 17' 4" (5.3 m)
MP = 548 lb. (249.1 kg)
BW = 174 lb. (79.1 kg)
BAW = 835 lb. (379.5 kg)

MOW = 2,364 lb. (1,074.5 kg)
ROW = 1,210 lb. (550 kg)
BR = 1 : 1.78
PMH = 75" (1.9 m)
UW = 661 lb. (300.5 kg)

△ = CABLE SYSTEM MANDATORY ON THIS CONFIGURATION.

IMD = 16"

16'

9'

34. 5234

MH = 22' 8" (6.9 m)
MR = 20' 1" (6.1 m)
MP = 432 lb. (196.4 kg)
BW = 265 lb. (120.4 kg)
BAW = 968 lb. (440 kg)

MOW = 2,290 lb. (1,040.9 kg)
ROW = 1,381 lb. (627.7 kg)
BR = 1 : 2.06
PMH = 75" (1.9 m)
UW = 703 lb. (319.5 kg)

(CSR) = Cable System Recommended on this configuration **for payloads over 400 lb.**

IMD = 19"

18' 6"

9'

35. 5235

MH = 24' (7.3 m)
MR = 21' 8" (6.6 m)
MP = 377 lb. (190 kg)
BW = 317 lb. (144.1 kg)
BAW = 1,038 lb. (471.8 kg)

MOW = 2,251 lb. (1,042.7 kg)
ROW = 1,473 lb. (655.9 kg)
BR = 1 : 2.22
PMH = 75" (1.9 m)
UW = 721 lb. (327.7 kg)

(CSR) = Cable System Recommended on this configuration **for payloads over 150 lb.**

IMD = 20"

20'

9'

36. 5236

MH = 26' 2" (7.9 m)
MR = 24' 5" (7.4 m)
MP = 288 lb. (130.9 kg)
BW = 427 lb. (194.1 kg)
BAW = 1,190 lb. (540.9 kg)

MOW = 2,206 lb. (1,002.7 kg)
ROW = 1,663 lb. (755.7 kg)
BR = 1 : 2.50
PMH = 75" (1.9 m)
UW = 763 lb. (346.8 kg)

(CSR) = Cable System Recommended on this configuration **for payloads over 150 lb.**

IMD = 23"

22' 6"

9'

Figure 76 *continued*

Lenny Arm II Plus® Assembly Configurations

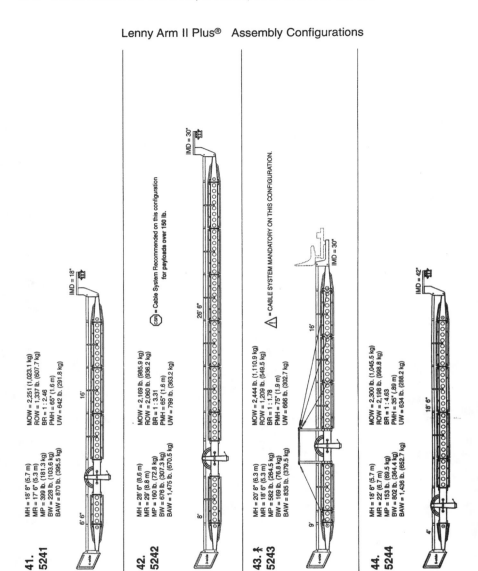

41.
5241

MH = 18' 8" (5.7 m)
MR = 17' 6" (5.3 m)
MP = 399 lb. (181.3 kg)
BW = 228 lb. (103.6 kg)
BAW = 870 lb. (395.5 kg)

MOW = 2,251 (1,023.1 kg)
ROW = 1,337 lb. (607.7 kg)
BR = 1 : 2.46
PMH = 65" (1.6 m)
UW = 642 lb. (291.8 kg)

IMD = 18"

16'

6' 6"

42.
5242

MH = 28' 6" (8.6 m)
MR = 29' (8.8 m)
MP = 160 lb. (72.8 kg)
BW = 676 lb. (307.3 kg)
BAW = 1,475 lb. (670.5 kg)

MOW = 2,169 lb. (985.9 kg)
ROW = 2,060 lb. (936.2 kg)
BR = 1 : 3.31
PMH = 65" (1.6 m)
UW = 799 lb. (363.2 kg)

(CSR) = Cable System Recommended on this configuration
for payloads over 150 lb.

IMD = 30"

26' 6"

8'

43.
5243

MH = 20' 8" (6.3 m)
MR = 18' 6" (5.3 m)
MP = 582 lb. (264.5 kg)
BW = 169 lb. (76.8 kg)
BAW = 835 lb. (379.5 kg)

MOW = 2,444 lb. (1,110.9 kg)
ROW = 1,209 lb. (549.5 kg)
BR = 1 : 1.78
PMH = 75" (1.9 m)
UW = 666 lb. (302.7 kg)

△ = CABLE SYSTEM MANDATORY ON THIS CONFIGURATION.

IMD = 30"

16'

9'

44.
5244

MH = 18' 6" (5.7 m)
MR = 22' (6.7 m)
MP = 153 lb. (69.5 kg)
BW = 802 lb. (364.4 kg)
BAW = 1,436 lb. (652.7 kg)

MOW = 2,300 lb. (1,045.5 kg)
ROW = 2,198 lb. (998.8 kg)
BR = 1 : 4.63
PMH = 35" (.89 m)
UW = 634 lb. (288.2 kg)

IMD = 42"

18' 6"

4'

Figure 76 *continued*

Lenny Arm II Plus® Assembly Configurations

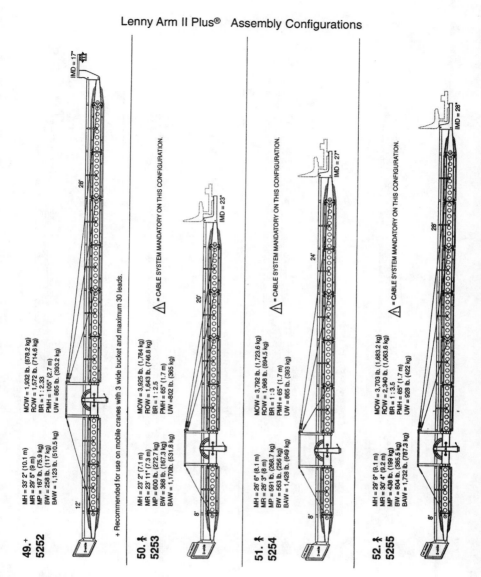

49.⁺
5252

IMD = 17"
28'
12'

MH = 33' 2" (10.1 m)
MR = 29' 5" (9 m)
MP = 167 lb. (75.9 kg)
BW = 258 lb. (117 kg)
BAW = 1,123 lb. (510.5 kg)

MOW = 1,932 lb. (878.2 kg)
ROW = 1,572 lb. (714.6 kg)
BR = 1 : 2.33
PMH = 105" (2.7 m)
UW = 865 lb. (393.2 kg)

+ Recommended for use on mobile cranes with 3 wide bucket and maximum 30 leads.

50.
5253

IMD = 23"
20'
8'

⚠ = CABLE SYSTEM MANDATORY ON THIS CONFIGURATION.

MH = 23' 2" (7.1 m)
MR = 23' 11" (7.3 m)
MP = 600 lb. (272.7 kg)
BW = 368 lb. (167.3 kg)
BAW = 1,170lb. (531.8 kg)

MOW = 3,925 lb. (1,784 kg)
ROW = 1,643 lb. (746.8 kg)
BR = 1 : 2.5
PMH = 65" (1.7 m)
UW =802 lb. (365 kg)

51.
5254

IMD = 27"
24'
8'

⚠ = CABLE SYSTEM MANDATORY ON THIS CONFIGURATION.

MH = 26' 6" (8.1 m)
MR = 26' 3" (8 m)
MP = 591 lb. (268.7 kg)
BW = 563 lb. (256 kg)
BAW = 1,428 lb. (649 kg)

MOW = 3,792 lb. (1,723.6 kg)
ROW = 1,968 lb. (894.5 kg)
BR = 1 : 3
PMH = 65" (1.7 m)
UW = 865 lb. (393 kg)

52.
5255

IMD = 28"
28'
8'

⚠ = CABLE SYSTEM MANDATORY ON THIS CONFIGURATION.

MH = 29' 9" (9.1 m)
MR = 30' 4" (9.2 m)
MP = 438 lb. (199 kg)
BW = 804 lb. (366.5 kg)
BAW = 1,732 lb. (787.3 kg)

MOW = 3,703 lb. (1,683.2 kg)
ROW = 2,340 lb. (1,063.6 kg)
BR = 1 : 3.5
PMH = 65" (1.7 m)
UW = 929 lb. (422 kg)

Figure 76 *continued*

Lenny Arm II Plus® Assembly Configurations

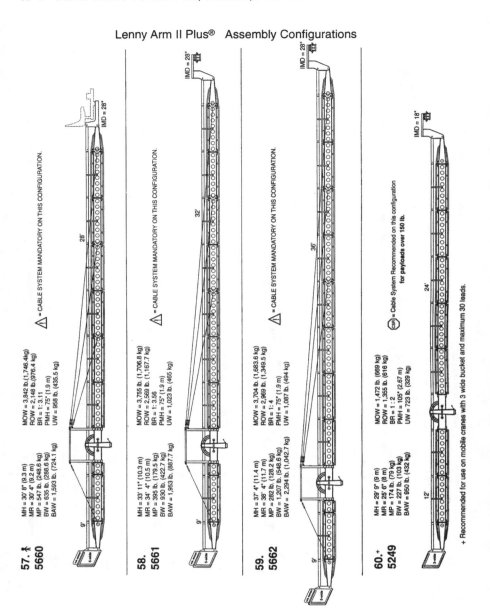

57. **5660**
MH = 30' 8" (9.3 m)
MR = 30' 4" (9.2 m)
MP = 547 lb. (248.6 kg)
BW = 635 lb. (288.6 kg)
BAW = 1,593 lb. (724.1 kg)
MOW = 3,842 lb. (1,746.4kg)
ROW = 2,148 lb.(976.4 kg)
BR = 1 : 3.11
PMH = 75" (1.9 m)
UW = 958 lb. (435.5 kg)
△ = CABLE SYSTEM MANDATORY ON THIS CONFIGURATION.

58. **5661**
MH = 33' 11" (10.3 m)
MR = 34' 4" (10.5 m)
MP = 395 lb. (179.5 kg)
BW = 930 lb. (422.7 kg)
BAW = 1,953 lb. (887.7 kg)
MOW = 3,755 lb. (1,706.8 kg)
ROW = 2,569 lb. (1,167.7 kg)
BR = 1: 3.56
PMH = 75" (1.9 m)
UW = 1,023 lb. (465 kg)
△ = CABLE SYSTEM MANDATORY ON THIS CONFIGURATION.

59. **5662**
MH = 37' 4" (11.4 m)
MR = 38' 4" (11.7 m)
MP = 282 lb. (128.2 kg)
BW = 1,207 lb. (548.6 kg)
BAW = 2,294 lb. (1,042.7 kg)
MOW = 3,704 lb. (1,683.6 kg)
ROW = 2,969 lb. (1,349.5 kg)
BR = 1 : 4
PMH = 75" (1.9 m)
UW = 1,087 lb. (494 kg)
△ = CABLE SYSTEM MANDATORY ON THIS CONFIGURATION.

60.+ **5249**
MH = 29' 9" (9 m)
MR = 25' 6" (8 m)
MP = 174 lb. (79 kg)
BW = 227 lb. (103 kg)
BAW = 950 lb. (432 kg)
MOW = 1,472 lb. (669 kg)
ROW = 1,355 lb. (616 kg)
BR = 1 : 2
PMH = 105" (2.67 m)
UW = 723 lb. (329 kg)
(CSR) = Cable System Recommended on this configuration for payloads over 150 lb.

+ Recommended for use on mobile cranes with 3 wide bucket and maximum 30 leads.

Figure 76 *continued*

Lenny Arm II Plus® Mounting Choices

The Lenny Arm II Plus can be mounted on these Chapman/Leonard products:

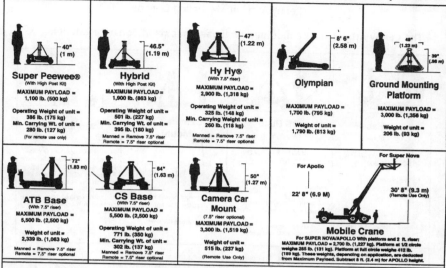

Super Peewee®
(With High Post Kit)

MAXIMUM PAYLOAD =
1,100 lb. (500 kg)

Operating Weight of unit =
386 lb. (175 kg)
Min. Carrying Wt. of unit =
280 lb. (127 kg)
(For remote use only)

Hybrid
(With High Post Kit)

MAXIMUM PAYLOAD =
1,900 lb. (863 kg)

Operating Weight of unit =
501 lb. (227 kg)
Min. Carrying Wt. of unit =
395 lb. (180 kg)
Manned = Remove 7.5" riser
Remote = 7.5" riser optional

Hy Hy®
(With 7.5" riser)

MAXIMUM PAYLOAD =
2,900 lb. (1,318 kg)

Operating Weight of unit =
325 lb. (148 kg)
Min. Carrying Weight of unit =
260 lb. (118 kg)
Manned = Remove 7.5" riser
Remote = 7.5" riser optional

Olympian

MAXIMUM PAYLOAD =
1,700 lb. (795 kg)

Weight of unit =
1,790 lb. (813 kg)

Ground Mounting Platform

MAXIMUM PAYLOAD =
3,000 lb. (1,356 kg)

Weight of unit =
206 lb. (93 kg)

ATB Base
(With 7.5" riser)

MAXIMUM PAYLOAD =
5,500 lb. (2,500 kg)

Weight of unit =
2,339 lb. (1,063 kg)
Manned = Remove 7.5" riser
Remote = 7.5" riser optional

CS Base
(With 7.5" riser)

MAXIMUM PAYLOAD =
5,500 lb. (2,500 kg)

Operating Weight of unit =
771 lb. (350 kg)
Min. Carrying Wt. of unit =
302 lb. (137 kg)
Manned = Remove 7.5" riser
Remote = 7.5" riser optional

Camera Car Mount
(7.5" riser optional)

MAXIMUM PAYLOAD =
3,300 lb. (1,519 kg)

Weight of unit =
515 lb. (237 kg)

(Remote Use Only)

Mobile Crane
For SUPER NOVA/APOLLO With platform and 2 ft. riser:
MAXIMUM PAYLOAD = 2,700 lb. (1,227 kg). Platform at 1/2 circle
weighs 285 lb. (131 kg). Platform at full circle weighs 412 lb.
(189 kg). These weights, depending on application, are deducted
from Maximum Payload. Subtract 8 ft. (2.4 m) for APOLLO height.

The maximum height for the LENNY ARM II PLUS is calculated by using the bearings at both ends of the arm as points of reference. Assuming that the arm is at its maximum angle of elevation (56°) and that the rear bucket touches the ground, the max. height is calculated by multiplying the arm length by sin56°(.829). The forward bearing height is approximately the same as the camera lens height when the camera is underslung Additional height can be achieved by the use of risers, overslinging or by manned use.

The maximum payloads and operational weights for the LENNY ARM II PLUS have been calculated by assuming the configurations include the REMOTE NOSE (13.5 lb.) and a 24" CAMERA PLATE + LEVELING HEAD (26.5 lb.). Using other noses in addition to or without a 24" CAMERA PLATE + LEVELING HEAD will affect the figures for operational weights and maximum payloads. - Please consider these facts while deciding which configuration is to be chosen for a given task.

To calculate specific operational weight for any given configuration, please use the following formula:

Specific Operational Weight = BAW (Balanced arm weight, no payload.) + payload (camera weight, risers, etc.) + payload x balance ratio (Weight in bucket required to balance the given payload.)

SPECIFIC OPERATIONAL HEIGHT ON ELEVATED PLATFORMS =

PLATFORM MOUNT HEIGHT (Ground to mount) + FORWARD LENGTH OF ARM x .829 (Center post to fwd. bearing) + 1.1 ft. (.35 m) (Center post bearing to mount)

Actual Height (H) = MH - (PMH x BR - Actual Mount Height x BR)

WEST COAST:
12950 RAYMER STREET
NO. HOLLYWOOD, CA. 91605
.88) 88 DOLLY or (888) 883-6559
FAX: (888) 50 CRANE or(888) 502-7623

**TIME SAVING CAMERA
CRANES, DOLLIES, REMOTE ARMS,**

EAST COAST:
9460 DELEGATES DRIVE
ORLANDO, FL. 32837
(888) 33 STAGE or (888) 337-8243
FAX: (407) 855-1653

*It is advised that the user of Chapman/Leonard equipment check with the manufacturer for the latest updates on *all* equipment.

Figure 76 *continued*

Lenny Arm III

Lenny Arm® III   Mounting Options

The Lenny Arm III can be mounted on these Chapman/Leonard products:

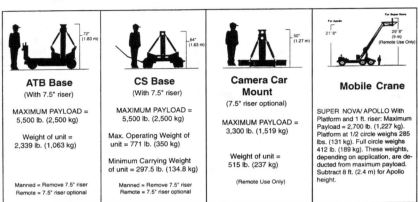

ATB Base	CS Base	Camera Car Mount	Mobile Crane
(With 7.5" riser)	(With 7.5" riser)	(7.5" riser optional)	
MAXIMUM PAYLOAD = 5,500 lb. (2,500 kg)	MAXIMUM PAYLOAD = 5,500 lb. (2,500 kg)	MAXIMUM PAYLOAD = 3,300 lb. (1,519 kg)	SUPER NOVA/ APOLLO With Platform and 1 ft. riser: Maximum Payload = 2,700 lb. (1,227 kg). Platform at 1/2 circle weighs 285 lbs. (131 kg). Full circle weighs 412 lb. (189 kg). These weights, depending on application, are deducted from maximum payload. Subtract 8 ft. (2.4 m) for Apollo height.
Weight of unit = 2,339 lb. (1,063 kg)	Max. Operating Weight of unit = 771 lb. (350 kg)	Weight of unit = 515 lb. (237 kg)	
	Minimum Carrying Weight of unit = 297.5 lb. (134.8 kg)	(Remote Use Only)	
Manned = Remove 7.5" riser Remote = 7.5" riser optional	Manned = Remove 7.5" riser Remote = 7.5" riser optional		

The maximum height for the LENNY ARM III is calculated by using the bearings at both ends of the arm as points of reference. Assuming that the arm is at its maximum angle of elevation (51°) and that the rear bucket touches the ground, the maximum height is calculated by multiplying the arm length by sin 51° (.777). The forward bearing height is approximately the same as the camera lens height when the camera is underslung. Additional height can be achieved by the use of risers or by overslinging, and in manned use.

The maximum payloads and operational weights for the LENNY ARM III have been calculated by assuming the configurations include the REMOTE NOSE (17 lb.), a 24" CAMERA PLATE + LEVELING HEAD (26.5 lb.) and NOSE SEGMENT   (82 lb.). Using other noses in addition to or without a 24" CAMERA PLATE + LEVELING HEAD will affect the figures for operational weights and maximum payloads. - Please consider these facts while deciding which configuration is to be chosen for a given task.

To calculate specific operational weight for any given configuration, please use the following formula:

SPECIFIC OPERATIONAL HEIGHT ON ELEVATED PLATFORMS =

Specific Operational Weight	BAW (Balanced arm weight, no payload.)	+	payload (camera weight, risers, etc.)	+	payload x balance ratio (Weight in bucket required to balance the given payload.)

PLATFORM MOUNT HEIGHT (Ground to mount)	+	FORWARD LENGTH OF ARM x .777 (Center post to fwd. bearing)	+	1.5 Ft. (.45 m) (Center post bearing to mount)

Actual Height (H) = MH - (PMH x BR - Actual Mount Height x BR)

Figure 77 Lenny Arm III.

Lenny Arm® III Configurations

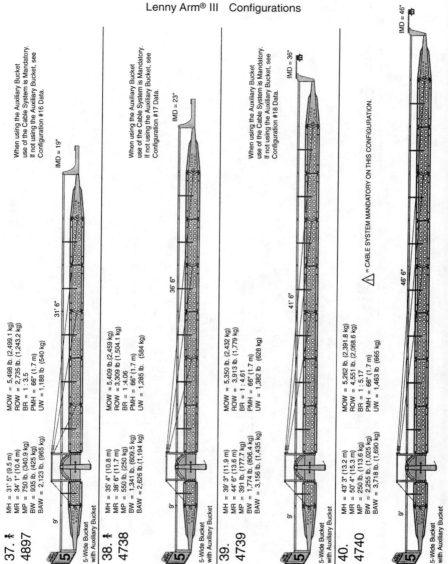

37. **4897**

5-Wide Bucket
with Auxiliary Bucket

MH = 31' 5" (9.5 m)
MR = 34' 1" (10.4 m)
MP = 750 lb. (340.9 kg)
BW = 935 lb. (425 kg)
BAW = 2,123 lb. (965 kg)

MOW = 5,498 lb. (2,499.1 kg)
ROW = 2,735 lb. (1,243.2 kg)
BR = 1 : 3.5
PMH = 66" (1.7 m)
UW = 1,188 lb (540 kg)

31' 6"

IMD = 19"

When using the Auxiliary Bucket
use of the Cable System is Mandatory.
If not using the Auxiliary Bucket, see
Configuration #16 Data.

38. **4738**

5-Wide Bucket
with Auxiliary Bucket

MH = 35' 4" (10.8 m)
MR = 38' 6" (11.7 m)
MP = 550 lb. (250 kg)
BW = 1,341 lb. (609.5 kg)
BAW = 2,626 lb. (1,194 kg)

MOW = 5,409 lb. (2,459)
ROW = 3,309 lb. (1,504.1 kg)
BR = 1 :4.06
PMH = 66" (1.7 m)
UW = 1,285 lb. (584 kg)

36' 6"

IMD = 23"

When using the Auxiliary Bucket
use of the Cable System is Mandatory.
If not using the Auxiliary Bucket, see
Configuration #17 Data.

39. **4739**

5-Wide Bucket
with Auxiliary Bucket

MH = 39' 3" (11.9 m)
MR = 44' 6" (13.6 m)
MP = 391 lb. (177.7 kg)
BW = 1,774 lb. (806.4 kg)
BAW = 3,156 lb. (1,435 kg)

MOW = 5,350 lb. (2,432 kg)
ROW = 3,913 lb. (1,779 kg)
BR = 1 : 4.61
PMH = 66" (1.7 m)
UW = 1,382 lb (628 kg)

41' 6"

IMD = 36"

When using the Auxiliary Bucket
use of the Cable System is Mandatory.
If not using the Auxiliary Bucket, see
Configuration #18 Data.

40. **4740**

5-Wide Bucket
with Auxiliary Bucket

MH = 43' 3" (13.2 m)
MR = 50' 4" (15.3 m)
MP = 250 lb. (113.6 kg)
BW = 2,255 lb. (1,025 kg)
BAW = 3,718 lb. (1,690 kg)

MOW = 5,262 lb. (2,391.8 kg)
ROW = 4,551 lb. (2,068.6 kg)
BR = 1 : 5.17
PMH = 66" (1.7 m)
UW = 1,463 lb (665 kg)

46' 6"

IMD = 46"

⚠ = CABLE SYSTEM MANDATORY ON THIS CONFIGURATION.

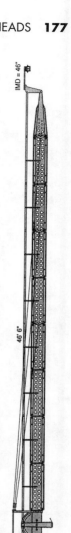

Figure 77 *continued*

Lenny Arm® III Configurations

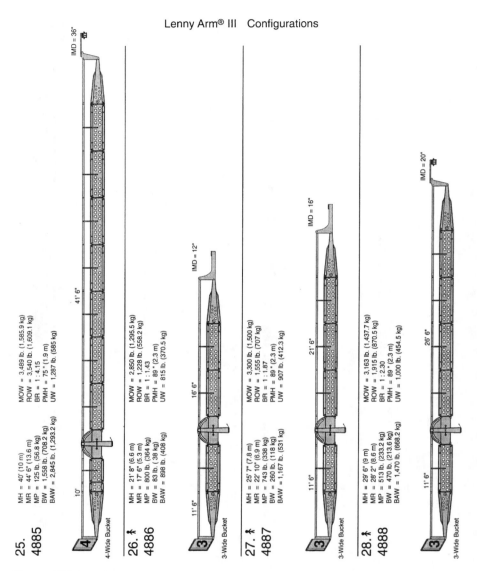

Figure 77 *continued*

Lenny Arm® III   Configurations

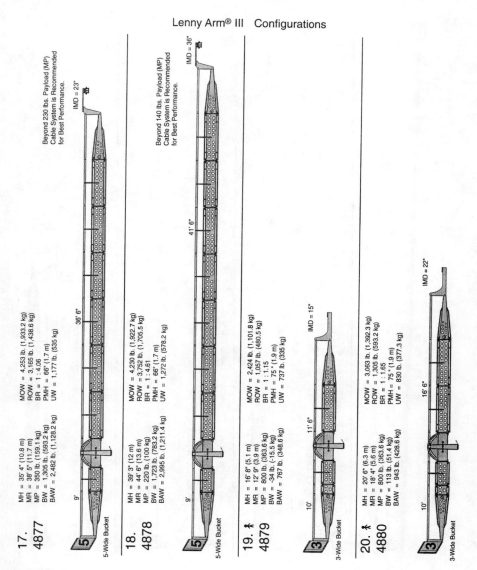

17.
4877

MH = 35' 4" (10.8 m)
MR = 38' 5" (11.7 m)
MP = 350 lb. (159.1 kg)
BW = 1,305 lb. (593.2 kg)
BAW = 2,482 lb. (1,128.2 kg)

MOW = 4,253 lb. (1,933.2 kg)
ROW = 3,165 lb. (1,436.6 kg)
BR = 1 : 4.06
PMH = 66" (1.7 m)
UW = 1,177 lb. (535 kg)

Beyond 230 lbs. Payload (MP)
Cable System is Recommended
for Best Performance.

IMD = 23"

36' 6"

9'

5-Wide Bucket

18.
4878

MH = 39' 3" (12 m)
MR = 44' 6" (13.6 m)
MP = 220 lb. (100 kg)
BW = 1,723 lb. (783.2 kg)
BAW = 2,995 lb. (1,211.4 kg)

MOW = 4,230 lb. (1,922.7 kg)
ROW = 3,752 lb. (1,705.5 kg)
BR = 1 : 4.61
PMH = 66" (1.7 m)
UW = 1,272 lb. (578.2 kg)

Beyond 140 lbs. Payload (MP)
Cable System is Recommended
for Best Performance.

IMD = 36"

41' 6"

9'

5-Wide Bucket

19.
4879

MH = 16' 8" (5.1 m)
MR = 12' 9" (3.9 m)
MP = 800 lb. (363.6 kg)
BW = -34 lb. (-15.5 kg)
BAW = 767 lb. (348.6 kg)

MOW = 2,424 lb. (1,101.8 kg)
ROW = 1,057 lb. (480.5 kg)
BR = 1 : 1.15
PMH = 75" (1.9 m)
UW = 737 lb. (335 kg)

IMD = 15"

11' 6"

10'

3-Wide Bucket

20.
4880

MH = 20' 6" (6.3 m)
MR = 18' 4" (5.6 m)
MP = 800 lb. (363.6 kg)
BW = 113 lb. (51.4 kg)
BAW = 943 lb. (428.6 kg)

MOW = 3,063 lb. (1,392.3 kg)
ROW = 1,305 lb. (593.2 kg)
BR = 1 : 1.65
PMH = 75" (1.9 m)
UW = 830 lb. (377.3 kg)

IMD = 22"

16' 6"

10'

3-Wide Bucket

Figure 77   *continued*

Lenny Arm® III   Configurations

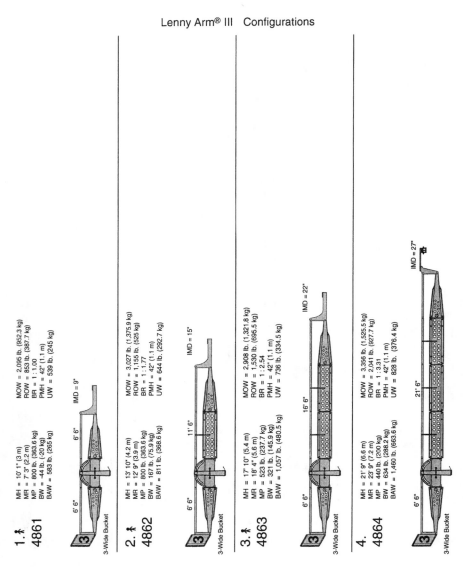

1.
4861

MH = 10' 1" (3 m)
MR = 7' 3" (2.2 m)
MP = 800 lb. (363.6 kg)
BW = –44 lb. (–20 kg)
BAW = 583 lb. (265 kg)

MOW = 2,095 lb. (952.3 kg)
ROW = 853 lb. (387.7 kg)
BR = 1 : 1.00
PMH = 42" (1.1 m)
UW = 539 lb. (245 kg)

IMD = 9"

6' 6"   6' 6"

3-Wide Bucket

2.
4862

MH = 13' 10' (4.2 m)
MR = 12' 9" (3.9 m)
MP = 800 lb. (363.6 kg)
BW = 167 lb. (75.9 kg)
BAW = 811 lb. (368.6 kg)

MOW = 3,027 lb. (1,375.9 kg)
ROW = 1,155 lb. (525 kg)
BR = 1 : 1.77
PMH = 42" (1.1 m)
UW = 644 lb. (292.7 kg)

IMD = 15"

6' 6"   11' 6"

3-Wide Bucket

3.
4863

MH = 17' 10' (5.4 m)
MR = 18' 4" (5.6 m)
MP = 523 lb. (237.7 kg)
BW = 321 lb. (145.9 kg)
BAW = 1,057 lb. (480.5 kg)

MOW = 2,908 lb. (1,321.8 kg)
ROW = 1,530 lb. (695.5 kg)
BR = 1 : 2.54
PMH = 42" (1.1 m)
UW = 736 lb. (334.5 kg)

IMD = 22"

6' 6"   16' 6"

3-Wide Bucket

4.
4864

MH = 21' 9" (6.6 m)
MR = 23' 9" (7.2 m)
MP = 440 lb. (200 kg)
BW = 634 lb. (288.2 kg)
BAW = 1,460 lb. (663.6 kg)

MOW = 3,356 lb. (1,525.5 kg)
ROW = 2,041 lb. (927.7 kg)
BR = 1 : 3.31
PMH = 42" (1.1 m)
UW = 828 lb. (376.4 kg)

IMD = 27"

6' 6"   21' 6"

3-Wide Bucket

Figure 77 *continued*

Lenny Arm® III   Configurations

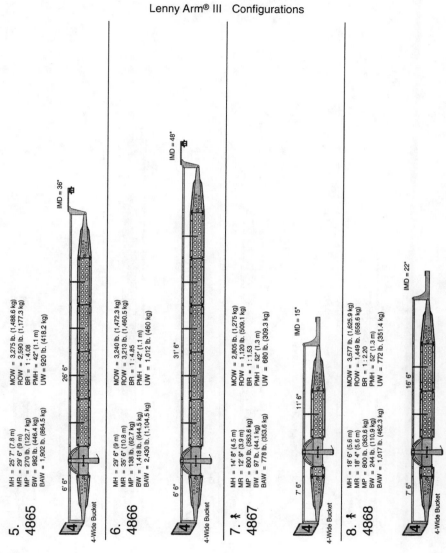

5.
4865

MH = 25' 7" (7.8 m)
MR = 29' 6" (9 m)
MP = 270 lb. (122.7 kg)
BW = 982 lb. (446.4 kg)
BAW = 1,902 lb. (864.5 kg)

MOW = 3,275 lb. (1,488.6 kg)
ROW = 2,590 lb. (1,177.3 kg)
BR = 1 : 4.08
PMH = 42" (1.1 m)
UW = 920 lb. (418.2 kg)

IMD = 36"
26' 6"
6' 6"
4-Wide Bucket

6.
4866

MH = 29' 6" (9 m)
MR = 35' 6" (10.8 m)
MP = 138 lb. (62.7 kg)
BW = 1,418 lb. (644.5 kg)
BAW = 2,430 lb. (1,104.5 kg)

MOW = 3,240 lb. (1,472.3 kg)
ROW = 3,213 lb. (1,460.5 kg)
BR = 1 : 4.85
PMH = 42" (1.1 m)
UW = 1,012 lb. (460 kg)

IMD = 48"
31' 6"
6' 6"
4-Wide Bucket

7. 🏃
4867

MH = 14' 8" (4.5 m)
MR = 12' 9" (3.9 m)
MP = 800 lb. (363.6 kg)
BW = 97 lb. (44.1 kg)
BAW = 778 lb. (353.6 kg)

MOW = 2,805 lb. (1,275 kg)
ROW = 1,120 lb. (509.1 kg)
BR = 1 : 1.53
PMH = 52" (1.3 m)
UW = 680 lb. (309.3 kg)

IMD = 15"
11' 6"
7' 6"
4-Wide Bucket

8. 🏃
4868

MH = 18' 6" (5.6 m)
MR = 18' 4" (5.6 m)
MP = 800 lb. (363.6 kg)
BW = 244 lb. (110.9 kg)
BAW = 1,017 lb. (462.3 kg)

MOW = 3,577 lb. (1,625.9 kg)
ROW = 1,449 lb. (658.6 kg)
BR = 1 : 2.20
PMH = 52" (1.3 m)
UW = 772 lb. (351.4 kg)

IMD = 22"
16' 6"
7' 6"
4-Wide Bucket

Figure 77   *continued*

Lenny Arm® III   Configurations

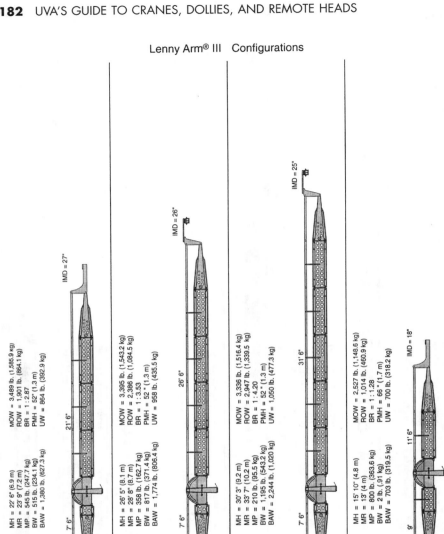

9. ⚡
4869

MH = 22' 6" (6.9 m)
MR = 23' 9" (7.2 m)
MP = 545 lb. (247.7 kg)
BW = 515 lb. (234.1 kg)
BAW = 1,380 lb. (627.3 kg)

MOW = 3,489 lb. (1,585.9 kg)
ROW = 1,901 lb. (864.1 kg)
BR = 1 : 2.87
PMH = 52" (1.3 m)
UW = 864 lb. (392.9 kg)

7' 6"   21' 6"   IMD = 27"

4-Wide Bucket

10.
4870

MH = 26' 5" (8.1 m)
MR = 28' 8" (8.7 m)
MP = 358 lb. (162.7 kg)
BW = 817 lb. (371.4 kg)
BAW = 1,774 lb. (806.4 kg)

MOW = 3,395 lb. (1,543.2 kg)
ROW = 2,386 lb. (1,084.5 kg)
BR = 1 : 3.53
PMH = 52" (1.3 m)
UW = 958 lb. (435.5 kg)

7' 6"   26' 6"   IMD = 26"

4-Wide Bucket

11.
4871

MH = 30' 3" (9.2 m)
MR = 33' 7" (10.2 m)
MP = 210 lb. (95.5 kg)
BW = 1,195 lb. (543.2 kg)
BAW = 2,244 lb. (1,020 kg)

MOW = 3,336 lb. (1,516.4 kg)
ROW = 2,947 lb. (1,339.5 kg)
BR = 1 : 4.20
PMH = 52" (1.3 m)
UW = 1,050 lb. (477.3 kg)

7' 6"   31' 6"   IMD = 25"

4-Wide Bucket

12. ⚡
4872

MH = 15' 10" (4.8 m)
MR = 13' (4 m)
MP = 800 lb. (363.6 kg)
BW = 2 lb. (.91 kg)
BAW = 703 lb. (319.5 kg)

MOW = 2,527 lb. (1,148.6 kg)
ROW = 1,014 lb. (460.9 kg)
BR = 1 : 1.28
PMH = 66" (1.7 m)
UW = 700 lb. (318.2 kg)

9'   11' 6"   IMD = 18"

3-Wide Bucket

Figure 77   *continued*

Lenny Arm® III   Configurations

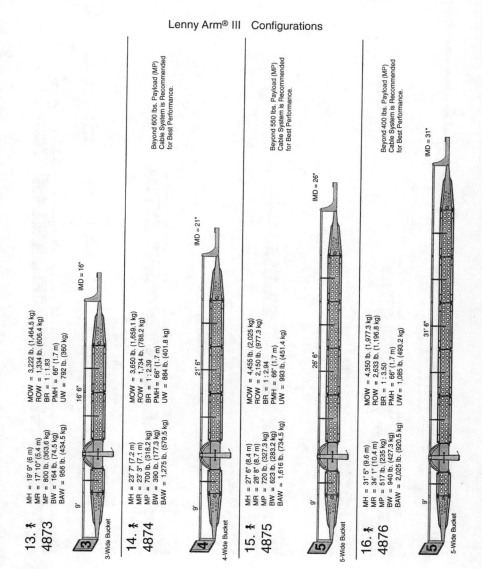

13. 4873
3-Wide Bucket

MH = 19' 9" (6 m)
MR = 17' 10" (5.4 m)
MP = 800 lb. (363.6 kg)
BW = 164 lb. (74.5 kg)
BAW = 956 lb. (434.5 kg)

MOW = 3,222 lb. (1,464.5 kg)
ROW = 1,334 lb. (606.4 kg)
BR = 1 : 1.83
PMH = 66" (1.7 m)
UW = 792 lb. (360 kg)

IMD = 16"
16' 6"
9'

14. 4874
4-Wide Bucket

MH = 23' 7" (7.2 m)
MR = 23' 3" (7.1 m)
MP = 700 lb. (318.2 kg)
BW = 390 lb. (177.3 kg)
BAW = 1,275 lb. (579.5 kg)

MOW = 3,650 lb. (1,659.1 kg)
ROW = 1,734 lb. (788.2 kg)
BR = 1 : 2.39
PMH = 66" (1.7 m)
UW = 884 lb. (401.8 kg)

Beyond 600 lbs. Payload (MP)
Cable System is Recommended
for Best Performance.

IMD = 21"
21' 6"
9'

15. 4875
5-Wide Bucket

MH = 27' 6" (8.4 m)
MR = 28' 8" (8.7 m)
MP = 720 lb. (327.3 kg)
BW = 623 lb. (283.2 kg)
BAW = 1,616 lb. (734.5 kg)

MOW = 4,455 lb. (2,025 kg)
ROW = 2,150 lb. (977.3 kg)
BR = 1 : 2.94
PMH = 66" (1.7 m)
UW = 993 lb. (451.4 kg)

Beyond 550 lbs. Payload (MP)
Cable System is Recommended
for Best Performance.

IMD = 26"
26' 6"
9'

16. 4876
5-Wide Bucket

MH = 31' 5" (9.6 m)
MR = 34' 1" (10.4 m)
MP = 517 lb. (235 kg)
BW = 940 lb. (427.3 kg)
BAW = 2,025 lb. (920.5 kg)

MOW = 4,350 lb. (1,977.3 kg)
ROW = 2,633 lb. (1,196.8 kg)
BR = 1 : 3.50
PMH = 66" (1.7 m)
UW = 1,085 lb. (493.2 kg)

Beyond 400 lbs. Payload (MP)
Cable System is Recommended
for Best Performance.

IMD = 31"
31' 6"
9'

Figure 77 *continued*

Lenny Arm® III   Configurations

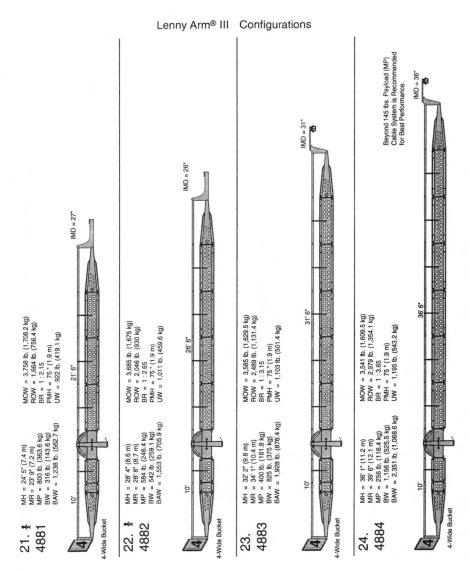

21.
4881

MH = 24' 5" (7.4 m)
MR = 23' 9" (7.2 m)
MP = 800 lb. (363.6 kg)
BW = 316 lb. (143.6 kg)
BAW = 1,238 lb. (562.7 kg)

MOW = 3,758 lb. (1,708.2 kg)
ROW = 1,664 lb. (756.4 kg)
BR = 1 : 2.15
PMH = 75" (1.9 m)
UW = 922 lb. (419.1 kg)

IMD = 27"

21' 6"

10'

4-Wide Bucket

22.
4882

MH = 28' 4" (8.6 m)
MR = 28' 8" (8.7 m)
MP = 584 lb. (246.4 kg)
BW = 542 lb. (259.1 kg)
BAW = 1,553 lb. (705.9 kg)

MOW = 3,685 lb. (1,675 kg)
ROW = 2,046 lb. (930 kg)
BR = 1 : 2.65
PMH = 75" (1.9 m)
UW = 1,011 lb. (459.6 kg)

IMD = 26"

26' 6"

10'

4-Wide Bucket

23.
4883

MH = 32' 2" (9.8 m)
MR = 34' 1" (10.4 m)
MP = 400 lb. (181.8 kg)
BW = 825 lb. (375 kg)
BAW = 1,928 lb. (876.4 kg)

MOW = 3,585 lb. (1,629.5 kg)
ROW = 2,489 lb. (1,131.4 kg)
BR = 1 : 3.15
PMH = 75" (1.9 m)
UW = 1,103 lb. (501.4 kg)

IMD = 31"

31' 6"

10'

4-Wide Bucket

24.
4884

MH = 36' 1" (11.2 m)
MR = 39' 6" (12.1 m)
MP = 256 lb. (116.4 kg)
BW = 1,156 lb. (525.5 kg)
BAW = 2,351 lb. (1,068.6 kg)

MOW = 3,541 lb. (1,609.5 kg)
ROW = 2,979 lb. (1,354.1 kg)
BR = 1 : 3.65
PMH = 75" (1.9 m)
UW = 1,195 lb. (543.2 kg)

IMD = 36"

36' 6"

Beyond 145 lbs. Payload (MP)
Cable System is Recommended
for Best Performance.

10'

4-Wide Bucket

Figure 77 *continued*

Lenny Arm® III   Configurations

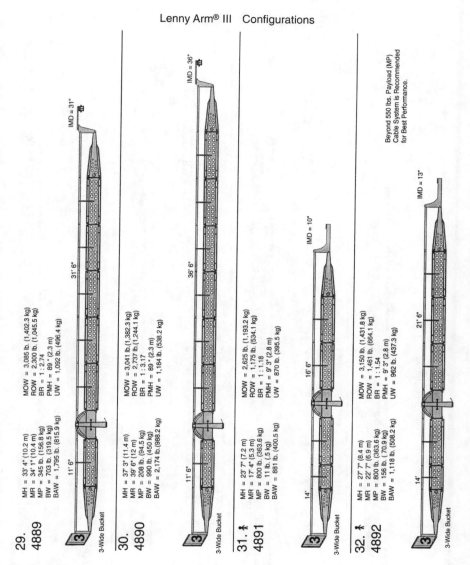

29.
4889

MH = 33' 4" (10.2 m)
MR = 34' 1" (10.4 m)
MP = 345 lb. (156.8 kg)
BW = 703 lb. (319.5 kg)
BAW = 1,795 lb. (815.9 kg)

MOW = 3,085 lb. (1,402.3 kg)
ROW = 2,300 lb. (1,045.5 kg)
BR = 1 : 2.74
PMH = 89˝ (2.3 m)
UW = 1,092 lb. (496.4 kg)

3-Wide Bucket

IMD = 31"
31' 6"
11' 6"

30.
4890

MH = 37' 3" (11.4 m)
MR = 39' 6" (12 m)
MP = 208 lb. (94.5 kg)
BW = 990 lb. (450 kg)
BAW = 2,174 lb.(988.2 kg)

MOW = 3,041 lb.(1,382.3 kg)
ROW = 2,737 lb.(1,244.1 kg)
BR = 1 : 3.17
PMH = 89˝ (2.3 m)
UW = 1,184 lb. (538.2 kg)

3-Wide Bucket

IMD = 36"
36' 6"
11' 6"

31.
4891

MH = 23' 7" (7.2 m)
MR = 17' 4" (5.3 m)
MP = 800 lb. (363.6 kg)
BW = 11 lb. (.5 kg)
BAW = 881 lb. (400.5 kg)

MOW = 2,625 lb. (1,193.2 kg)
ROW = 1,175 lb. (534.1 kg)
BR = 1 : 1.18
PMH = 9'3" (2.8 m)
UW = 870 lb. (395.5 kg)

3-Wide Bucket

IMD = 10"
16' 6"
14'

32.
4892

MH = 27' 7" (8.4 m)
MR = 22' 7" (6.9 m)
MP = 800 lb. (363.6 kg)
BW = 156 lb. (70.9 kg)
BAW = 1,118 lb. (508.2 kg)

MOW = 3,150 lb. (1,431.8 kg)
ROW = 1,461 lb. (664.1 kg)
BR = 1 : 1.54
PMH = 9' 3" (2.8 m)
UW = 962 lb. (437.3 kg)

3-Wide Bucket

IMD = 13"
21' 6"
14'

Beyond 550 lbs. Payload (MP)
Cable System is Recommended
for Best Performance.

Figure 77 *continued*

Lenny Arm® III   Configurations

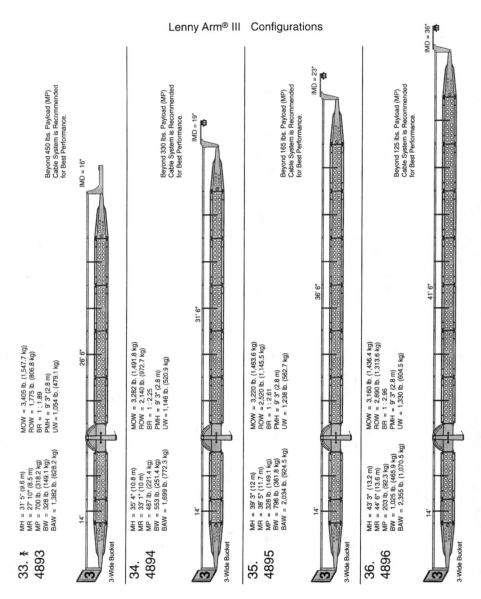

Figure 77   *continued*

Lenny Arm® III Warnings

In all configurations keep the crane arm balanced at all times. Avoid sudden disembarking of personnel or equipment removal.

The Lenny Arm rear section combination should be configurated so that the bucket touches the ground before the Lenny Arm vertical travel limits are obtained.

Bucket reaches ground.
(RECOMMENDED)

Bucket does not reach ground.
(NOT RECOMMENDED)

WARNING: DO NOT EXCEED THE LISTED POST MOUNT HEIGHT (PMH) VALUES TO AVOID INVALIDATING OUR SAFETY RECOMMENDATIONS.

WARNING: The 7 1/2" Riser should **NOT** be used with Manned Configurations.

WARNING

- It is NOT Permitted and is Unlawful to Operate This Equipment Within 10 Feet of High-Voltage Line of 50,000 Volts or Less.

- For Minimum Clearances of High-Voltage Line in Excess of 50,000 Volts. See California Code of Regulations, Title 8, Article 37, High-Voltage Electrical Safety Orders.

Source Title 8, California Code of Regulations, Subchapter 5, Group 2, Article 37, §2946, 29 Code of Federal Regulations 1926.451 (F)(6)

Nominal Voltage	Minimum Required Clearance (Feet)	(Meters)
600 up to 50,000	10	3
Over 50,000 to 75,000	11	3.4
Over 75,000 to 125,000	13	4
Over 125,000 to 175,000	15	4.6
Over 175,000 to 250,000	17	4.6
Over 250,000 to 370,000	21	6.4
Over 370,000 to 550,000	27	8.2
Over 550,000 to 1,000,000	42	12.8

Figure 77 *continued*

Lenny Arm® III

Parts and Accessories

All weights are based on scale accuracy of 2%

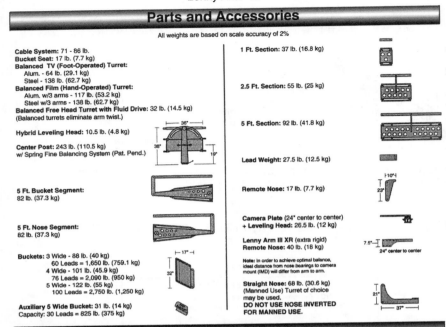

Cable System: 71 - 86 lb.
Bucket Seat: 17 lb. (7.7 kg)
Balanced TV (Foot-Operated) Turret:
Alum. - 64 lb. (29.1 kg)
Steel - 138 lb. (62.7 kg)
Balanced Film (Hand-Operated) Turret:
Alum. w/3 arms - 117 lb. (53.2 kg)
Steel w/3 arms - 138 lb. (62.7 kg)
Balanced Free Head Turret with Fluid Drive: 32 lb. (14.5 kg)
(Balanced turrets eliminate arm twist.)

Hybrid Leveling Head: 10.5 lb. (4.8 kg)

Center Post: 243 lb. (110.5 kg)
w/ Spring Fine Balancing System (Pat. Pend.)

5 Ft. Bucket Segment:
82 lb. (37.3 kg)

5 Ft. Nose Segment:
82 lb. (37.3 kg)

Buckets: 3 Wide - 88 lb. (40 kg)
60 Leads = 1,650 lb. (759.1 kg)
4 Wide - 101 lb. (45.9 kg)
76 Leads = 2,090 lb. (950 kg)
5 Wide - 122 lb. (55 kg)
100 Leads = 2,750 lb. (1,250 kg)

Auxiliary 5 Wide Bucket: 31 lb. (14 kg)
Capacity: 30 Leads = 825 lb. (375 kg)

1 Ft. Section: 37 lb. (16.8 kg)

2.5 Ft. Section: 55 lb. (25 kg)

5 Ft. Section: 92 lb. (41.8 kg)

Lead Weight: 27.5 lb. (12.5 kg)

Remote Nose: 17 lb. (7.7 kg)

Camera Plate (24" center to center)
+ **Leveling Head:** 26.5 lb. (12 kg)

Lenny Arm III XR (extra rigid)
Remote Nose: 40 lb. (18 kg)

Note: In order to achieve optimal balance, ideal distance from nose bearings to camera mount (IMD) will differ from arm to arm.

Straight Nose: 68 lb. (30.6 kg)
(Manned Use) Turret of choice may be used.
DO NOT USE NOSE INVERTED FOR MANNED USE.

Terms and Definitions

MH = Maximum Height. (From lens to ground in underslung mode. Additional height may be achieved by inverting remote head.) Note: In manned configurations add 2 to 4 feet to MH.

MR = Maximum Reach. (As measured from center post to ideal camera position.)

MP = Maximum Payload.

BW = Bucket Weight for balanced arm. (No payload.)

BAW = Balanced Arm Weight. (No payload.)

MOW = Maximum Operating Weight of unit. (With maximum payload and a full lead bucket.)

ROW = Remote Operational Weight of unit. (With 135 lb. payload.)

BR = Balance Ratio. (Determines the weight required in bucket to balance a payload after arm has been balanced.)

PMH = Post Mount Height needed to obtain maximum height on level ground. (Do not exceed.)

UW = Unit Weight.

IMD = Ideal camera Mount Distance. (From bearing to camera mount.)

BAW + (BR + 1) X Nose Load = Operating Weight for any given nose load.

🚶 = These configurations can be considered for manned use. Check payload.

In General: For Manned use, we recommend the Cable System for best performance.

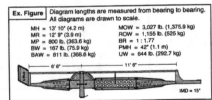

| Ex. Figure | Diagram lengths are measured from bearing to bearing. All diagrams are drawn to scale. |

MH = 13' 10" (4.2 m)   MOW = 3,027 lb. (1,375.9 kg)
MR = 12' 9" (3.9 m)   ROW = 1,155 lb. (525 kg)
MP = 800 lb. (363.6 kg) BR = 1 : 1.77
BW = 167 lb. (75.9 kg)   PMH = 42" (1.1 m)
BAW = 811 lb. (368.6 kg) UW = 644 lb. (292.7 kg)

*It is advised that the user of Chapman/Leonard equipment check with the manufacturer for the latest updates on *all* equipment.

Figure 77 *continued*

Dollies

The dollies described in this section are only a few of the types available. I believe that the chosen examples are the best the industry has to offer. Each dolly has its own characteristics, but all of the dollies do one basic thing—they are a mobile platform for the camera. This invention has saved the grip and camera department many hours of pain from carrying the tripod with the camera on it. As you look through the charts and specifications for each dolly, decide for yourself which dolly is best suited for the job you are about to do.

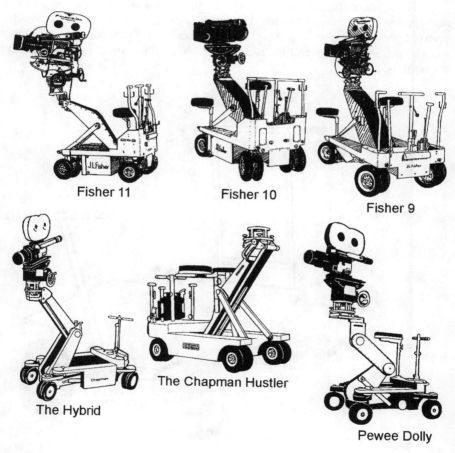

Fisher 11

Fisher 10

Fisher 9

The Hybrid

The Chapman Hustler

Pewee Dolly

Figure 78 A sampling of dollies.

Doorway Dolly

As the name suggests, the doorway dolly was designed to be an inexpensive camera dolly. It is narrow enough to fit through most standard doorways. Over the years, doorway dollies have been used not only for this purpose but also as efficient equipment transporters for camera cases, lighting fixtures, cable, and so forth.

Pneumatic tires are standard, but the doorway can be fitted with track wheels for use on straight dolly track. Steering is accomplished by using a pull handle (like a wagon). A new steering feature has been added that allows the operator to steer from onboard the dolly. This is accomplished by inserting the pull handle through the push bar on the front of the dolly. A recent addition available for the push bar is an angled fitting to allow the bar to tilt down 34 degrees for more clearance between the dolly and dolly operator. The basic construction is a wooden platform attached to a steel tubing frame.

The platform is fitted with a recessed camera tiedown and is carpeted for a nonslip, low-maintenance surface. For extra-low-angle shots, the dolly can be inverted, thereby positioning the platform closer to the ground. This dolly also includes the ability to extend the rear wheels outward to provide greater operating stability.

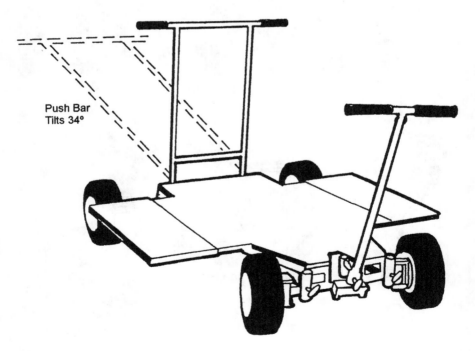

Push Bar
Tilts 34°

Figure 79 The doorway dolly.

T.O.T.

Use whatever is available to get the shot. On one job, I needed a long dolly shot in front of a *peru* (small swamp boat) in the Louisiana swamps. The actor would stand in his small craft and push himself off the bottom of the swamp floor with a long rod. It's a slow-paced movement. The director wanted a long, slow move down the center of this bayou. A boat would rock, giving an unwanted camera action. I used two floating platforms that were square and flat-bottomed. I placed the camera, the cameraperson, and the camera assistant only on the camera platform. This was tied to the front platform, where excess camera gear and two grips were stationed. A 600-foot rope was tied to a tree down the bayou. I pulled the rope, setting the pace asked for by the director.

Western Dolly

Somewhat similar in design to the doorway dolly, the western is much larger and is capable of transporting a heavier load. Larger wheels offer a smoother, steadier ride than the smaller dollies. The western can be fitted with flotation track wheels and (unlike the doorway) can be operated on curved track. You can use this dolly as a camera dolly, an equipment transporter, or a low platform behind a camera car.

For operator convenience, the push bar can be tilted down 34 degrees by using the tilt adapter. The bar can also be side-mounted for close shots. When the

Figure 80   The western dolly.

western dolly is used inverted, the platform clearance is raised for use over rough terrain.

Two recent additions to the western dolly include the turret assembly and the pop-off wheels. The turret assembly allows for mounting two seats and a complete camera configuration supported by a Mitchell base. The pop-off wheels allow for quick removal of the dolly wheels for easy storage. The axle is captivated into the wheel assembly to prevent it from becoming separated from the wheel upon removal.

> **T.O.T.**
> Most dollies either fold or remove the grips working end for a 360 degree shot.

Tube Dolly

A tube dolly is a specialized dolly originally designed to ride on sections of straight standard dolly track or tubing. The tube dolly was created to serve as a tracking platform for the older conventional-type crab dollies, which were not capable of being adapted for track use. The crab dolly would be physically loaded onto the tube dolly. The rear carriage of the tube dolly is adjustable back and forth to compensate for differing wheel lengths of crab dollies. Another application of the adjustable rear carriage is to serve as an outrigger platform for lighting or sound when the camera is riding on the main platform.

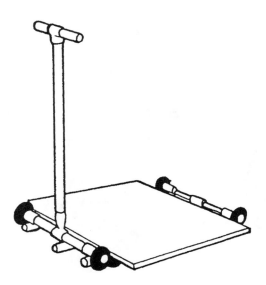

Figure 81 The tube dolly.

T.O.T.
Always replace the rubber tips on the track before transporting the dolly. This prevents damage.

The Fisher #11 Crab Dolly

Specifications

Maximum elevation (without riser)		
Head up	51½ in.	(131 cm)
Head down	49½ in.	(126 cm)
Minimum elevation (down position)		
Head up	17½ in.	(44 cm)
Head down	15½ in.	(37 cm)
Minimum elevation (low-level head)	3½ in.	(9 cm)
Vertical beam travel	34 in.	(86 cm)
Lift beam capacity	200 lbs.	(91 kg)
Lifts per system charge	6	6
Length (level head forward)	44¾ in.	(114 cm)
Length (level head reversed)	39⅜ in.	(101 cm)
Width for fully operational steering (wheels in)	20⅜ in.	(52 cm)
Width for fully operational steering (wheels out)	25¾ in.	(65 cm)
Height (operating)	39⅝ in.	(101 cm)
Height (folded)	23¼ in.	(59 cm)
Minimum turn radius (round steering)	16³⁄₁₆ in.	(41 cm)
Minimum turn radius (conventional steering)	33½ in.	(85 cm)
Carrying weight	320 lbs.	(145 kg)

Features

- Three-way steering system: crab, conventional, and round
- 80 to 240 volts AC or DC
- Multi-position level head
- Rotary knob or up-down lever
- Camera battery compartment
- Self-contained track system

T.O.T.
Rule of thumb: Never arm more than four times without a pump up. Some dollies may arm up seven to eight times, but you do not want to run out of pressure in the middle of the shot.

Figure 82a   Fisher #11 crab dolly.

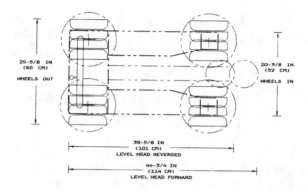

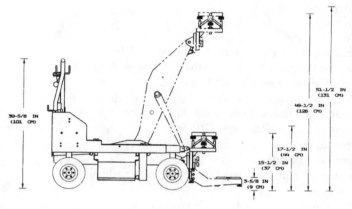

Figure 82b   Specifications for Fisher #11 crab dolly.

Fisher #11 Dolly Order

Standard Accessories

NOTE: These accessories will/should come with the Fisher #11 dolly.

(2) Seats
(2) Front boards (elephant ears or porkchops)
(2) High-side boards (31½ in. long) (79 cm)
(2) Low-side boards (11 in. long) (28 cm)
(1) Battery rack
(2) Push posts
(2) Carry handles (nickname: can openers)
(1) Knee bumper
(1) Power cord
Front Pins

Optional Accessories

Straight (Square)Track
20 ft.
16 ft.
10 ft.
8 ft.
4 ft.
3 ft.
2 ft.

Curved Track
10-ft. diameter
20-ft. diameter
30-ft. diameter
70-ft. diameter

Rotating offsets (There are four models to choose from.)
Low-level heads (two- or four-way level-type models)
45-degree seat offset
90 degree seat offset
Seat riser
Rotating seats
Camera offsets: 10 in. or 24 in. (nickname: Ubangie)
Universal adapter (makes a Mitchell base into a Ball base)
Camera risers: 3 in., 6 in., or 12 in.
90-degree camera angle plate
Round track adapter wheel set (boggie wheels)
Diving boards (42 in. long) (107 cm)
Lamp adapter
Front board bridge
Front track platform (low board with roller wheels)
Ice skates
Center mount kit (for large jib arms)
Soft wheels (used as a softening effect)
Monitor rack
Cue board

Fisher #10 Crab Dolly

Specifications

Maximum elevation (without riser)	160 cm	63 in.
Minimum elevation (unaided)	41 cm	16 in.
Minimum elevation (low-level head)	12 cm	$4\frac{3}{4}$ in.
Vertical beam travel	119 cm	47 in.
Lift capacity	227 kg	500 lbs.
Lifts per charge	7	7
Length	137 cm	54 in.
Width (wheels in)	68 cm	$26\frac{5}{8}$ in.
Width (wheels out)	81 cm	32 in.
Height (operating)	98 cm	$38\frac{1}{2}$ in.
Height (folded)	64 cm	25 in.

Figure 83a   Fisher #10 crab dolly.

Minimum turning radius (for round steering)	56 cm	22 in.
Minimum turning radius (for conventional steering)	112 cm	44 in.
Carrying weight	190 kg	420 lbs.
Maximum load capacity	408 kg	900 lbs.
High side boards	91 cm	36 in.
Low side boards	52 cm	$20\frac{1}{2}$ in.

Standard Accessories

Interchangeable front boards
(2) Adjustable seats
(2) Push posts
(2) Carry handles

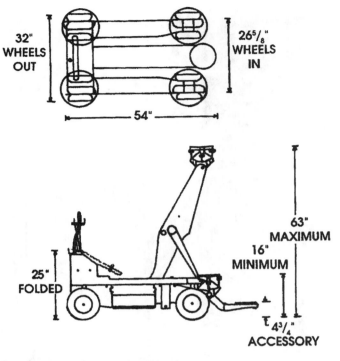

Figure 83b Specifications for Fisher #10 dolly.

(1) Power cord
(1) Battery rack
(2) Front pins
(1) Knee bumper

Optional Accessories

(1) Battery tray
6-in. and 12-in. risers (one each)
10-in. and 24-in. camera offsets and Fisher rotating (nickname: Ubangie)
    (one each)
Seat offset: 45 degree and 90 degree (one each)
(1) Seat riser
(2) Diving boards
(1) Monitor rack
(1) Low-level head (nickname: shovel nose)
(1) Seat platform
Straight track: comes in 8-ft. and 4-ft. sections (one each)
Curved track: 10-ft. and 20-ft. diameter (one each)

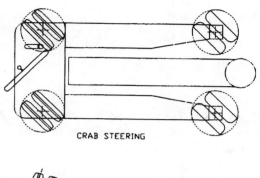

CRAB STEERING

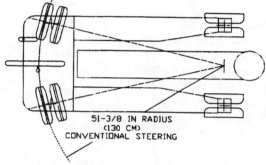

51-3/8 IN RADIUS
(130 CM)
CONVENTIONAL STEERING

Figure 83c   Fisher #10 dolly steering capacities.

Track ramps (one pair)
(1) Shipping case

Fisher #10 Dolly Order

Standard Accessories

NOTE: These accessories will/should come with the Fisher #10 dolly.

(2) Seats
(2) Front boards (elephant ears or porkchops)
(2) High side boards (36 in. long)
(2) Low side boards (20½ in. long)
(1) Battery rack
(2) Push posts
(2) Carry handles (nickname: can openers)
(1) Knee bumper
(1) Power cord
Front pins

Optional Accessories

Straight (Square) Track
20 ft.

Curved Track
10-ft. diameter

16 ft.	20-ft. diameter
10 ft.	30-ft. diameter
8 ft.	70-ft. diameter
4 ft.	
3 ft.	
2 ft.	

Rotating offsets (There are four models to choose from.)
Low-level heads (two- or four-way level-type models)
45-degree seat offset
90-degree seat offset
Seat riser
Rotating seat
Beam step standing platform
Camera offsets: 10 in. or 24 in. (nickname: Ubangie)
Universal adapter (makes a Mitchell base into a Ball base)
Camera risers: 3 in., 6 in., or 12 in.
90-degree camera angle plate
Round track adapter wheel set (boggie wheels)
Diving boards (48 in. long)
Lamp adapter
Front track platform (low board with roller wheels)
Front porch (high board that hooks on front of the dolly)
Ice skates
Center mount kit (for large jib arms)
Soft wheels (used as a softening effect)
Monitor rack
Cue board

Fisher #9 Crab Dolly

Specifications

Maximum elevation (without riser)	157 cm	61¾ in.
Minimum elevation (unaided)	37 cm	14½ in.
Minimum elevation (low-level head)	12 cm	4¾ in.
Vertical beam travel	120 cm	47¼ in.
Lift capacity	227 kg	500 lbs.
Lifts per charge	5	5
Length	170 cm	67 in.
Width	77 cm	30½ in.
Height (operating)	94 cm	37 in.
Height (folded)	50 cm	19½ in.
Minimum turning radius (for conventional steering)	130 cm	61⅜ in.
Carrying weight	202 kg	445 lbs.
Maximum load capacity	454 kg	1,000 lbs.

Figure 84   Fisher #9 crab dolly.

Features

- Three-way steering system: crab, conventional, and steering
- 80 to 240 volts AC or DC

Standard Accessories

High, 36 in., and low; $20\frac{1}{2}$ in. (52 cm), side boards
Interchangeable front boards
Adjustable seats
Push posts
Carry handles

Power cord
Front pins
Battery rack
Knee board

Optional Accessories

3-in., 6-in., and 12-in. risers
10-in. and 24-in. camera offsets and Fisher rotating (nickname: Ubangie)
90-degree angle plates
Pan/tilt adapters
Monitor rack
Low-level head
Seat offset
Seat risers
Seat platform
Extended high side boards
Track trucks (for Fisher, Matthews, Elemack, and Dexter straight tracks)
Straight track (round or square)
Track ramps
Shipping case

Fisher #9 Dolly Order

Standard Accessories

NOTE: These accessories will/should come with the Fisher #9 dolly.

(2) Seats
(2) Front boards (elephant ears or porkchops)
(2) High side boards (36 in. long)
(2) Low side boards (20$\frac{1}{2}$ in. long)
(1) Battery rack
(2) Push posts
(2) Carry handles (nickname: can openers)
(1) Knee bumper
(1) Power cord
Front pins

Optional Accessories

Straight (Square) Track	Curved Track
20 ft.	10-ft. diameter
16 ft.	20-ft. diameter
10 ft.	30-ft. diameter
8 ft.	70-ft. diameter
4 ft.	
3 ft.	
2 ft.	

Rotating offsets (There are four models to choose from.)
Low-level heads (two- or four-way level-type models)
45-degree seat offset
90-degree seat offset
Seat riser
Rotating seat
Beam step standing platform
Camera offsets: 10 in. or 24 in. (nickname: Ubangie)
Universal adapter (makes a Mitchell base into a Ball base)
Camera risers: 3 in., 6 in., or 12 in.
90-degree camera angle plate
Round track adapter wheel set (boggie wheels)
Diving boards (48 in. long)
Lamp adapter
Front track platform (low board with roller wheels)
Front porch (high board that hooks on front of the dolly)
Ice skates
Center mount kit (for large jib arms)
Soft wheels (used as a softening effect)
Monitor rack
Cue board

Fisher Camera Dolly Accessories

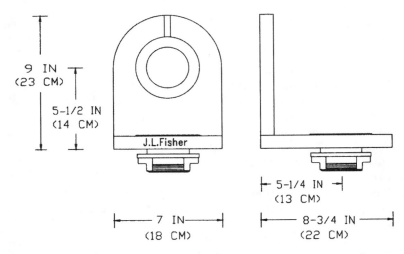

Figure 85 *Angle plate.* The 90-degree camera angle plate has a standard Mitchell mount and is designed for use with all dollies.

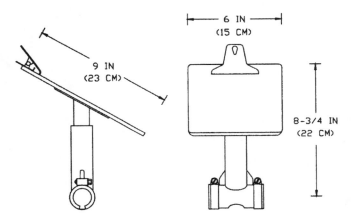

Figure 86 *Cue board.* Mounts firmly on the steering post of J. L. Fisher #10 and #9 camera dollies, keeping the cue board in view of the dolly grip at all times. Adjustable height and rotation positions.

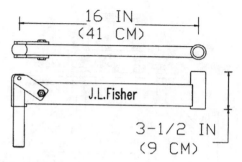

Seat Offset Straight

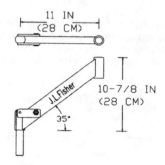

Seat Offset High

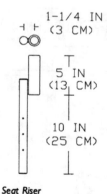

Seat Riser

Figure 87 *Seat accessories.* J. L. Fisher camera dollies offer two seat offsets and one seat riser. These accessories allow you to safely and securely adjust the seats to nearly any desirable position. Rotating seats are also available (not shown).

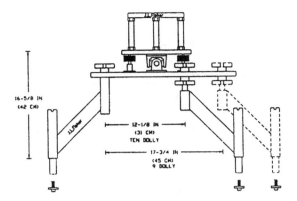

Figure 88 *Center mount kit.* The center mount adapter kit is designed and built to support jib arms, lightweight booms, and counterbalance cranes on the J. L. Fisher #10 and #9 camera dollies. Easy to install, the center mount increases the load capacity and versatility of the camera dollies. Maximum load capacity is 900 lbs. (408 kg).

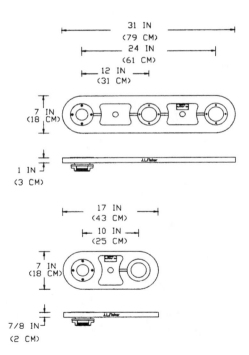

Figure 89 *Camera offsets.* Camera offsets are available in two lengths: 10 in. and 24 in. center to center. The 24-in. model may also be used to support two cameras or as a 12-in. offset. The camera offsets are constructed of high-grade lightweight aluminum for stability.

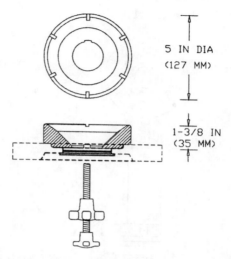

Figure 90 *Universal adapter.* The universal adapter converts the Mitchell mount on J. L. Fisher dollies and accessories for use with Clawball, Sachtler, Miller, and O'Conner heads.

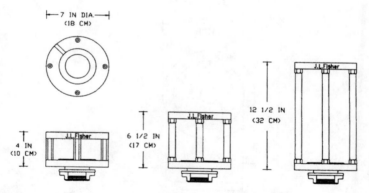

Figure 91 *Camera risers.* Camera risers are available in three sizes: 3 in., 6 in., and 12 in., allowing configuring of various heights by stacking. Constructed of high-grade lightweight aluminum for stability, the standard Mitchell mount (24 in. and 36 in.) fits all J. L. Fisher dollies, Elemack dollies, and most other makes. Jimmy Fisher Company risers are also available in 24 in. and 26 in.

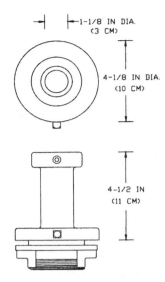

Figure 92 *Mitchell mount lamp adapter.* This adapter converts the standard Mitchell mount on all J. L. Fisher dollies and accessories to accept $1\frac{1}{8}$ in. lamp pins.

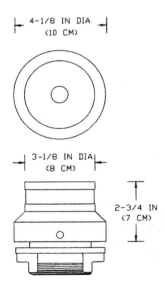

Figure 93 *Mitchell Euro mount adapter.* This adapter converts the standard Mitchell mount on all J. L. Fisher dollies and accessories to the European-style camera mount.

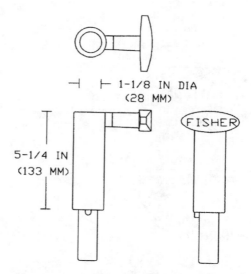

Figure 94 *Lamp adapter.* This adapter converts the seat sockets and push post sockets on a J. L Fisher dolly to hold a lamp riser. The adapter allows for mounting of standard $1\frac{1}{8}$ in. lamp pins.

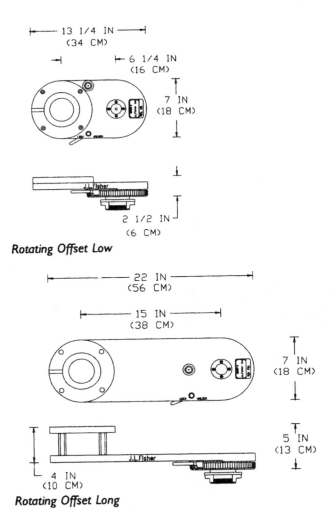

Rotating Offset Low

Rotating Offset Long

Figure 95 *Rotating offsets.* Rotating offsets allow the camera position to be easily changed with the lockable, smooth, rotating mechanism. All four models feature a 360-degree range with 84 lock positions (every 4.3 degrees) and a leveling indicator. It is constructed of high-grade aluminum alloy with multiple lubricated bearings.

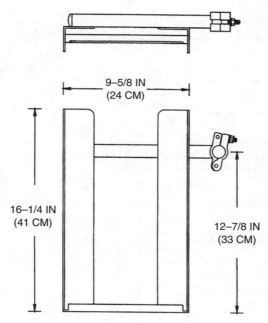

Figure 96 *Monitor rack.* This rack mounts on the push post of J. L. Fisher #9 and #10 dollies for supporting video monitors. It fits most monitors in use today.

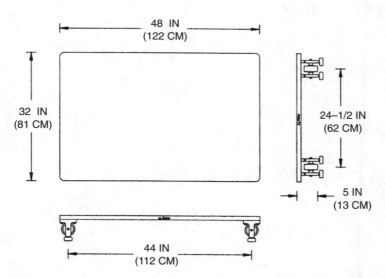

Figure 97 *Scooter board.* The scooter board is for use on straight track only, square or round. The Scooter board can be used to support tripods, light stands, or other devices and personnel. Polyurethane wheels and rollers give this accessory a smooth, steady ride.

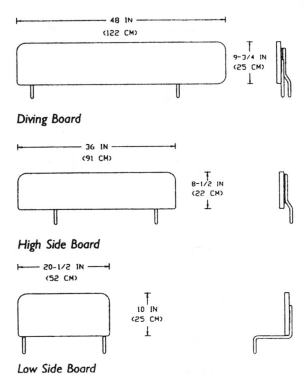

Diving Board

High Side Board

Low Side Board

Figure 98 Model #10 dolly boards.

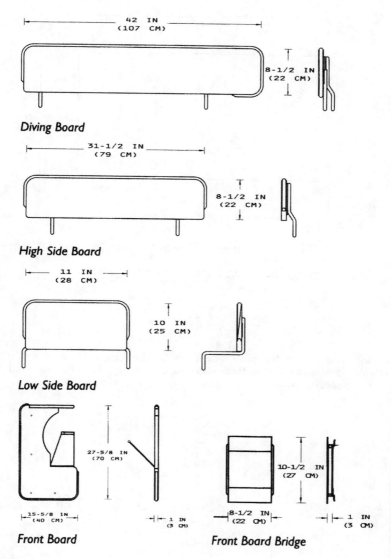

Figure 99 Model #11 dolly boards.

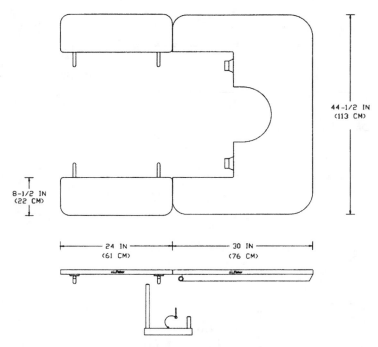

Figure 100 *Front porch.* This piece mounts on the front of J. L. Fisher #9 and #10 camera dollies, creating a large platform at the walk plate level. The #10 dolly front porch comes with two short high boards, providing additional area to stand on.

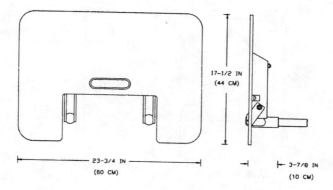

Model 9 Dolly Platform

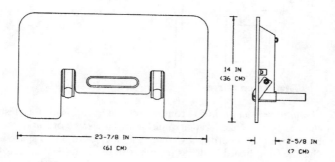

Model Ten Dolly Platform

Figure 101 *Beam step standing platform.* The beam steps are for J. L. Fisher #9 and #10 camera dollies. These accessories mount near the midpoint of the lift beam in the seat mounts and are designed for the camera operator to stand on.

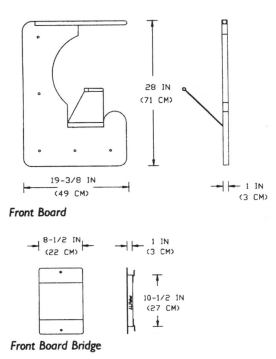

Front Board

Front Board Bridge

Figure 102 *Front boards and bridge.* Front boards are for use with J. L. Fisher #9 and #10 camera dollies. They provide a large area just above the stage or top of the track to stand on. When used with low boards, they create 180 degrees of board space around the front of the dolly. The front board bridge is for use with the front boards on a J. L. Fisher #10 dolly.

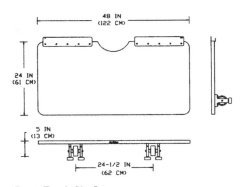

Front Track Platform

Figure 103 *Front track platform.* This platform is for use with J. L. Fisher #9 and #10 camera dollies in conjunction with front boards to ride on straight track, square or round. The platform creates a large space for personnel, light stands, tripods, or other equipment just above the track surface. Polyurethane wheels and rollers give smooth, steady performance.

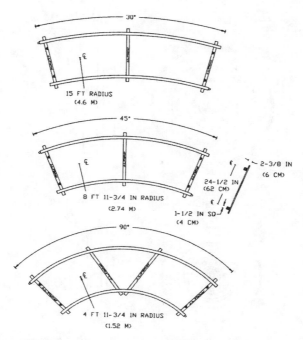

Figure 104 *Camera dolly track.* This is low-friction, square-tube curved track for J. L. Fisher #10 and Elemack dollies: Low-maintenance 1½ in. stainless steel tubing with alloy crossties. Available in precision manufactured 5-, 10-, and 15-ft. radius sections, allowing configuration of 10-, 20-, and 30-ft. diameter, full tested circles; 10-ft. circle requires four pieces of 5-ft. radius track; 20-ft. circle requires eight pieces of 10-ft. radius track; 30-ft. circle requires 12 pieces of 15-ft. radius track.

Because there is less friction, camera dollies are more stable and operate more easily on the Fisher square track than on the round tube track. Track sections connect and disconnect to the straight or curved track quickly with the Track Buckle System (width: 24½ in. center to center). Track ramps and wedges are available. Special wheels are also available to convert other makes of dollies to operate easily on the Fisher square track.

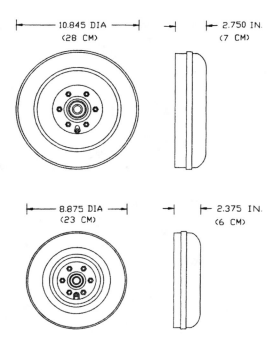

Figure 105 *Soft wheels.* These wheels are available to fit J. L. Fisher #9 and #10 camera dollies. These polyurethane tires are made so that the surface area with the floor is reduced significantly, adding a cushion effect. Large and small #10 dolly wheels are shown.

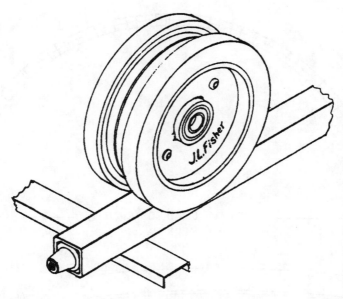

Figure 106 *P Wheels.* Designed and manufactured for the Peewee dolly to operate on straight and curved track.

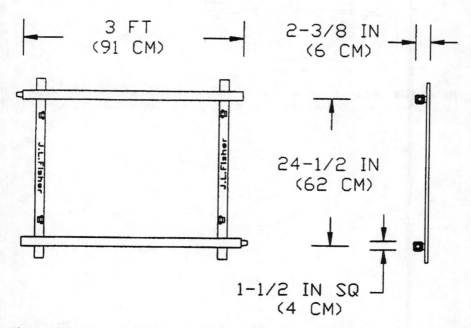

Figure 107 *Three-foot square straight track.* This track is manufactured with the same materials and high-quality workmanship as the square track. Complements all other Fisher track.

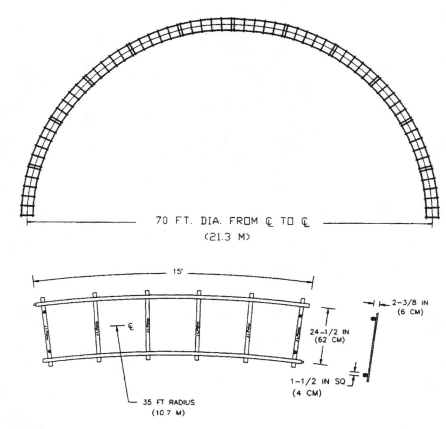

Figure 108 *Seventy-foot-diameter curved square track.* This track is designed for use in automobile commercials. Twelve pieces are required for a half-circle, and 24 pieces for a full circle.

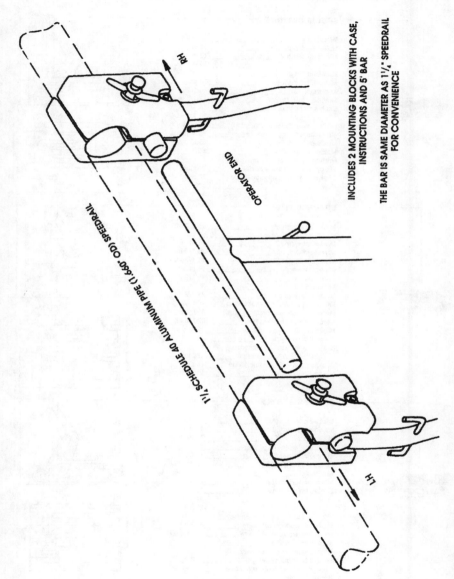

RH

INCLUDES 2 MOUNTING BLOCKS WITH CASE, INSTRUCTIONS AND 5' BAR

THE BAR IS SAME DIAMETER AS 1¼" SPEEDRAIL FOR CONVENIENCE

OPERATOR END

1¼" SCHEDULE 40 ALUMINUM PIPE (1.660" OD) SPEEDRAIL

LH

Figure 109 Push rod for a Fisher dolly.

Shotmaker Blue

Shotmaker Blue Goes Above and Beyond You Know Who.

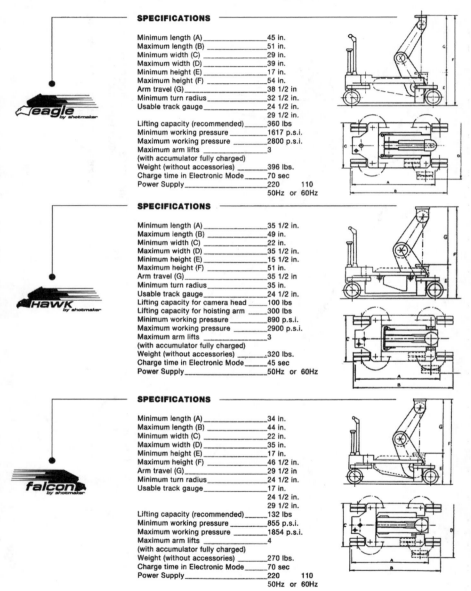

SPECIFICATIONS

eagle *by shotmaker*

Minimum length (A)	45 in.
Maximum length (B)	51 in.
Minimum width (C)	29 in.
Maximum width (D)	39 in.
Minimum height (E)	17 in.
Maximum height (F)	54 in.
Arm travel (G)	38 1/2 in
Minimum turn radius	32 1/2 in.
Usable track gauge	24 1/2 in.
	29 1/2 in.
Lifting capacity (recommended)	360 lbs
Minimum working pressure	1617 p.s.i.
Maximum working pressure	2800 p.s.i.
Maximum arm lifts	3
(with accumulator fully charged)	
Weight (without accessories)	396 lbs.
Charge time in Electronic Mode	70 sec
Power Supply	220 110
	50Hz or 60Hz

SPECIFICATIONS

hawk *by shotmaker*

Minimum length (A)	35 1/2 in.
Maximum length (B)	49 in.
Minimum width (C)	22 in.
Maximum width (D)	35 1/2 in.
Minimum height (E)	15 1/2 in.
Maximum height (F)	51 in.
Arm travel (G)	35 1/2 in.
Minimum turn radius	35 in.
Usable track gauge	24 1/2 in.
Lifting capacity for camera head	100 lbs
Lifting capacity for hoisting arm	300 lbs
Minimum working pressure	890 p.s.i.
Maximum working pressure	2900 p.s.i.
Maximum arm lifts	3
(with accumulator fully charged)	
Weight (without accessories)	320 lbs.
Charge time in Electronic Mode	45 sec
Power Supply	50Hz or 60Hz

SPECIFICATIONS

falcon *by shotmaker*

Minimum length (A)	34 in.
Maximum length (B)	44 in.
Minimum width (C)	22 in.
Maximum width (D)	35 in.
Minimum height (E)	17 in.
Maximum height (F)	46 1/2 in.
Arm travel (G)	29 1/2 in
Minimum turn radius	24 1/2 in.
Usable track gauge	17 in.
	24 1/2 in.
	29 1/2 in.
Lifting capacity (recommended)	132 lbs
Minimum working pressure	855 p.s.i.
Maximum working pressure	1854 p.s.i.
Maximum arm lifts	4
(with accumulator fully charged)	
Weight (without accessories)	270 lbs.
Charge time in Electronic Mode	70 sec
Power Supply	220 110
	50Hz or 60Hz

Figure 110   Shotmaker Blue.

Falcon II

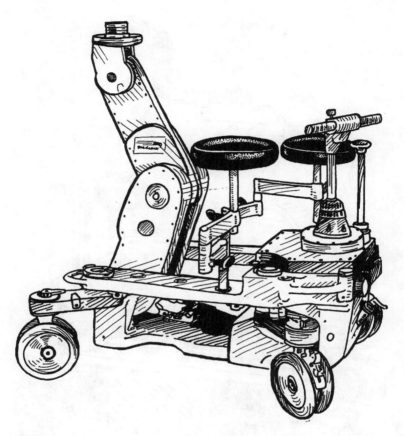

Figure 111 Falcon II.

Eagle II

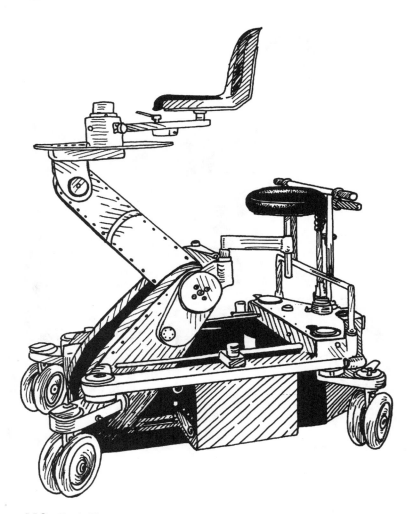

Figure 112 Eagle II.

Fraser Dolly

Specifications

A	Wheel track centers	$24^{1/2}$	622.3 mm
B	Overall width MkII	27 in.	686.0 mm
C	Chassis height	15 in.	381.0 mm

Figure 113a Fraser dolly.

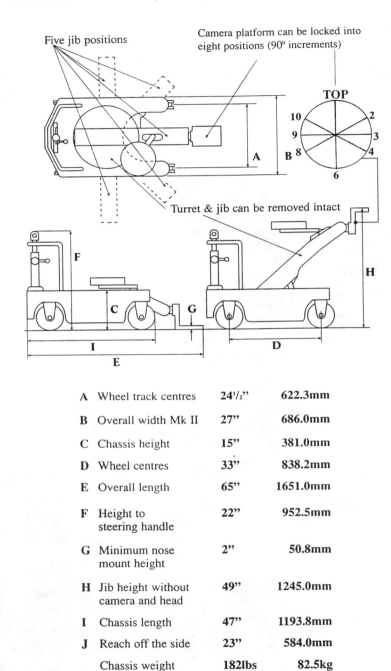

	A	Wheel track centres	24¹/₂"	622.3mm
	B	Overall width Mk II	27"	686.0mm
	C	Chassis height	15"	381.0mm
	D	Wheel centres	33"	838.2mm
	E	Overall length	65"	1651.0mm
	F	Height to steering handle	22"	952.5mm
	G	Minimum nose mount height	2"	50.8mm
	H	Jib height without camera and head	49"	1245.0mm
	I	Chassis length	47"	1193.8mm
	J	Reach off the side	23"	584.0mm
		Chassis weight	182lbs	82.5kg
		Turret weight	198lbs	89.9kg

Figure 113b   Fraser dolly.

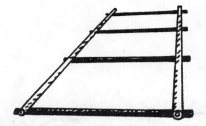

Figure 114 Straight tube-type track.

D	Wheel centers	33 in.	838.2 mm
E	Overall length	65 in.	1,651.0 mm
F	Height to steering handle	22 in.	952.5 mm
G	Minimum nose mount height	2 in.	50.8 mm
H	Jib height without camera and head	49 in.	1,245.0 mm
I	Chassis length	47 in.	1,193.8 mm
J	Reach off the side	23 in.	584.0 mm
	Chassis weight	182 lbs.	82.5 kg
	Turret weight	198 lbs.	89.9 kg

Filou

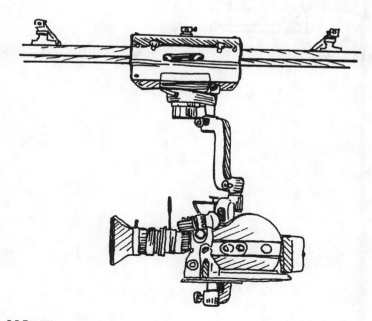

Figure 115 Filou.

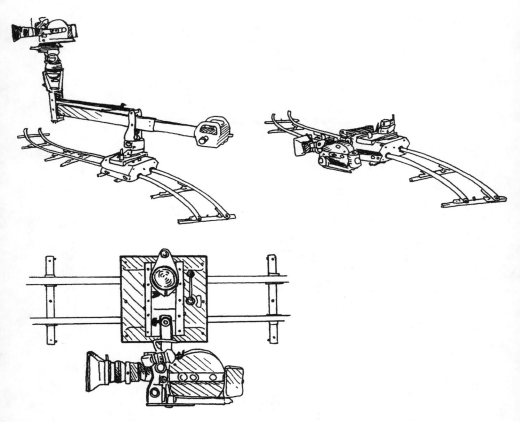

Figure 116   Filou.

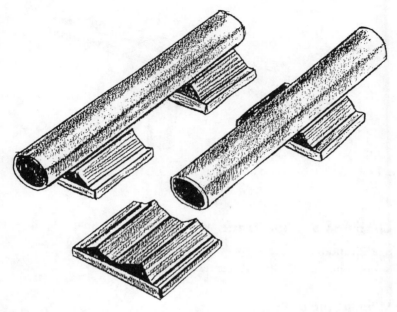

Figure 117 Speed-Rail® rubber flange, by Modern Studio Equipment.

Figure 118 Portable track wheels.

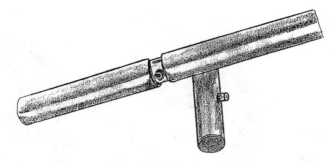

Figure 119   Track joiner (pipe/tube dolly).

Chapman Straight Track

Specifications

8-foot round track with 24$\frac{1}{2}$ center to center

Wheelchair Dolly

Specifications

Adjusts to just above ground level to approximately 5-feet high camera positions

Channel Wheels Dolly

Specifications

Will fit 24$\frac{1}{2}$ center to center straight or curved track

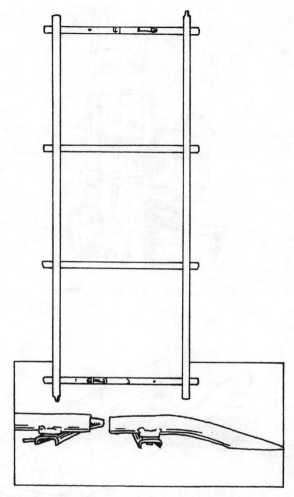

Figure 120 Chapman straight track 8-foot section (tube type).

Figure 121 Wheelchair dolly from Modern Studio Equipment.

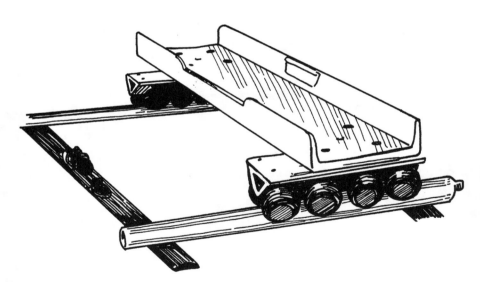

Figure 122 Channel wheels dolly from Modern Studio Equipment.

Backstage Action Dolly

ACTION DOLLY WIDTH ADJUSTMENTS:

ACTION DOLLY TURNING RADIUS:

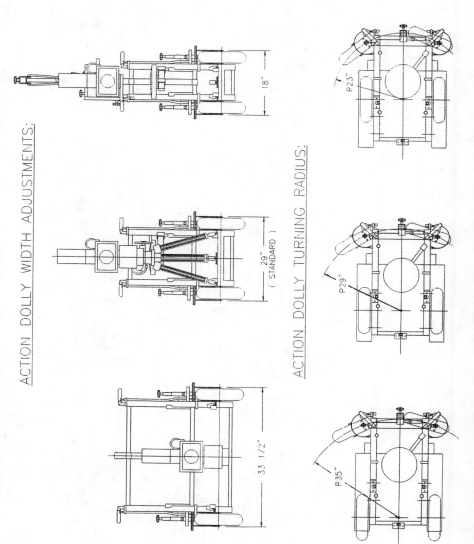

18"

29" (STANDARD)

33 1/2"

R23"

R29"

R35"

Figure 123 Backstage action dolly width adjustments.

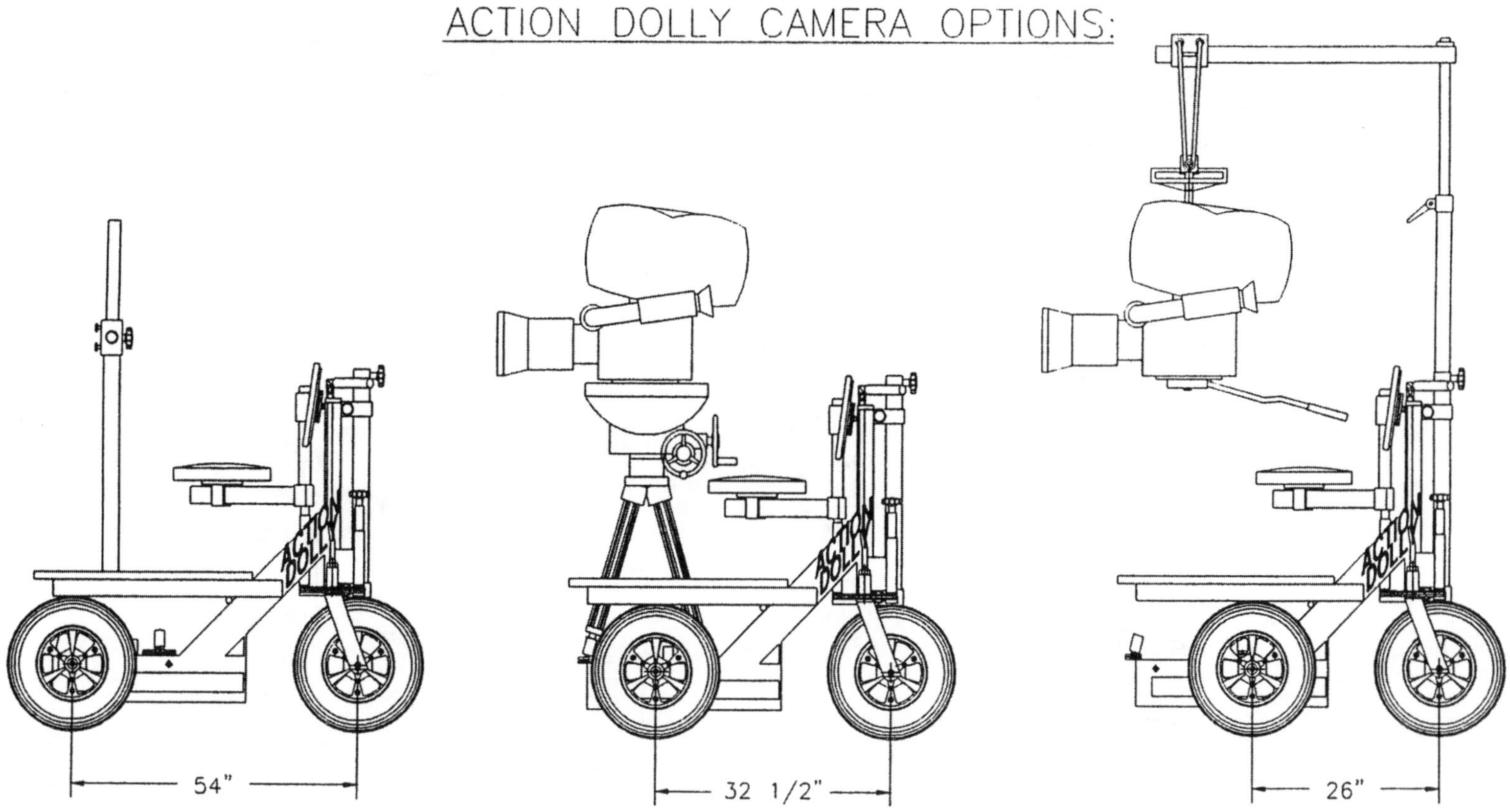

ACTION DOLLY CAMERA OPTIONS:

Figure 124 Backstage action dolly camera options.

Panther Bazooka

Figure 125 Panther Bazooka base with risers.

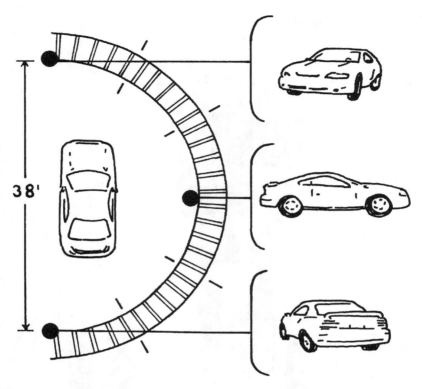

Figure 126 Precision I Beam.

Precision I Beam

Specifications

Use 38 foot

Precision Cadillac Track

Specifications

3-ft. straight	5 ft. 1 in.	1.5 m
5-ft. straight	7 ft. 2 in.	2.1 m
8-ft. straight	10 ft. 2 in.	3.0 m
10-ft. straight	12 ft. 2 in.	3.7 m
12-ft. straight	14 ft. 2 in.	4.3 m

30-degree curve, 2- to 5-ft. sections = 20-ft.-diameter circle

With standard sleepers	24½ in.	.6 m
With expandable sleepers		
First position	24½ in.	.6 m

Precision Cadillac Track

Precision Cadillac Track is extruded from structural marine alloy. Rigidity is 10 times greater than conventional tube track. Precision Cadillac Track is available in 2½" and 3" heights. Having a twin-pin joining system, it offers zero gap and deflection, thus giving you the smoothest tracking shots ever, particularly with long lenses.

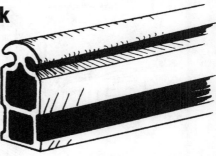

Specifications	Folding Length	
	Feet	Meters
3' Straight	5'1"	1.5
5' Straight	7'2"	2.1
8' Straight	10'2"	3.0
10' Straight	12'2"	3.7
12' Straight	14'2"	4.3
30° Curve	6'6"	1.98
2-5' Sections =		
20' Dia. Circlei		

	Track Width	
	Feet	Meters
With Standard Sleepers	24½"	0.6
With Expandable Sleepers		
1st Position	24½"	0.6
2nd Position	28"	0.7
3rd Position	34½"	0.8

Precision Cadillac Track offers unique custom curves, folding 30 degree curves and non-folding 45 degree curves. It is a low profile, multi-wheel dolly and crane track that is compatible with Fisher and standard wheel applications. This large curve track is ideal for shooting car commercials and music videos.

Precision Cadillac Track is lower, lighter, stronger and more cost effective than other track

Figure 127 Precision Cadillac Track-Shotmaker.

Second position	28 in.	.7 m
Third position	34¾ in.	.8 m

Magnum Dolly

Specifications

Magnum Dolly with Duo Jib and TV Platform

Maximum payload capacity	220 kg/484 lbs.
Maximum platform height (Euro adapter)	209 cm/6 ft. 10 in.
Minimum platform height (Euro adapter)	59 cm/1 ft. 11 in.

Magnum Dolly with Duo Jib

Maximum payload capacity with high rig mode	220 kg/440 lbs.
With low rig mode	220 kg/484 lbs.
Standard mode	250 kg/550 lbs.
Maximum platform height (Euro adapter)	272 cm/8 ft. 11 in.
Minimum platform height (Euro adapter)	26 cm/10 in.
Lift range	150 cm/4 ft. 11 in.

Magnum Dolly with Mini Jib Arm

Maximum payload capacity	80 kg/176 lbs.
Maximum height (Euro adapter)	235 cm/7 ft. 9 in.
Minimum height (Euro adapter)	70 cm/2 ft. 3 in.
Minimum height with mini low rig	9 cm/3 in.
Lift range	165 cm/5 ft. 5 in.

Figure 128 Magnum duo jib.

Magnum Dolly with Low Rig

Maximum payload capacity	130 kg/286 lbs.
Maximum platform height (Euro adapter)	78 cm/2 ft. 6 in.
Minimum platform height (Euro adapter)	10 cm/4 in.
Lift range	68 cm/2 ft. 4 in.

Basic Dolly with Felix Crane System

Maximum payload capacity	220 kg/484 lbs.
Maximum platform height	275 cm/9 ft.
Lift range	275 cm/9 ft.

T.O.T.

Mark a small "V" with tape on your dolly control knobs. When one side of the "V" is directly in line where the dolly arm begins to move up, the other edge is inline when it moves down. This technique is a great eyeball reference.

Master Track System

Foldable track width is 0.62 m/24 ft. 5 in.

Specifications

	Length*	Weight	Transp. Length
Master track	0.9 m/3 ft.	7 kg/15 lbs.	1.6 m/5 ft.
Master track straight	1.6 m/5 ft.	13 kg/28 lbs.	2.3 m/7 ft. 5 in.
Master track straight	2.3 m/7 ft. 5 in.	18 kg/39 lbs.	3 m/10 ft.

NOTE: *Other lengths are available upon request.

Fixed track width is 0.62 m/24 ft. 5 in.

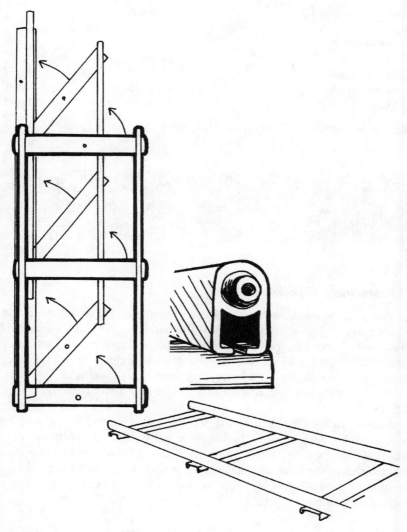

Figure 129   Master track system.

Specifications

	Length*	Weight
Master track	0.9 m/3 ft.	7 kg/15 lbs
Master track	1.6 m/5 ft.	13 kg/28 lbs.
Master track	2.3 m/7 ft. 5 in.	18 kg/39 lbs.
Master track curved 45 degrees		20 kg/44 lbs.

NOTE: *Other lengths are available upon request.

Track width is 1 m/39 in.

Specifications

	Length*	Height
Master track	0.9 m/3 ft.	10 kg/22 lbs.
Master track	1.6 m/5 ft.	14 kg/30 lbs.
Master track	2.3 m/7 ft. 5 in.	19 kg/41 lbs.

NOTE: *Other lengths are available upon request.

T.O.T.

Most "dolly track" is 24½ inches wide from the center of the track rail to the center of the opposite track rail.

Losmandy Flex Trak

This amazing seamless dolly track can be configured in straight runs that can suddenly curve in any radius or direction. The basic unit is 40 feet, which will loop to make one 18-foot run. Two pieces side by side will create a 40-foot run. Each section rolls up into a 2-foot-diameter bundle and weights 40 pounds, creating unprecedented portability for a track rigid enough to support an operator and assistant on a dolly, yet flexible enough to curve into a 90-degree turn with a 2-foot radius.

The key to the Flex Trak's success lies in the unique capability of its track wheels, which are designed with double articulating arms that create the ability to negotiate dollies; however, it can also work with other dolly systems because the outer diameter of the Flex Trak is the same as that of standard steel track. Other dolly systems generally are not able to make the tight radius turns that are a feature of the Losmandy system.

Losmandy Spider Dolly

The Losmandy Spider comes with either leveling floor wheels or track wheels capable of making 2-foot radius turns. It can be configured with either three legs for easier leveling or four legs for stability. The Spider, when combined with the SD or DV adjustable column, creates the easiest and safest way to move heavy cameras and jib arms. It supports 400 pounds (182 kg). The legs fold up for shipping.

Specifications

Platform height with wheels	6.25 in.	15.9 cm
Platform height without wheels	16 lbs.	7.3 kg

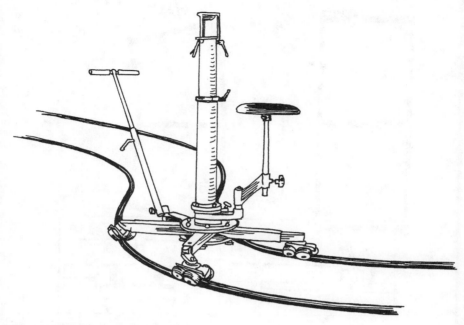

Figure 130 Losmandy flex track.

T.O.T

When pushing the dolly, watch the actor with your peripheral vision. Look at your stop marks and watch the camera operator.

Egripment Track

Steel Track Specifications

			Steel Track Standard	
154 starter			3.5 kg	7.7 lbs.
15⁵/₄ straight	120 cm	4 ft.	10 kg	22 lbs.
15⁵/₆ straight	180 cm	6 ft.	15 kg	33 lbs.
15⁵/₈ straight	240 cm	8 ft.	17 kg	37 lbs.
15⁵/₁₀ straight	300 cm	10 ft.	20 kg	44 lbs.
153 curved	240 cms	8 ft.	17 kg	37 lbs.
Width of track rail to rail	62 cm	2 ft. 8 in.		
Diameter full circle	520 cm	17 ft. 4 in.		

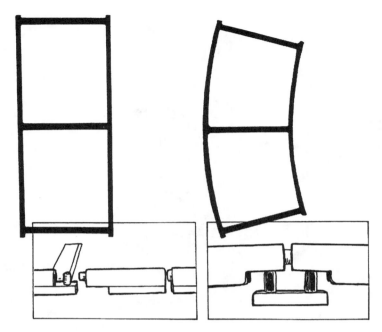

Figure 131   Egripment track.

Focus Track Specifications

Length	150 cm	5 ft.
Width rail to rail	62 cm	2 ft. 1 in.
Weight	4.5 kg	10 lbs.
Diameter full circle	540 cm	18 ft.

Pack Track Specifications

Length	150 cm	5 ft.
Width rail to rail	62 cm	2 ft. 1 in.
Weight	3 kg	6½ lbs.
Diameter full circle	540 cm	18 ft.

T.O.T.

Spray oil or talcum powder on dolly wheels while on the track as you roll the dolly up and down the track. This will transfer the lubricant to the needed areas while making less of a mess.

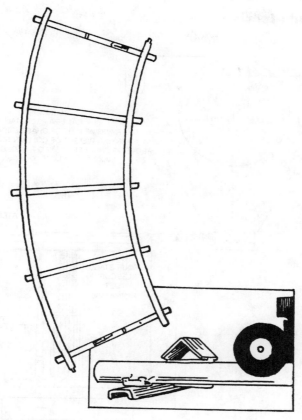

Figure 132 Egripment tracker.

Chapman Lencin

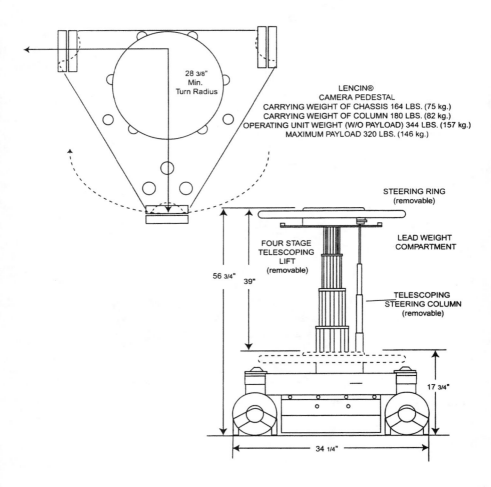

28 3/8"
Min.
Turn Radius

LENCIN®
CAMERA PEDESTAL
CARRYING WEIGHT OF CHASSIS 164 LBS. (75 kg.)
CARRYING WEIGHT OF COLUMN 180 LBS. (82 kg.)
OPERATING UNIT WEIGHT (W/O PAYLOAD) 344 LBS. (157 kg.)
MAXIMUM PAYLOAD 320 LBS. (146 kg.)

STEERING RING
(removable)

FOUR STAGE
TELESCOPING
LIFT
(removable)

LEAD WEIGHT
COMPARTMENT

56 3/4"   39"

TELESCOPING
STEERING COLUMN
(removable)

17 3/4"

34 1/4"

LENCIN ACCESSORIES
Lencin Seat Offset with Wheel
Lencin Wood Crate (Shipping & Storage)
Lencin Soft Tires - (Set of 6)
Lencin Battery Tray
Lencin Weather Cover
Pedestal Mitchell Adapter - 3"
Pedestal Mitchell Adapter - 6"
Pedestal Nitrogen Bottle-Large

Pedestal Mini Monitor Bracket
Pedestal 18" Column Riser
Pedestal Center Post Insert
Pedestal Column Star Base
Pedestal Pressure Regulator & Hose
Pedestal Nitrogen Bottle
Pedestal Small Steering Ring
Pedestal 4 Bolt 6" Riser
Pedestal Nitrogen Bottle Kit

Figure 133 Chapman Lencin.

SPECIFICATIONS

Minimum Camera Mount Height	17 3/4 in.	45 cm
Maximum Camera Mount Height	56 3/4 in.	1.4 m
Vertical Travel	39 in.	1 m
*Payload Range	20-320 lbs.	9 - 146 kg
**Maximum Payload with Center Post Insert	1,100 lbs.	500 kg
Steering Ring Diameter	30 in.	76 cm
Number of Stages in Column	4	
Carrying Weight of Chassis	164 lbs.	75 kg
Carrying Weight of Column	180 lbs.	82 kg
Total Weight	344 lbs.	157 kg
Operational Weight of Unit w/ Center Post Insert (w/o Payload)	245 lbs.	111 kg
Minimum Chassis Width	34 1/4 in.	87 cm
Minimum Turning Radius	28 3/8 in.	72 cm
Column Diameter (when Removed)	16 5/8 in.	42 cm
Chassis Minimum Height (without Column)	14 1/2 in.	37 cm
Column Minimum Height (when Removed)	16 1/2 in.	42 cm

OTHER LENCIN FEATURES

- Open Access to Wheels for Maintenance
- Lock Column at Any Height (Optional Cam Lock)
- Special Performance Enhancing Tire Compound
- Can Be Used Indoors and Outdoors
- Track Ready, for Use on Straight Track Only
- Incorporates Both Crab and Conventional Steering
- Low Maintenance
- 22 Inch Steering Ring Available

- Removable Column
- Securable to Floors or Platforms
- Interchangeable Wheels-Hard or Soft
- Easily Adjusted Cable Guards
- Easily Replaced Steering Column
- Virtually Silent Operation
- LENCIN Has A Wheel Brake

*Payload Includes All Items (i.e. Man, Camera, Platform, Turret, Crane Arm, etc.) on Column.

**Payload Includes All Items (i.e. Man, Camera, Platform, Turret, Crane Arm, etc.) on Base Mount.

*It is advised that the user of Chapman/Leonard equipment check with the manufacturer for the latest updates on *all* equipment.

Figure 133   *continued*

Chapman Pedolly

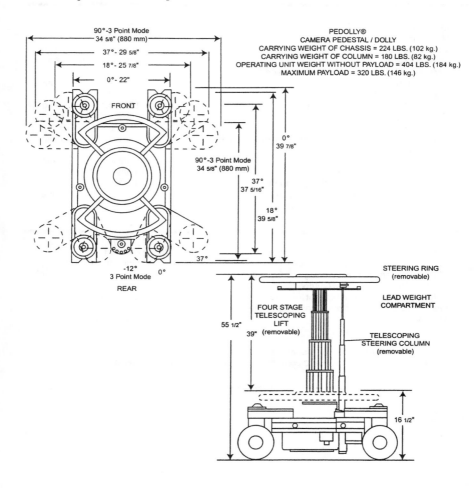

PEDOLLY ACCESSORIES
Pedolly Wood Crate (Shipping & Storage)
Pedolly 7" Seat Offset
Pedolly Full Support Seat w/Back
Pedolly Steering Attachment
Pedolly Push Bar
Pedolly Battery Tray
Pedolly Adjustable Battery Tray - (3 Pieces)
Pedolly Precision Seat Offset
Pedolly Soft Tires - (Set of 8)
Pedolly Electronic Shifter
Pedolly Push Bar Offset
Pedolly Sideboards - (Set of 3)

Pedolly Sideboard Extension - (Set of 6)
Pedolly Weather Cover
Pedestal Mitchell Adapter - 3"
Pedestal Mitchell Adapter - 6"
Pedestal Mini Monitor Bracket
Pedestal 18" Column Riser
Pedestal Center Post Insert
Pedestal Column Star Base
Pedestal Pressure Regulator & Hose
Pedestal Nitrogen Bottle-Large
Pedestal Nitrogen Bottle Kit
Pedestal Small Steering Ring
Pedestal 4 Bolt 6" Riser

Figure 134 Chapman Pedolly.

SPECIFICATIONS

Minimum Camera Mount Height	16 1/2 in.	42 cm
Maximum Camera Mount Height	55 1/2 in.	1.4 m
Vertical Travel	39 in.	99 cm
*Payload Range	20 - 320 lbs.	9 - 145 kg
**Maximum Payload with Center Post Insert	1,100 lbs.	500 kg
Number of Stages in Column	4	
Steering Ring Diameter	28 in.	71 cm
Column Diameter (when Removed)	16 5/8 in.	42 cm
Column Charging Pressure	70 - 385 psi	
Chassis Width - Legs at 0 Degree Position	22 in.	56 cm
Chassis Width - Legs at 18 Degree Position	25 7/8 in.	66 cm
Chassis Width - Legs at 37 Degree Position (Track Position)	29 5/8 in.	75 cm
Chassis Width - Legs at 90 Degree Position (3 Point Mode)	34 5/8 in.	880 mm
Minimum Chassis Width	22 in.	56 cm
Minimum Chassis Length	33 5/16 in.	85 cm
Minimum Turning Radius	27 1/2 in.	70 cm
Carrying Weight of Chassis	224 lbs.	102 kg
Carrying Weight of Column	180 lbs.	82 kg
Total Weight	404 lbs.	184 kg
Operational Weight of Unit w/ Center Post Insert (w/o Payload)	305 lbs.	139 kg

OTHER PEDOLLY FEATURES

- Longer Tilt Line
- Open Access To Wheels for Maintenance
- Lock Column at Any Height (Cam Lock)
- Special Tire Compound Reduces Squeaking
- Can Be Used Indoors and Outdoors
- PEDOLLY Has Wheel Brakes
- Easily Replaced Steering Column
- Split Chassis Is Adjustable for Different Loads
- Split Chassis - with Dampened 3 Point Suspension and 4 Wheeled Stability

- Electronic Shifting of Steering
- Removable Lift Columns
- Securable to Floors or Platforms
- Can Be Used on Standard Track
- Interchangeable Hard or Soft Tires
- Virtually Silent Operation
- Changeable Leg Positions
- Easily Adjusted Cable Guards
- 22 Inch Steering Ring Available
- Seating Capability

*Payload Includes All Items (i.e. Man, Camera, Platform, Turret, Crane Arm, etc.) on Column.
**Payload Includes All Items (i.e. Man, Camera, Platform, Turret, Crane Arm, etc.) on Base Mount.

*It is advised that the user of Chapman/Leonard equipment check with the manufacturer for the latest updates on *all* equipment.

Figure 134 *continued*

Chapman Peewee

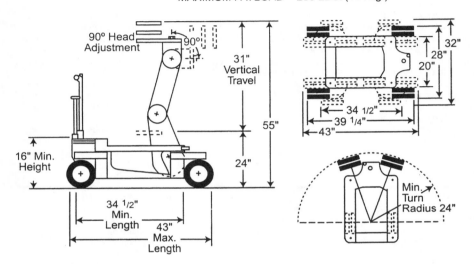

PEEWEE®
CAMERA DOLLY
CARRYING WEIGHT = 280 LBS. (127 kg.)
MAXIMUM PAYLOAD = 250 LBS. (114 kg.)

PEEWEE ACCESSORIES

PeeWee Grip Pouch	12" Mitchell Riser with 12" Offset
PeeWee Front Board	16" Camera Extension / 2 Cam Plate
PeeWee Narrow Sideboard	24" Camera Extension / 2 Cam Plate
PeeWee Wide Sideboard	36" Camera Extension / 2 Cam Plate
PeeWee Standing Board	Dolly Seat Pocket Light Adapter - 1 1/8"
PeeWee Drop Down Sideboard	3" Mitchell/Mitchell Male Adapter
PeeWee Battery Box	3" Mitchell/Mitchell Female Adapter
PeeWee Levon Tracking Bar (Narrow)	3' Variable Extension - Panther
PeeWee Tracking Bar (Wide)	Euro / Mitchell Swing Head
PeeWee Rader Walk-Around Package	Dolly Swivel Seat with Back Rest (Long Post)
PeeWee Excalibur Case - (Set of 2)	Dolly Swivel Seat with Back Rest (Short Post)
PeeWee Soft Tires - (Set of 8)	Dolly Swivel Seat
PeeWee Pneumatic Tires - (Set of 8)	Dolly Seat Complete
PeeWee Lifting Bars - (Set of 2)	12" Dolly Seat Riser
PeeWee Square Track Tires - (Set of 8)	Seat Offset Arm Short Post
PeeWee Accessory Cart	Camera Swing Head & Case
PeeWee Heating System	Euro Camera Swing Head & Case
3" Camera Riser - Mitchell 100	EVA (Electronic Valve Actuator)
6" Camera Riser - Mitchell 100	Vibration Isolator & Case
12" Camera Riser - Mitchell 100	Speed Rail Push Bar Adapter - (Set of 2)
18" Camera Riser - Mitchell 100	Box of Wedges (FLORIDA ONLY)
24" Camera Riser - Mitchell 100	Box of Shims (FLORIDA ONLY)
38" Camera Riser - Mitchell 100	Box of Cribbing (FLORIDA ONLY)
3" Mitchell Riser with 24" Offset	Tire Holder - Short
Dolly Rain House	Tire Holder - Tall
Open 4" Mitchell 4-Way Leveling Head	Underslung Seat Offset Arm

Figure 135 Chapman Peewee.

SPECIFICATIONS

Maximum Camera Mount Height (without Risers)	55 in.	1.4 m
Maximum Camera Mount Height (with Standard 12" Riser)	67 in.	1.7 m
Minimum Camera Mount Height (without Riser)	24 in.	61 cm
Minimum Camera Mount Height with PeeWee 90 Degree Plate	3 in.	8 cm
Vertical Travel	31 in.	79 cm
*Maximum Payload	250 lbs.	114 kg
**Maximum Payload with High Post Kit	1,100 lbs.	500 kg
Maximum Boom Lifts (Fully Charged)	4 Lifts	
Chassis Maximum Length (Wheels Fully Extended)	43 in.	109 cm
Chassis Minimum Length (Wheels Fully Retracted)	34 1/2 in.	88 cm
Minimum Chassis Height for Transportation	16 in.	41 cm
Chassis Width - Legs at 0° Position	20 in.	51 cm
Chassis Width - Legs at 17° Position (Pneumatic Tire Position)	23 1/2 in.	60 cm
Chassis Width - Legs at 45° Position	28 1/2 in.	71 cm
Chassis Width - Legs at 90° Position (Sideways or Scissor Track Position)	32 in.	81 cm
Steering Post Height	35 in.	89 cm
Minimum Turn Radius	24 in.	61 cm
Minimum Door Width PeeWee Can Be Carried Through	16 in.	41 cm
Carrying Weight	280 lbs.	127 kg
Standard Operational Weight	329 lbs.	150 kg
Operational Weight w/ High Post Kit (w/o Payload)	386 lbs.	178 kg

OTHER PEEWEE FEATURES

- PEEWEE Incorporates Brakes on Rear Wheels
- Variable Chassis Leg Adjustment Cam-Lock Chassis
- Hardened Stainless Steel Bushings
- Compact and Lightweight for Travel and Storage

- Vertical Arm Travel
- Planetary Gear-Driven Arm
- Rear Controlled Steering
- Corrected Steering Geometry

*Payload Includes All Items (i.e. Man, Camera, Platform, Turret, Crane Arm, etc.) on Arm.
**Payload Includes All Items (i.e. Man, Camera, Platform, Turret, Crane Arm, etc.) on Base Mount.

*It is advised that the user of Chapman/Leonard equipment check with the manufacturer for the latest updates on *all* equipment.

Figure 135 *continued*

Chapman Super Peewee

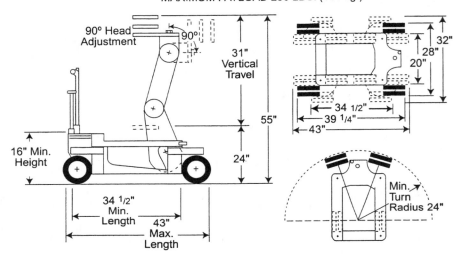

SUPER PEEWEE®
CAMERA DOLLY
CARRYING WEIGHT 280 LBS. (127 kg.)
MAXIMUM PAYLOAD 250 LBS. (114 kg.)

PEEWEE ACCESSORIES

PeeWee Grip Pouch	12" Mitchell Riser with 12" Offset
PeeWee Front Board	16" Camera Extension / 2 Cam Plate
PeeWee Narrow Sideboard	24" Camera Extension / 2 Cam Plate
PeeWee Wide Sideboard	36" Camera Extension / 2 Cam Plate
PeeWee Standing Board	Dolly Seat Pocket Light Adapter - 1 1/8"
PeeWee Drop Down Sideboard	3" Mitchell/Mitchell Male Adapter
PeeWee Battery Box	3" Mitchell/Mitchell Female Adapter
PeeWee Levon Tracking Bar (Narrow)	3' Variable Extension - Panther
PeeWee Tracking Bar (Wide)	Euro / Mitchell Swing Head
PeeWee Rader Walk-Around Package	Dolly Swivel Seat with Back Rest (Long Post)
PeeWee Excalibur Case - (Set of 2)	Dolly Swivel Seat with Back Rest (Short Post)
PeeWee Soft Tires - (Set of 8)	Dolly Swivel Seat
PeeWee Pneumatic Tires - (Set of 8)	Dolly Seat Complete
PeeWee Lifting Bars - (Set of 2)	12" Dolly Seat Riser
PeeWee Square Track Tires - (Set of 8)	Seat Offset Arm Short Post
PeeWee Accessory Cart	Camera Swing Head & Case
PeeWee Heating System	Euro Camera Swing Head & Case
3" Camera Riser - Mitchell 100	EVA (Electronic Valve Actuator)
6" Camera Riser - Mitchell 100	Vibration Isolator & Case
12" Camera Riser - Mitchell 100	Speed Rail Push Bar Adapter - (Set of 2)
18" Camera Riser - Mitchell 100	Box of Wedges (FLORIDA ONLY)
24" Camera Riser - Mitchell 100	Box of Shims (FLORIDA ONLY)
38" Camera Riser - Mitchell 100	Box of Cribbing (FLORIDA ONLY)
3" Mitchell Riser with 24" Offset	Tire Holder - Short
Dolly Rain House	Tire Holder - Tall
Open 4" Mitchell 4-Way Leveling Head	Underslung Seat Offset Arm

Figure 136 Chapman Super Peewee.

NEW SPECIFICATIONS

Maximum Camera Mount Height (without Risers)	55 in.	1.4 m
Maximum Camera Mount Height (with Standard 12" Riser)	67 in.	1.7 m
Minimum Camera Mount Height (without Riser)	24 in.	61 cm
Minimum Camera Mount Height with PeeWee 90 Degree Plate	3 in.	8 cm
Vertical Travel	31 in.	79 cm
*Maximum Payload	250 lbs.	114 kg
**Maximum Payload with High Post Kit	1,100 lbs.	500 kg
Maximum Boom Lifts (Fully Charged)	4 Lifts	
Chassis Maximum Length (Wheels Fully Extended)	43 in.	109 cm
Chassis Minimum Length (Wheels Fully Retracted)	34 1/2 in.	88 cm
Minimum Chassis Height for Transportation	16 in.	41 cm
Chassis Width - Legs at 0° Position	20 in.	51 cm
Chassis Width - Legs at 17° Position (Pneumatic Tire Position)	23 1/2 in.	60 cm
Chassis Width - Legs at 45° Position	28 1/2 in.	71 cm
Chassis Width - Legs at 90° Position (Sideways or Scissor Track Position)	32 in.	81 cm
Steering Post Height	35 in.	89 cm
Minimum Turn Radius	24 in.	61 cm
Accumulator Charging Time (Empty to Full)	60 sec.	
Minimum Door Width PeeWee Can Be Carried Through	16 in.	41 cm
Carrying Weight	280 lbs.	127 kg
Standard Operational Weight	329 lbs.	150 kg
Operational Weight w/ High Post Kit (w/o Payload)	386 lbs.	178 kg

OTHER SUPER PEEWEE FEATURES

- SUPER PEEWEE Incorporates Brakes on Rear Wheels
- Variable Chassis Leg Adjustment Cam-Lock Chassis
- Enclosed King Pin System
- Hardened Stainless Steel Bushings
- Compact and Lightweight for Travel and Storage
- Works on Both Straight and Curved Tubular Track

- Rear Controlled Steering
- Planetary Gear-Driven Arm
- Electric Pump
- Auxiliary Air Tank
- Vertical Arm Travel
- Variety of Tires Available

*Payload Includes All Items (i.e. Man, Camera, Platform, Turret, Crane Arm, etc.) on Arm.

**Payload Includes All Items (i.e. Man, Camera, Platform, Turret, Crane Arm, etc.) on Base Mount.

*It is advised that the user of Chapman/Leonard equipment check with the manufacturer for the latest updates on *all* equipment.

Figure 136 *continued*

Chapman Super Peewee II

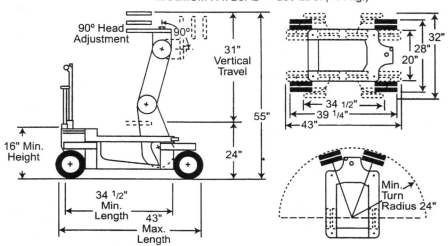

SUPER PEEWEE® II
CAMERA DOLLY
CARRYING WEIGHT = 280 LBS. (127 kg.)
MAXIMUM PAYLOAD = 250 LBS. (114 kg.)

PEEWEE ACCESSORIES

PeeWee Grip Pouch
PeeWee Front Board
PeeWee Narrow Sideboard
PeeWee Wide Sideboard
PeeWee Standing Board
PeeWee Drop Down Sideboard
PeeWee Battery Box
PeeWee Levon Tracking Bar (Narrow)
PeeWee Tracking Bar (Wide)
PeeWee Rader Walk-Around Package
PeeWee Excalibur Case - (Set of 2)
PeeWee Soft Tires - (Set of 8)
PeeWee Pneumatic Tires - (Set of 8)
PeeWee Lifting Bars - (Set of 2)
PeeWee Square Track Tires - (Set of 8)
PeeWee Accessory Cart
PeeWee Heating System
3" Camera Riser - Mitchell 100
6" Camera Riser - Mitchell 100
12" Camera Riser - Mitchell 100
18" Camera Riser - Mitchell 100
24" Camera Riser - Mitchell 100
38" Camera Riser - Mitchell 100
3" Mitchell Riser with 24" Offset
Dolly Rain House
Open 4" Mitchell 4-Way Leveling Head

12" Mitchell Riser with 12" Offset
16" Camera Extension / 2 Cam Plate
24" Camera Extension / 2 Cam Plate
36" Camera Extension / 2 Cam Plate
Dolly Seat Pocket Light Adapter - 1 1/8"
3" Mitchell/Mitchell Male Adapter
3" Mitchell/Mitchell Female Adapter
3' Variable Extension - Panther
Euro / Mitchell Swing Head
Dolly Swivel Seat with Back Rest (Long Post)
Dolly Swivel Seat with Back Rest (Short Post)
Dolly Swivel Seat
Dolly Seat Complete
12" Dolly Seat Riser
Seat Offset Arm Short Post
Camera Swing Head & Case
Euro Camera Swing Head & Case
EVA (Electronic Valve Actuator)
Vibration Isolator & Case
Speed Rail Push Bar Adapter - (Set of 2)
Box of Wedges (FLORIDA ONLY)
Box of Shims (FLORIDA ONLY)
Box of Cribbing (FLORIDA ONLY)
Tire Holder - Short
Tire Holder - Tall
Underslung Seat Offset Arm

Figure 137 Chapman Super Peewee II.

SPECIFICATIONS

Maximum Camera Mount Height (without Risers)	55 in.	1.4 m
Maximum Camera Mount Height (with Standard 12" Riser)	67 in.	1.7 m
Minimum Camera Mount Height (without Riser)	24 in.	61 cm
Minimum Camera Mount Height with PeeWee 90 Degree Plate	3 in.	8 cm
Vertical Travel	31 in.	79 cm
*Maximum Payload	250 lbs.	114 kg
**Maximum Payload with High Post Kit	1,100 lbs.	500 kg
Maximum Boom Lifts (Fully Charged)	4 Lifts	
Chassis Maximum Length (Wheels Fully Extended)	43 in.	109 cm
Chassis Minimum Length (Wheels Fully Retracted)	34 1/2 in.	88 cm
Minimum Chassis Height for Transportation	16 in.	41 cm
Chassis Width - Legs at 0° Position	20 in.	51 cm
Chassis Width - Legs at 17° Position (Pneumatic Tire Position)	23 1/2 in.	60 cm
Chassis Width - Legs at 45° Position	28 1/2 in.	71 cm
Chassis Width - Legs at 90° Position (Sideways or Scissor Track Position)	32 in.	81 cm
Steering Post Height	35 in.	89 cm
Minimum Turn Radius	24 in.	61 cm
Accumulator Charging Time (Empty to Full)	60 sec.	
Minimum Door Width PeeWee Can Be Carried Through	16 in.	41 cm
Carrying Weight	280 lbs.	127 kg
Standard Operational Weight	329 lbs.	150 kg
Operational Weight w/ High Post Kit (w/o Payload)	386 lbs.	178 kg

OTHER SUPER PEEWEE II FEATURES

- SUPER PEEWEE II Is Nickel Plated for Less Maintenance
- SUPER PEEWEE II Incorporates the Universal Stop Valve System
- Variable Chassis Leg Adjustment Cam-Lock Chassis
- SUPER PEEWEE II Incorporates Brakes on Rear Wheels
- Hardened Stainless Steel Bushings
- Compact and Lightweight for Travel and Storage
- Works on Both Straight and Curved Tubular Track
- Rear-Controlled Steering
- Vertical Arm Travel
- Planetary Gear Driven Arm
- Electric Pump
- Auxiliary Air Tank
- Enclosed King Pin System
- Variety of Tires Available

*Payload Includes All Items (i.e. Man, Camera, Platform, Turret, Crane Arm, etc.) on Arm.
**Payload Includes All Items (i.e. Man, Camera, Platform, Turret, Crane Arm, etc.) on Base Mount.

*It is advised that the user of Chapman/Leonard equipment check with the manufacturer for the latest updates on *all* equipment.

Figure 137 *continued*

Chapman Super Peewee III

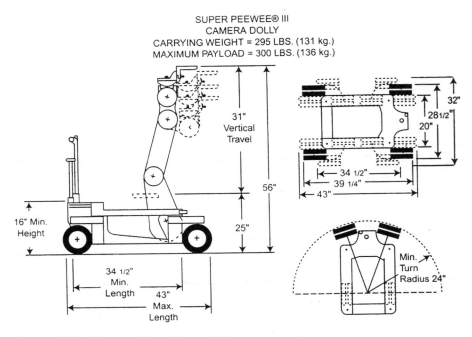

Figure 138 Chapman Super Peewee III.

SPECIFICATIONS

Maximum Camera Mount Height (Position 1-High Mode-Head Is in Upright Position)	56 in.	1.4 m
Minimum Camera Mount Height (Position 1-High Mode-Head Is in Upright Position)	25 in.	64 cm
Vertical Travel (Position 1-High Mode-Head Is in Upright Position)	31 in.	79 cm
Maximum Camera Mount Height (Position 2-45° Mode)	54 in.	1.4 m
Minimum Camera Mount Height (Position 2-45° Mode)	23 in.	58 cm
Vertical Travel (Position 2-45° Mode)	31 in.	79 cm
Maximum Camera Mount Height (Position 3-Extender Mode)	55 1/2 in.	1.4 m
Minimum Camera Mount Height (Position 3-Extender Mode)	17 1/2 in.	45 cm
Vertical Travel (Position 3-Extender Mode)	38 in.	97 cm
Max. Camera Mount Height (Position 4-Low Mode -Head Is in Lowest Position)	46 3/4 in.	1.2 m
Min. Camera Mount Height (Position 4-Low Mode -Head Is in Lowest Position)	15 3/4 in.	40 cm
Vertical Travel (Position 4 -Low Mode-Head Is in Lowest Position)	31 in.	79 cm
Chassis Width - Legs at 0° Position	20 in.	51 cm
Chassis Width - Legs at 17° Position (Pneumatic Tire Position)	23 1/2 in.	60 cm
Chassis Width - Legs at 45° Position	28 1/2 in.	72 cm
Chassis Width - Legs at 90° Position (Sideways or Scissor Track Position)	32 in.	81 cm
Steering Post Height	35 1/4 in.	90 cm
Minimum Chassis Length	34 1/2 in.	88 cm
Maximum Chassis Length	43 in.	109 cm
*Maximum Payload	300 lbs.	136 kg
**Maximum Payload with High Post Kit	1,100 lbs.	500 kg
Maximum Number of Lifts on a Single Charge	4 Lifts	
Accumulator Charging Time (Empty to Full)	60 sec.	
Carrying Weight	295 lbs.	131 kg
Operational Weight w/ High Post Kit (w/o Payload)	391 lbs.	178 kg

OTHER SUPER PEEWEE III FEATURES

UNIVERSAL STOP VALVE
• Works in Conjunction with, as Well as Back up to Control Valve • Stops Are Feathered
• Ability to Set Upper and Lower Stops • Repetitive Stops, at All Speeds
• Valve Is Well Protected within Frame Dimensions

UNIVERSAL HEAD MOUNT WITH 'XOX' LEVELING
• New XOX Leveling ... Locks into 4 Different Positions
• Adjustable Built-In Riser Adjusts without Removing the Camera

NEW CONTROL VALVE DESIGN
• Faster and Quieter

NEW COMPOSITION FOR HARD & SOFT TIRES
• New Arm Design Increases Vertical Travel and Rigidity • Increases Rigidity
• Hardened Stainless Steel Bushings • Virtually Silent Operation on Track
• Compact and Lightweight for Travel and Storage • Easier Steering and Maneuverability

*Payload Includes All Items (i.e. Man, Camera, Platform, Turret, Crane Arm, etc.) on Arm.
**Payload Includes All Items (i.e. Man, Camera, Platform, Turret, Crane Arm, etc.) on Base Mount.

*It is advised that the user of Chapman/Leonard equipment check with the manufacturer for the latest updates on *all* equipment.

Figure 138 *continued*

Chapman Super Peewee IV

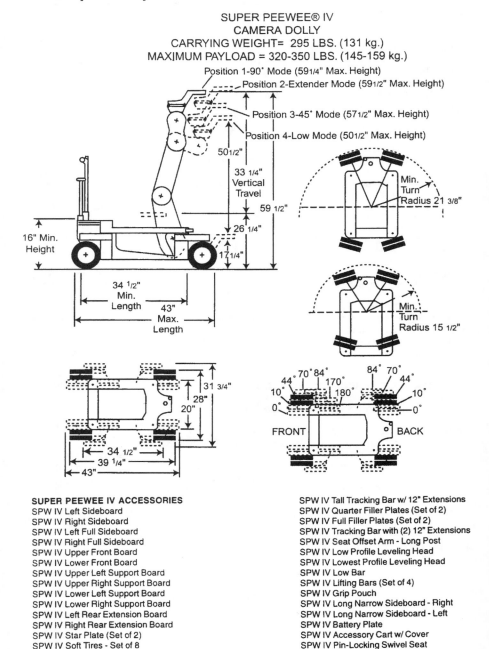

SUPER PEEWEE® IV
CAMERA DOLLY
CARRYING WEIGHT= 295 LBS. (131 kg.)
MAXIMUM PAYLOAD = 320-350 LBS. (145-159 kg.)

Position 1-90° Mode (591/4" Max. Height)
Position 2-Extender Mode (591/2" Max. Height)
Position 3-45° Mode (571/2" Max. Height)
Position 4-Low Mode (501/2" Max. Height)

501/2"
33 1/4" Vertical Travel
59 1/2"
26 1/4"
171/4"
16" Min. Height
34 1/2" Min. Length
43" Max. Length

Min. Turn Radius 21 3/8"
Min. Turn Radius 15 1/2"

31 3/4"
28"
20"
34 1/2"
39 1/4"
43"

44° 70° 84° 170° 84° 70° 44°
10° 180° 10°
0° 0°
FRONT   BACK

SUPER PEEWEE IV ACCESSORIES

SPW IV Left Sideboard
SPW IV Right Sideboard
SPW IV Left Full Sideboard
SPW IV Right Full Sideboard
SPW IV Upper Front Board
SPW IV Lower Front Board
SPW IV Upper Left Support Board
SPW IV Upper Right Support Board
SPW IV Lower Left Support Board
SPW IV Lower Right Support Board
SPW IV Left Rear Extension Board
SPW IV Right Rear Extension Board
SPW IV Star Plate (Set of 2)
SPW IV Soft Tires - Set of 8
SPW IV Pneumatic Tires - Set of 8
SPW IV Quick Release Wheel Cap - Set of 8

SPW IV Tall Tracking Bar w/ 12" Extensions
SPW IV Quarter Filler Plates (Set of 2)
SPW IV Full Filler Plates (Set of 2)
SPW IV Tracking Bar with (2) 12" Extensions
SPW IV Seat Offset Arm - Long Post
SPW IV Low Profile Leveling Head
SPW IV Lowest Profile Leveling Head
SPW IV Low Bar
SPW IV Lifting Bars (Set of 4)
SPW IV Grip Pouch
SPW IV Long Narrow Sideboard - Right
SPW IV Long Narrow Sideboard - Left
SPW IV Battery Plate
SPW IV Accessory Cart w/ Cover
SPW IV Pin-Locking Swivel Seat
SPW IV MI Boards - Set of 3
Dolly Rain House

Figure 139 Chapman Super Peewee IV.

SPECIFICATIONS

Maximum Camera Mount Height (Position 1-90º Mode)	59 1/2 in.	1.5 m
Minimum Camera Mount Height (Position 1-90º Mode)	26 1/4 in.	67 cm
Vertical Boom Travel (Position 1-90º Mode)	33 1/4 in.	85 cm
Maximum Camera Mount Height (Position 2-Extender Mode)	59 1/2 in.	1.5 m
Minimum Camera Mount Height (Position 2-Extender Mode)	18 1/4 in.	46 cm
Vertical Boom Travel (Position 2-Extender Mode)	41 1/4 in.	1 m
Maximum Camera Mount Height (Position 3- 45º Mode)	57 1/2 in.	1.5 m
Minimum Camera Mount Height (Position 3- 45º Mode)	24 1/4 in.	62 cm
Vertical Boom Travel (Position 3- 45º Mode)	33 1/4 in.	85 cm
Maximum Camera Mount Height (Position 4-Low Mode)	50 1/2 in.	1.3 m
Minimum Camera Mount Height (Position 4-Low Mode)	17 1/4 in.	44 cm
Vertical Boom Travel (Position 4-Low Mode)	33 1/4 in.	85 cm
Minimum Camera Mount Height (Low Bar Setup w/ Lowest 4-Way Leveling Head)	4 in.	10 cm
Maximum Camera Mount Height (Low Bar Setup w/ Lowest 4-Way Leveling Head)	37 1/4 in.	95 cm
NOTE: LOWEST SETUP 1 1/2" REFER TO SPW IV USERS GUIDE		
Chassis Width - All Legs at 0º (Use in Tight Quarters)	20 in.	51 cm
Chassis Width - All Legs at 10º (Pneumatic or 880 mm Track Position)	25 in.	64 cm
Chassis Width - All Legs at 44º (Track Position)	28 in.	71 cm
Chassis Width - All Legs at 70º (Tread and Wheel Base are Equal -'S' Position)	31 in.	79 cm
Chassis Width - All Legs at 84º (Sideways or Scissor Track Position)	31 3/4 in.	81 cm
Chassis Width - Front Legs at 84º/Rear at 0º (3 Point Solid Tire Position)	31 3/4 in.	81 cm
Chassis Width - Front Legs at 84º/Rear at 10º (3 Point Pneumatic Tire Position)	31 3/4 in.	81 cm
Chassis Width - Front Legs at 180º/Rear at 0º (Compact Solid Tire Position)	20 in.	51 cm
Chassis Width - Front Legs at 170º/Rear at 10º (Compact Pneumatic Tire Position)	25 in.	64 cm
Steering Post Height	38 in.	97 cm
Minimum Chassis Length	34 1/2 in.	88 cm
Maximum Chassis Length	43 in.	109 cm
*Maximum Payload with Accumulator Charge at 2,400psi	320 lbs.	145 kg
*Maximum Payload with Accumulator Charge at 2,600psi	350 lbs,	159 kg
**Maximum Payload with High Post Kit	1,100 lbs.	500 kg
Maximum Number of Lifts on a Single Charge	5 Lifts	
Accumulator Charging Time (Empty to Full)	60 sec.	
Carrying Weight	295 lbs.	131 kg
Operational Weight w/ High Post Kit (w/o Payload)	391 lbs.	178 kg

*Payload Includes All Items (i.e. Man, Camera, Platform, Turret, Crane Arm, etc.) on Arm.
**Payload Includes All Items (i.e. Man, Camera, Platform, Turret, Crane Arm, etc.) on Base Mount.

- Revolutionary new three mode transmission featuring conventional, crab and round steering that can be shifted while the dolly is moving or stationary, without the dolly operator's hands leaving the steering handle. This transmission has the ability to be adjusted to provide perfect steering geometry when re-configuring the chassis to its various leg positions. No other transmission has been able to do this.
- The Super PeeWee® IV now provides for much less maintenance.
  (a) The need for air bleeding has been eliminated.
  (b) Corrosion resistance has been dramatically improved.

Figure 139 *continued*

OTHER SUPER PEEWEE IV FEATURES (CONTINUED)

(c) All exposed working joints have been sealed.

(d) Far greater precision greatly reduces the need for adjustments. All adjustments, if required by operator's specific desires, can be done externally without removing bolted covers or lids.

(e) Steering chain adjustments have been virtually eliminated, dramatically reducing maintenance time.

(f) Larger hydraulic capacity requires less recharging.

(g) Greater strength reduces the possibility of damage.

(h) Modular design of steering transmission and shifting linkage facilitates quick and easy replacements.

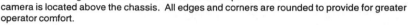

Above: New convenient location of Universal Stop Valve controls.

- New arm design provides greater operator clearance, while assuring greater rigidity, smoothness, speed and added vertical travel. This new trim arm design also allows for lower camera setups when the camera is located above the chassis. All edges and corners are rounded to provide for greater operator comfort.

- New valve concept gives the operator much improved control, providing for greater speed with added precision.

- Stop valve now requires no tools to make adjustments. Accessibility is now directly in front of the dolly operator, providing for quick and easy adjustments.

- Improved Universal Head performance is now achieved. Added arm precision, a control cylinder and a middle rib, provides major gains in safety and rigidity.

- Improved arm performance is exhibited with five full strokes of the arm on a single charge, while still achieving added vertical travel. The rigidity has been dramatically increased. The profile has been streamlined, providing added clearance for lower lens levels when operating over the chassis. This new design also adds to operator comfort. The new internal drive mechanism is smoother and maintenance free.

- Improved valve design provides for smoother, faster and quieter arm control. The dolly operator control has been significantly improved.

- The Super PeeWee® IV has a new sideboard system. Feedback from thousands of users and our own survey has led to this new design that provides complete walk-a-round ability at both the high and low levels.

- The Super PeeWee® IV now comes with built-in heat control for the hydraulic system to maintain a minimum hydraulic oil temperature of 70º F, thus providing constant performance even in the coldest environment.

- Leg positions have been improved to enhance performance by providing:

    (a) **0º** position for **narrowest configuration with standard tires.**

    (b) **10º** position for **narrowest configuration with pneumatic tires** OR for **side mounting the dolly on 880mm track.**

    (c) **44º** position for **standard 24½" track** alignment and **general all-around use.**

    (d) **84º** position for **maximum lateral stability** or for **side mounting dolly on 24½" track.**

    (e) **Front legs at 84º, rear legs at 0º.** This is the **three point contact position** for standard tires which is great for outdoor use on rough terrain.

    (f) **70º** position where Tread and Wheel Base are Equal, called the **S** position.

    (g) **Front legs at 84º, rear legs at 10º.** This is the **three point contact position** for pneumatic tires which is great for outdoor use on rough terrain.

    (h) **Front legs at 180º** and the **rear legs at 0º** provides the **most compact dolly configuration with Standard Solid Tires**, making the Super PeeWee® IV efficient, even in especially tight quarters.

    (i) **Front Legs at 170º** and **rear legs at 10º** provides the **most compact dolly configuration with Pneumatic Tires**, making the Super PeeWee® IV efficient, even in especially tight quarters.

*It is advised that the user of Chapman/Leonard equipment check with the manufacturer for the latest updates on *all* equipment.

Figure 139 *continued*

Chapman Hustler

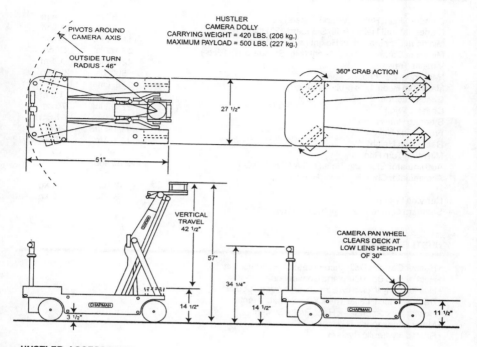

HUSTLER ACCESSORIES

Drop Down / Z Plate
Hustler Steering Extension
Hustler Mitchell 4-Way Leveling Head
Hustler Grip Pouch
Hustler Short Sideboard Pin
Hustler Medium Sideboard Pin
Hustler High Level Front Board
Hustler Front Board
Hustler Standing Board
Hustler Narrow Sideboard
Hustler Wide Sideboard
Hustler Grease Gun
Hustler Large Grease Gun
Hustler Push Bar - (Set of 2)
Hustler AR Battery Tray
Hustler Extended Push Bar (Set of 2)
Hustler Track Wheel Attachment & Ramps
Hustler Steadicam Z Plate
Hustler III Steadicam Platform Package
Hustler Heating System (Advanced Notice Required)
3" Camera Riser - Mitchell 100
6" Camera Riser - Mitchell 100
12" Camera Riser - Mitchell 100
18" Camera Riser - Mitchell 100
24" Camera Riser - Mitchell 100
38" Camera Riser - Mitchell 100
Open 4" Mitchell 4-Way Leveling Head

3" Mitchell Riser with 24" Offset
12" Mitchell Riser with 12" Offset
16" Camera Extension / 2 Cam Plate
24" Camera Extension / 2 Cam Plate
36" Camera Extension / 2 Cam Plate
Dolly Seat Pocket Light Adapter - 1 1/8"
3" Mitchell/Mitchell Male Adapter
3" Mitchell/Mitchell Female Adapter
3' Variable Extension - Panther
Euro / Mitchell Swing Head
Dolly Swivel Seat with Back Rest
Dolly Swivel Seat
Dolly Seat Complete
12" Dolly Seat Riser
Seat Offset Arm Short Post
Camera Swing Head & Case
Euro Camera Swing Head & Case
EVA (Electronic Valve Actuator)
Vibration Isolator & Case
Speed Rail Push Bar Adapter - (Set of 2)
Box of Wedges (FLORIDA ONLY)
Box of Shims (FLORIDA ONLY)
Box of Cribbing (FLORIDA ONLY)
Tire Holder - Short
Tire Holder - Tall
Underslung Seat Offset Arm
Dolly Rain House

Figure 140 Chapman Hustler.

SPECIFICATIONS

Camera Mount Height (without Risers)	57 in.	1.4 m
Camera Mount Height (with Standard 12" Riser)	69 in.	1.8 m
Minimum Camera Mount Height (without Risers)	14 1/2 in.	37 cm
Minimum Camera Mount Height (with Standard 12" Riser)	26 1/2 in.	67 cm
Vertical Travel	42 1/2 in.	1.1 m
*Maximum Payload	500 lbs.	227 kg
Maximum Boom Lifts (Fully Charged)	6 Lifts	
Chassis Length	51 in.	1.3 m
Chassis Width	27 1/2 in.	70 cm
Steering Post Height	34 1/4 in.	87 cm
Front Deck Height	11 1/4 in.	29 cm
Rear Deck Height	14 1/2 in.	37 cm
Minimum Turn Radius	46 in.	1.2 m
Accumulator Charging Time (110 A.C. and D.C.)	under 60 sec.	
Accumulator Charging Time (Hand Pump)	2 min.	
	420 lbs.	191 kg
Carrying Weight	454 lbs.	206 kg
Standard Operational Weight (w/o Payload)		

HUSTLER FEATURES

- Hustler Camera Dolly Incorporates a Hydraulic Lift
- Hustler Has Both Crab and Conventional Steering
- Hustler Dolly Works on Straight or Curved Tubular
  Track with the Hustler Track Wheel Attachments
- Hustler II Incorporates a Hand Brake System
- Many Accessories Available
- Sealed Hydraulic System

*Payload Includes All Items (i.e. Man, Camera, Platform, Turret, Crane Arm, etc.) on Arm.

*It is advised that the user of Chapman/Leonard equipment check with the manufacturer for the latest updates on *all* equipment.

Figure 140 *continued*

Chapman Hustler II

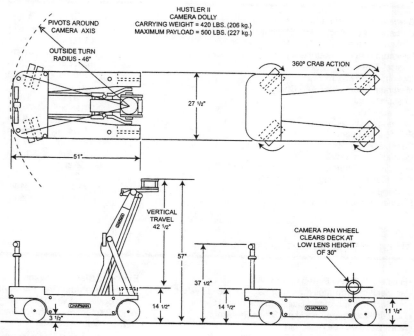

HUSTLER ACCESSORIES

Drop Down / Z Plate
Hustler Steering Extension
Hustler Mitchell 4-Way Leveling Head
Hustler Grip Pouch
Hustler Short Sideboard Pin
Hustler Medium Sideboard Pin
Hustler High Level Front Board
Hustler Front Board
Hustler Standing Board
Hustler Narrow Sideboard
Hustler Wide Sideboard
Hustler Grease Gun
Hustler Large Grease Gun
Hustler Push Bar - (Set of 2)
Hustler AR Battery Tray
Hustler Extended Push Bar (Set of 2)
Hustler Track Wheel Attachment & Ramps
Hustler Steadicam Z Plate
Hustler III Steadicam Platform Package
Hustler Heating System (Advanced Notice Required)
3" Camera Riser - Mitchell 100
6" Camera Riser - Mitchell 100
12" Camera Riser - Mitchell 100
18" Camera Riser - Mitchell 100
24" Camera Riser - Mitchell 100
38" Camera Riser - Mitchell 100
Open 4" Mitchell 4-Way Leveling Head

3" Mitchell Riser with 24" Offset
12" Mitchell Riser with 12" Offset
16" Camera Extension / 2 Cam Plate
24" Camera Extension / 2 Cam Plate
36" Camera Extension / 2 Cam Plate
Dolly Seat Pocket Light Adapter - 1 1/8"
3" Mitchell/Mitchell Male Adapter
3" Mitchell/Mitchell Female Adapter
3' Variable Extension - Panther
Euro / Mitchell Swing Head
Dolly Swivel Seat with Back Rest
Dolly Swivel Seat
Dolly Seat Complete
12" Dolly Seat Riser
Seat Offset Arm Short Post
Camera Swing Head & Case
Euro Camera Swing Head & Case
EVA (Electronic Valve Actuator)
Vibration Isolator & Case
Speed Rail Push Bar Adapter - (Set of 2)
Box of Wedges (FLORIDA ONLY)
Box of Shims (FLORIDA ONLY)
Box of Cribbing (FLORIDA ONLY)
Tire Holder - Short
Tire Holder - Tall
Underslung Seat Offset Arm
Dolly Rain House

Figure 141 Chapman Hustler II.

SPECIFICATIONS

Camera Mount Height (without Risers)	57 in.	1.4 m
Camera Mount Height (with Standard 12" Riser)	69 in.	1.8 m
Minimum Camera Mount Height (without Risers)	14 1/2 in.	37 cm
Minimum Camera Mount Height (with Standard 12" Riser)	26 1/2 in.	67 cm
Vertical Travel	42 1/2 in.	1.1 m
*Maximum Payload	500 lbs.	227 kg
Maximum Boom Lifts (Fully Charged)	6 Lifts	
Chassis Length	51 in.	1.3 m
Chassis Width	27 1/2 in.	70 cm
Steering Post Height	37 1/2 in.	95 cm
Front Deck Height	11 1/4 in.	29 cm
Rear Deck Height	14 1/2 in.	37 cm
Minimum Turn Radius	46 in.	1.2 m
Accumulator Charging Time (110 A.C. and D.C.)	under 60 sec.	
Accumulator Charging Time (Hand Pump)	2 min.	
Carrying Weight	420 lbs.	191 kg
Standard Operational Weight (w/o Payload)	454 lbs.	206 kg

OTHER HUSTLER II FEATURES

- Hustler II Is Nickel Plated for Easy Maintenance
- Hustler II Incorporates the Universal Stop Valve System
- Hustler II Incorporates a Built-In Track Wheel System
- Hustler II Incorporates a Hand Brake System
- Many Accessories Available
- Operates in Both Crab and Conventional Steering
- **Optional AR Battery Tray Accessory**

- Extended Steering Column
- Hustler II Has Improved Faster Arm
- Swift Brake and Valve Controls
- Works on Standard Tubular Track
- Sealed Hydraulic System

*Payload Includes All Items (i.e. Man, Camera, Platform, Turret, Crane Arm, etc.) on Arm.

*It is advised that the user of Chapman/Leonard equipment check with the manufacturer for the latest updates on *all* equipment.

Figure 141   *continued*

Chapman Hustler III

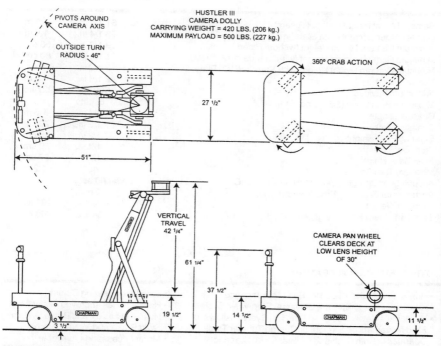

HUSTLER ACCESSORIES

Drop Down / Z Plate
Hustler Steering Extension
Hustler Mitchell 4-Way Leveling Head
Hustler Grip Pouch
Hustler Short Sideboard Pin
Hustler Medium Sideboard Pin
Hustler High Level Front Board
Hustler Front Board
Hustler Standing Board
Hustler Narrow Sideboard
Hustler Wide Sideboard
Hustler Grease Gun
Hustler Large Grease Gun
Hustler Push Bar - (Set of 2)
Hustler AR Battery Tray
Hustler Extended Push Bar (Set of 2)
Hustler Track Wheel Attachment & Ramps
Hustler Steadicam Z Plate
Hustler III Steadicam Platform Package
Hustler Heating System (Advanced Notice Required)
3" Camera Riser - Mitchell 100
6" Camera Riser - Mitchell 100
12" Camera Riser - Mitchell 100
18" Camera Riser - Mitchell 100
24" Camera Riser - Mitchell 100
38" Camera Riser - Mitchell 100
Open 4" Mitchell 4-Way Leveling Head

3" Mitchell Riser with 24" Offset
12" Mitchell Riser with 12" Offset
16" Camera Extension / 2 Cam Plate
24" Camera Extension / 2 Cam Plate
36" Camera Extension / 2 Cam Plate
Dolly Seat Pocket Light Adapter - 1 1/8"
3" Mitchell/Mitchell Male Adapter
3" Mitchell/Mitchell Female Adapter
3' Variable Extension - Panther
Euro / Mitchell Swing Head
Dolly Swivel Seat with Back Rest
Dolly Swivel Seat
Dolly Seat Complete
12" Dolly Seat Riser
Seat Offset Arm Short Post
Camera Swing Head & Case
Euro Camera Swing Head & Case
EVA (Electronic Valve Actuator)
Vibration Isolator & Case
Speed Rail Push Bar Adapter - (Set of 2)
Box of Wedges (FLORIDA ONLY)
Box of Shims (FLORIDA ONLY)
Box of Cribbing (FLORIDA ONLY)
Tire Holder - Short
Tire Holder - Tall
Underslung Seat Offset Arm
Dolly Rain House

Figure 142 Chapman Hustler III.

SPECIFICATIONS

Camera Mount Height (without Risers)	61 1/4 in.	1.6 m
Camera Mount Height (with Standard 12" Riser)	73 1/4 in.	1.9 m
Minimum Camera Mount Height (without Risers)	19 1/2 in.	50 cm
Minimum Camera Mount Height (with Standard 12" Riser)	31 1/2 in.	80 cm
Minimum Camera Mount Height with Standard 90º Plate	3 1/2 in.	9 cm
Vertical Travel	42 1/4 in.	1.1 m
*Maximum Payload	500 lbs.	227 kg
Maximum Boom Lifts (Fully Charged)	6 Lifts	
Chassis Length	51 in.	1.3 m
Chassis Width	27 1/2 in.	70 cm
Steering Post Height	37 1/2 in.	95 cm
Front Deck Height	11 1/4 in.	29 cm
Rear Deck Height	14 1/2 in.	37 cm
Minimum Turn Radius	46 in.	1.2 m
Accumulator Charging Time (110 A.C. and D.C.)	under 60 sec.	
Accumulator Charging Time (Hand Pump)	2 min.	
Carrying Weight	420 lbs.	191 kg
Standard Operational Weight (w/o Payload)	454 lbs.	206 kg

OTHER HUSTLER III FEATURES

- Hustler III Is Nickel Plated for Easy Maintenance
- Hustler III Incorporates the Universal Stop Valve System
- Hustler III's Newly Designed King Pin System Allows for Fluid Movement on Straight or Curved Tubular Track
- Operates in Both Crab and Conventional Steering
- **Optional Universal Head Mount** for Convenient, Quick Placement of the Camera

- Extended Steering Column
- Hustler III Has Improved Faster Arm
- Hustler III has a Hand Brake System
- Swift Brake and Valve Controls
- Many Accessories Available
- Sealed Hydraulic System

*Payload Includes All Items (i.e. Man, Camera, Platform, Turret, Crane Arm, etc.) on Arm.

*It is advised that the user of Chapman/Leonard equipment check with the manufacturer for the latest updates on *all* equipment.

Figure 142 *continued*

Chapman Hybrid

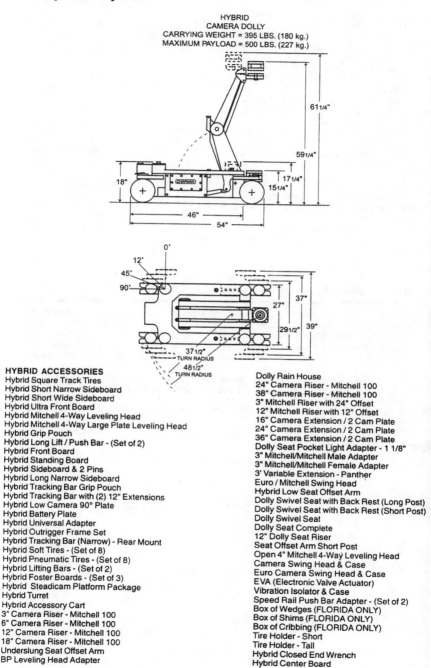

HYBRID
CAMERA DOLLY
CARRYING WEIGHT = 395 LBS. (180 kg.)
MAXIMUM PAYLOAD = 500 LBS. (227 kg.)

HYBRID ACCESSORIES
Hybrid Square Track Tires
Hybrid Short Narrow Sideboard
Hybrid Short Wide Sideboard
Hybrid Ultra Front Board
Hybrid Mitchell 4-Way Leveling Head
Hybrid Mitchell 4-Way Large Plate Leveling Head
Hybrid Grip Pouch
Hybrid Long Lift / Push Bar - (Set of 2)
Hybrid Front Board
Hybrid Standing Board
Hybrid Sideboard & 2 Pins
Hybrid Long Narrow Sideboard
Hybrid Tracking Bar Grip Pouch
Hybrid Tracking Bar with (2) 12" Extensions
Hybrid Low Camera 90° Plate
Hybrid Battery Plate
Hybrid Universal Adapter
Hybrid Outrigger Frame Set
Hybrid Tracking Bar (Narrow) - Rear Mount
Hybrid Soft Tires - (Set of 8)
Hybrid Pneumatic Tires - (Set of 8)
Hybrid Lifting Bars - (Set of 2)
Hybrid Foster Boards - (Set of 3)
Hybrid Steadicam Platform Package
Hybrid Turret
Hybrid Accessory Cart
3" Camera Riser - Mitchell 100
6" Camera Riser - Mitchell 100
12" Camera Riser - Mitchell 100
18" Camera Riser - Mitchell 100
Underslung Seat Offset Arm
BP Leveling Head Adapter

Dolly Rain House
24" Camera Riser - Mitchell 100
38" Camera Riser - Mitchell 100
3" Mitchell Riser with 24" Offset
12" Mitchell Riser with 12" Offset
16" Camera Extension / 2 Cam Plate
24" Camera Extension / 2 Cam Plate
36" Camera Extension / 2 Cam Plate
Dolly Seat Pocket Light Adapter - 1 1/8"
3" Mitchell/Mitchell Male Adapter
3" Mitchell/Mitchell Female Adapter
3' Variable Extension - Panther
Euro / Mitchell Swing Head
Hybrid Low Seat Offset Arm
Dolly Swivel Seat with Back Rest (Long Post)
Dolly Swivel Seat with Back Rest (Short Post)
Dolly Swivel Seat
Dolly Seat Complete
12" Dolly Seat Riser
Seat Offset Arm Short Post
Open 4" Mitchell 4-Way Leveling Head
Camera Swing Head & Case
Euro Camera Swing Head & Case
EVA (Electronic Valve Actuator)
Vibration Isolator & Case
Speed Rail Push Bar Adapter - (Set of 2)
Box of Wedges (FLORIDA ONLY)
Box of Shims (FLORIDA ONLY)
Box of Cribbing (FLORIDA ONLY)
Tire Holder - Short
Tire Holder - Tall
Hybrid Closed End Wrench
Hybrid Center Board

Figure 143 Chapman Hybrid.

Maximum Camera Mount Height (with Standard 12" Riser)	73 in.	1.9 m
Maximum Camera Mount Height (without Risers)	61 1/4 in.	1.6 m
Minimum Camera Mount Height	15 1/4 in.	39 cm
Minimum Camera Mount Height with Hybrid Low Camera 90 Degree Plate	1 in.	3 cm
Vertical Travel	44 in.	1.1 m
*Maximum Payload	500 lbs.	227 kg
**Maximum Payload with High Post Kit	1,900 lbs.	863 kg
Maximum Boom Lifts (Fully Charged)	5 Lifts	
Chassis Maximum Length (Wheels Fully Extended)	54 in.	1.4 m
Chassis Minimum Length (Wheels Fully Retracted)	46 in.	1.2 m
Minimum Chassis Height for Transportation	18 in.	46 cm
Chassis Variable Widths - Legs in	27 in.	69 cm
Chassis Variable Widths - Legs at 12 Degree Track Position	29 1/2 in.	75 cm
Chassis Variable Widths - Legs at 45 Degrees	37 in.	89 cm
Chassis Variable Widths - Legs at 90 Degrees	39 in.	99 cm
Steering Post Height	36 in.	91 cm
Minimum Turn Radius	37 1/2 in.	95 cm
Accumulator Charging Time (110 A.C. and D.C.)	under 60 sec.	
Accumulator Charging Time (Hand Pump)	2 1/2 min.	
Minimum Door Width Hybrid Can Be Carried Through	18 in.	46 cm
Carrying Weight	395 lbs.	180 kg
Standard Operational Weight (w/o Payload)	463 lbs.	210 kg
Hybrid w/ High Post Kit Operational Weight (w/o Payload)	501 lbs.	227 kg

OTHER HYBRID II FEATURES

- The Hybrid II Incorporates the Universal Stop Valve System
- The Hybrid II Is Nickel Plated for Less Maintenance
- Works on Both Straight or Curved Track
- Interchangeable Soft, Hard or Pneumatic Tires for Different Terrain
- Hybrid II Incorporates Brakes on Rear Wheels

- Cam-Lock Chassis Legs
- Enclosed King Pin System
- Variable Camera Head
- Variable Chassis Legs
- Compact and Lightweight

*Payload Includes All Items (i.e. Man, Camera, Platform, Turret, Crane Arm, etc.) on Arm.
**Payload Includes All Items (i.e. Man, Camera, Platform, Turret, Crane Arm, etc.) on Base Mount.

*It is advised that the user of Chapman/Leonard equipment check with the manufacturer for the latest updates on *all* equipment.

Figure 143 *continued*

Chapman Hybrid II

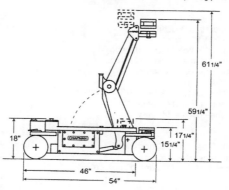

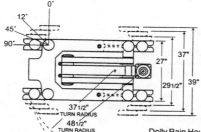

HYBRID ACCESSORIES

Hybrid Square Track Tires
Hybrid Short Narrow Sideboard
Hybrid Short Wide Sideboard
Hybrid Ultra Front Board
Hybrid Mitchell 4-Way Leveling Head
Hybrid Mitchell 4-Way Large Plate Leveling Head
Hybrid Grip Pouch
Hybrid Long Lift / Push Bar - (Set of 2)
Hybrid Front Board
Hybrid Standing Board
Hybrid Sideboard & 2 Pins
Hybrid Long Narrow Sideboard
Hybrid Tracking Bar Grip Pouch
Hybrid Tracking Bar with (2) 12" Extensions
Hybrid Low Camera 90° Plate
Hybrid Battery Plate
Hybrid Universal Adapter
Hybrid Outrigger Frame Set
Hybrid Tracking Bar (Narrow) - Rear Mount
Hybrid Soft Tires - (Set of 8)
Hybrid Pneumatic Tires - (Set of 8)
Hybrid Lifting Bars - (Set of 2)
Hybrid Foster Boards - (Set of 3)
Hybrid Steadicam Platform Package
Hybrid Turret
Hybrid Accessory Cart
3" Camera Riser - Mitchell 100
6" Camera Riser - Mitchell 100
12" Camera Riser - Mitchell 100
18" Camera Riser - Mitchell 100
Underslung Seat Offset Arm
BP Leveling Head Adapter

Dolly Rain House
24" Camera Riser - Mitchell 100
38" Camera Riser - Mitchell 100
3" Mitchell Riser with 24" Offset
12" Mitchell Riser with 12" Offset
16" Camera Extension / 2 Cam Plate
24" Camera Extension / 2 Cam Plate
36" Camera Extension / 2 Cam Plate
Dolly Seat Pocket Light Adapter - 1 1/8"
3" Mitchell/Mitchell Male Adapter
3" Mitchell/Mitchell Female Adapter
3' Variable Extension - Panther
Euro / Mitchell Swing Head
Hybrid Low Seat Offset Arm
Dolly Swivel Seat with Back Rest (Long Post)
Dolly Swivel Seat with Back Rest (Short Post)
Dolly Swivel Seat
Dolly Seat Complete
12" Dolly Seat Riser
Seat Offset Arm Short Post
Open 4" Mitchell 4-Way Leveling Head
Camera Swing Head & Case
Euro Camera Swing Head & Case
EVA (Electronic Valve Actuator)
Vibration Isolator & Case
Speed Rail Push Bar Adapter - (Set of 2)
Box of Wedges (FLORIDA ONLY)
Box of Shims (FLORIDA ONLY)
Box of Cribbing (FLORIDA ONLY)
Tire Holder - Short
Tire Holder - Tall
Hybrid Closed End Wrench
Hybrid Center Board

Figure 144   Chapman Hybrid II.

SPECIFICATIONS

Maximum Camera Mount Height (with Standard 12" Riser)	73 in.	1.9 m
Maximum Camera Mount Height (without Risers)	61 1/4 in.	1.6 m
Minimum Camera Mount Height	15 1/4 in.	39 cm
Minimum Camera Mount Height with Hybrid Low Camera 90 Degree Plate	1 in.	3 cm
Vertical Travel	44 in.	1.1 m
*Maximum Payload	500 lbs.	227 kg
**Maximum Payload with High Post Kit	1,900 lbs.	863 kg
Maximum Boom Lifts (Fully Charged)	5 Lifts	
Chassis Maximum Length (Wheels Fully Extended)	54 in.	1.4 m
Chassis Minimum Length (Wheels Fully Retracted)	46 in.	1.2 m
Minimum Chassis Height for Transportation	18 in.	46 cm
Chassis Variable Widths - Legs in	27 in.	69 cm
Chassis Variable Widths - Legs at 12 Degree Track Position	29 1/2 in.	75 cm
Chassis Variable Widths - Legs at 45 Degrees	37 in.	89 cm
Chassis Variable Widths - Legs at 90 Degrees	39 in.	99 cm
Steering Post Height	36 in.	91 cm
Minimum Turn Radius	37 1/2 in.	95 cm
Accumulator Charging Time (110 A.C. and D.C.)	under 60 sec.	
Accumulator Charging Time (Hand Pump)	2 1/2 min.	
Minimum Door Width Hybrid Can Be Carried Through	18 in.	46 cm
Carrying Weight	395 lbs.	180 kg
Standard Operational Weight (w/o Payload)	463 lbs.	210 kg
Hybrid w/ High Post Kit Operational Weight (w/o Payload)	501 lbs.	227 kg

OTHER HYBRID II FEATURES

- The Hybrid II Incorporates the Universal Stop Valve System
- The Hybrid II Is Nickel Plated for Less Maintenance
- Works on Both Straight or Curved Track
- Interchangeable Soft, Hard or Pneumatic Tires for Different Terrain
- Hybrid II Incorporates Brakes on Rear Wheels
- Cam-Lock Chassis Legs
- Enclosed King Pin System
- Variable Camera Head
- Variable Chassis Legs
- Compact and Lightweight

*Payload Includes All Items (i.e. Man, Camera, Platform, Turret, Crane Arm, etc.) on Arm.
**Payload Includes All Items (i.e. Man, Camera, Platform, Turret, Crane Arm, etc.) on Base Mount.

*It is advised that the user of Chapman/Leonard equipment check with the manufacturer for the latest updates on *all* equipment.

Figure 144 *continued*

Chapman Hybrid III

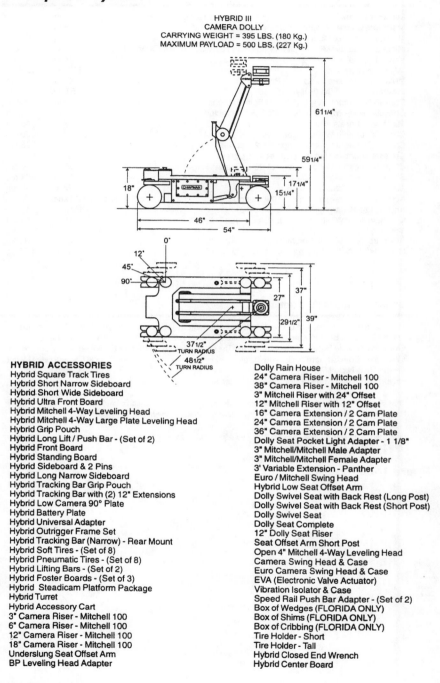

HYBRID III
CAMERA DOLLY
CARRYING WEIGHT = 395 LBS. (180 Kg.)
MAXIMUM PAYLOAD = 500 LBS. (227 Kg.)

HYBRID ACCESSORIES

Hybrid Square Track Tires
Hybrid Short Narrow Sideboard
Hybrid Short Wide Sideboard
Hybrid Ultra Front Board
Hybrid Mitchell 4-Way Leveling Head
Hybrid Mitchell 4-Way Large Plate Leveling Head
Hybrid Grip Pouch
Hybrid Long Lift / Push Bar - (Set of 2)
Hybrid Front Board
Hybrid Standing Board
Hybrid Sideboard & 2 Pins
Hybrid Long Narrow Sideboard
Hybrid Tracking Bar Grip Pouch
Hybrid Tracking Bar with (2) 12" Extensions
Hybrid Low Camera 90° Plate
Hybrid Battery Plate
Hybrid Universal Adapter
Hybrid Outrigger Frame Set
Hybrid Tracking Bar (Narrow) - Rear Mount
Hybrid Soft Tires - (Set of 8)
Hybrid Pneumatic Tires - (Set of 8)
Hybrid Lifting Bars - (Set of 2)
Hybrid Foster Boards - (Set of 3)
Hybrid Steadicam Platform Package
Hybrid Turret
Hybrid Accessory Cart
3" Camera Riser - Mitchell 100
6" Camera Riser - Mitchell 100
12" Camera Riser - Mitchell 100
18" Camera Riser - Mitchell 100
Underslung Seat Offset Arm
BP Leveling Head Adapter

Dolly Rain House
24" Camera Riser - Mitchell 100
38" Camera Riser - Mitchell 100
3" Mitchell Riser with 24" Offset
12" Mitchell Riser with 12" Offset
16" Camera Extension / 2 Cam Plate
24" Camera Extension / 2 Cam Plate
36" Camera Extension / 2 Cam Plate
Dolly Seat Pocket Light Adapter - 1 1/8"
3" Mitchell/Mitchell Male Adapter
3" Mitchell/Mitchell Female Adapter
3' Variable Extension - Panther
Euro / Mitchell Swing Head
Hybrid Low Seat Offset Arm
Dolly Swivel Seat with Back Rest (Long Post)
Dolly Swivel Seat with Back Rest (Short Post)
Dolly Swivel Seat
Dolly Seat Complete
12" Dolly Seat Riser
Seat Offset Arm Short Post
Open 4" Mitchell 4-Way Leveling Head
Camera Swing Head & Case
Euro Camera Swing Head & Case
EVA (Electronic Valve Actuator)
Vibration Isolator & Case
Speed Rail Push Bar Adapter - (Set of 2)
Box of Wedges (FLORIDA ONLY)
Box of Shims (FLORIDA ONLY)
Box of Cribbing (FLORIDA ONLY)
Tire Holder - Short
Tire Holder - Tall
Hybrid Closed End Wrench
Hybrid Center Board

Figure 145   Chapman Hybrid III.

SPECIFICATIONS

Maximum Camera Mount Height (with Standard 12" Riser)	73 in.	1.9 m
Maximum Camera Mount Height (without Risers)	61 1/4 in.	1.6 m
Minimum Camera Mount Height	15 1/4 in.	39 cm
Minimum Camera Mount Height with Hybrid Low Camera 90 Degree Plate	1 in.	3 cm
Vertical Travel	44 in.	1.1 m
*Maximum Payload	500 lbs.	227 kg
**Maximum Payload with High Post Kit	1,900 lbs.	863 kg
Maximum Boom Lifts (Fully Charged)	5 Lifts	
Chassis Maximum Length (Wheels Fully Extended)	54 in.	1.4 m
Chassis Minimum Length (Wheels Fully Retracted)	46 in.	1.2 m
Minimum Chassis Height for Transportation	18 in.	46 cm
Chassis Variable Widths - Legs in	27 in.	69 cm
Chassis Variable Widths - Legs at 12 Degree Track Position	29 1/2 in.	75 cm
Chassis Variable Widths - Legs at 45 Degrees	37 in.	89 cm
Chassis Variable Widths - Legs at 90 Degrees	39 in.	99 cm
Steering Post Height	36 in.	91 cm
Minimum Turn Radius	37 1/2 in.	95 cm
Accumulator Charging Time (110 A.C. and D.C.)	under 60 sec.	
Accumulator Charging Time (Hand Pump)	2 1/2 min.	
Minimum Door Width Hybrid Can Be Carried Through	18 in.	46 cm
Carrying Weight	395 lbs.	180 kg
Standard Operational Weight (w/o Payload)	463 lbs.	210 kg
Hybrid w/ High Post Kit Operational Weight (w/o Payload)	501 lbs.	227 kg

OTHER HYBRID III FEATURES

- Hybrid III Incorporates the Universal Stop Valve System
- Hybrid III has a Built-in Automatic Hydraulic Oil Heating System
- Interchangeable Soft, Hard or Pneumatic Tires for Different Terrain
- Works on Both Straight or Curved Track
- Hybrid III Is Nickel Plated
- Hybrid III Incorporates Brakes on Rear Wheels

- Cam-Lock Chassis Legs
- Compact and Lightweight
- Enclosed King Pin System
- Variable Camera Head Mount
- Variable Chassis Legs

*Payload Includes All Items (i.e. Man, Camera, Platform, Turret, Crane Arm, etc.) on Arm.
**Payload Includes All Items (i.e. Man, Camera, Platform, Turret, Crane Arm, etc.) on Base Mount.

*It is advised that the user of Chapman/Leonard equipment check with the manufacturer for the latest updates on *all* equipment.

Figure 145 *continued*

Chapman Sidewinder

Figure 146 Chapman Sidewinder.

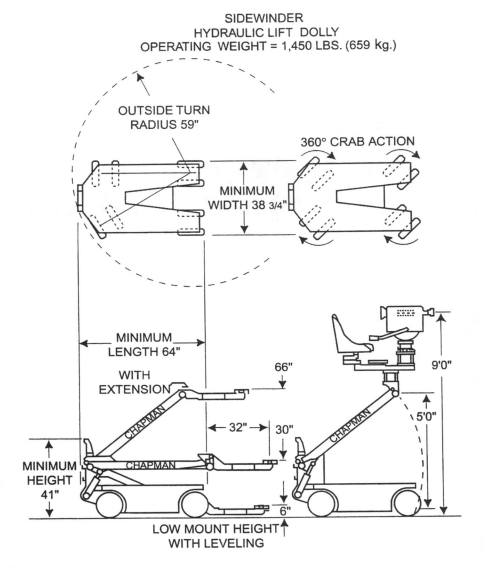

SIDEWINDER
HYDRAULIC LIFT DOLLY
OPERATING WEIGHT = 1,450 LBS. (659 kg.)

OUTSIDE TURN RADIUS 59"

360° CRAB ACTION

MINIMUM WIDTH 38 3/4"

MINIMUM LENGTH 64"

WITH EXTENSION

66"

9'0"

← 32" → | 30"

5'0"

MINIMUM HEIGHT 41"

CHAPMAN

6"

LOW MOUNT HEIGHT
WITH LEVELING

SIDEWINDER ACCESSORIES
6" Mitchell Riser
Sidewinder Sideboard
Sidewinder Pneumatic Tires - (Set of 8)
Sidewinder Solid Tires - (Set of 8)
Sidewinder Extension Arm - 2'
Rear 14" Seat Arm w/Seat - Sidewinder
Sidewinder Standing Board

*It is advised that the user of Chapman/Leonard equipment check with the manufacturer for the latest updates on *all* equipment.

Figure 146 *continued*

SPECIFICATIONS

Lens Height (Turret and Camera)	9 ft.	2.7 m
Base Mount Height	5 ft. 6 in.	1.7 m
Vertical Travel	5 ft.	1.5 m
Minimum Lens Height (Extension Setup) with Gear Head and Leveling Device	22 in.	56 cm
Minimum Lens Height (without Gear Head) Adapter Available	12 in.	30 cm
Maximum Lens Height with Sidewinder Setup (Leveling Head Only)	7 ft. 6 in.	2.3 m
Low Lens Height with Same Setup	30 in.	76 cm
*Maximum Payload	900 lbs.	409 kg
Maximum Horizontal Reach (with Extension)	38 in.	97 cm
Chassis Length	64 in.	1.6 m
Minimum Chassis Height	41 in.	1 m
Chassis Width (with Special or Pneumatic Tires)	38 3/4 in.	98 cm
Tread	26 in.	66 cm
Wheel Base	42 in.	1.1 m
Normal Operating Weight	1,450 lbs.	659 kg

OTHER SIDEWINDER FEATURES

- Operates on 8 Wheels (Power Delivered to 4)
- Dual Rocker Suspension (8 Wheels to 3 Point Suspension)
- Operates in Both Crab and Conventional Steering
- Selection of Turrets, Risers, Extensions and Aluminum Track
- On a Full Charge, Batteries Allow 24 Hours Use
- Built-In Battery Charger (110v/220v)
- Hydraulic Floor Locks
- Dual Steering Control
- Automatic Valve Control
- Silent Operation

*Payload Includes All Items (i.e. Man, Camera, Platform, Turret, Crane Arm, etc.) on Base Mount.

*It is advised that the user of Chapman/Leonard equipment check with the manufacturer for the latest updates on *all* equipment.

Figure 146 *continued*

T.O.T.

When you push the dolly, always put down a tape mark every time you park it. Many times the DP will say, "go to the last mark." I usually have three or four different-colored tapes pre-torn with tabs ready for such an occasion.

T.O.T.

If you are asked to work the dolly, don't roll over any cable because it may throw off the pin registry (the interior movement of the camera). It can also cause damage to the dolly.

FLUID AND REMOTE HEADS

Fluid heads in cameras gives hands-on control. They are designed with springs and lubricants that give the camera operator a pan and tilt movement. They usually have adjustment levers or collars that can restrict or lessen the friction of each head—sort of like an adjustable power steering unit. Each operator will like a certain "feel" to enhance his or her movement of the camera. There are several designs out there in the film world; I will show you some of what I see used daily.

Remote heads are electronic heads that attach to cranes, dollies, or rigs. They are fast becoming preferred over having a person riding a crane and operating the camera. They have either control wheels, a joystick, or even a fluid-type head with sensors on it to operate the remotely controlled head. They are sometimes located up to 100 feet from the operator.

T.O.T.

During installation of a remote head on a jib arm, or a crane arm in an under-slung position, I have found it easier to loosen all four leveling bolts, allowing the leveling head movement and four-way tilting freedom. Set the remote head on the ground (deck) with the threaded portion upward, if the head permits this method. With the arm balanced out, lower it to the threaded end of the remote and gently slide the receiver hole over the threads of the remote, making sure not to damage the threads. Align the keyway, then install the wing gland nut on the threads and rough level it in place. Add weight to the bucket end of the jib or crane to rebalance the pivot point of the arm. Raise the arm to a working height. (Usually, a six-step ladder under the arm will do nicely.) Now install the camera and safety. Rebalance the arm for the camera weight.

Kenworthy Snorkel Camera Systems

The Kenworthy Snorkel is the perfect device to maneuver. It's a tube with the mirror on the end through closed areas. For example, say you're shooting a McDonald's commercial and you want an extreme closeup of a burger, then rotate to a huge cup in frame, then to the fries. The snorkel will help you film in tight areas. The downside is its extremely heavy weight (about 350 pounds). You will probably need a small stage crane to mount it. Whatever you mount it on, make sure when you first set up the Snorkel system that the unit can handle the weight. The Snorkel system always comes with an able technician.

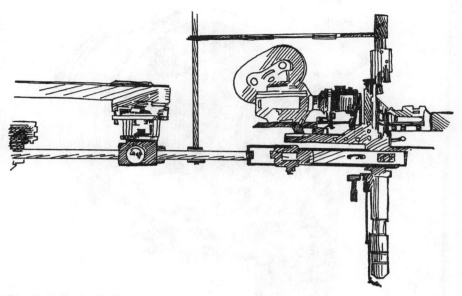

Figure 147   Kenworthy Snorkel.

T.O.T.

Not only does the snorkel get into tiny places, but it also delivers its own look (almost a three-dimensional effect) for film, I am told. Other pieces of equipment are available, but this one is a major problem solver.

Oppenheimer Spin-Axis 360 Head

The Spin-Axis 360 Head is the all-new motorized third-axis system from Oppenheimer Camera Products of Seattle. The system is lightweight, exceptionally robust, and is built to a standard that allows it to carry virtually any modern 35-mm, 16-mm, or video camera.

Remote Heads

On a set, I am often asked what remote heads I want to use because the production personnel want to place an order to hold a particular piece of equipment. I give them my standard answer: I'll tell you as soon as I talk to the DP and find out what camera they are using and how high a crane or jib is supposed to be. The weight of each camera is usually not the main factor—it is one of a few factors. Another factor is the length (or how high the camera is supposed to go). The longer the arm of a crane, the less weight can be put on the receiving end. You

Figure 148   Oppenheimer spin-axis 360 head.

have to know the weight of the remote head and the weight of the camera—always use your worst-case scenario (e.g., the heaviest the remote might be rigged with extensions; the heaviest the camera will be with zoom and the largest film magazine). Plan for the worst and then design for the best.

Some cranes may take a lot of weight, but they must have an added cable strength. This is wonderful for safety, but it makes the crane wider, which could be a problem in a tight spot. You may not get the desired movement on the crane shot. The remote head may be the type that can be reduced in overall size; by using certain remotes, you can squeeze down the size (adjust the unit to a smaller size) for use on a shot. For example, if you want a high shot on a set that drops as the actor approaches the walk up to a door, opens it, and walks in, then the remote head used could actually enter an adjoining living room window and go inside with the actor.

So now you can see why there is no one easy answer to the question of which remote heads should be used. First, you have to know what shots are desired. So after you have planned out the shot, you now have to find out what equipment is available. Sometimes shots may have to be reconsidered because of the unavailability of equipment or money. I have worked with production companies when, by no fault of their own, equipment suddenly does not show up, and then they are told "oh, by the way, we do not have *this* in stock." As the grip in this situation, you have to ensure that the substituted equipment will work and is safe.

HOT HEAD
REMOTE CAMERA
(with Preston System)

SPECIFICATIONS

	Hot Head S/NTS		HD Hot Head	
Height	2 ft. 3 in.	68 cm	2 ft. 3 in.	68 cm
Width	1 ft. 3 in.	37 cm	1 ft. 7 in.	47 cm
Depth	11 in.	27 cm	11 in.	27 cm
Weight	44 lbs.	20 kg	48 lbs.	22 kg
Total Shipping Weight	374 lbs.	170 kg	410 lbs.	186 kg
Load Capacity	154 lbs.	70 kg	176 lbs.	80 kg
Voltage	24v DC		24v DC	
Maximum Speed	2.5 sec. per 360°		2.5 sec. per 360°	
Minimum Speed	17 min. per 360°		17 min. per 360°	
Number of Slip Rings	34		34	
Number of Limit Switches	2 Tilt & Pan		2 Tilt & Pan	
Riser Size	4.38 in.	11.11 cm	4.38 in.	11.11 cm
Riser Size	8.63 in.	21.9 cm	8.63 in.	21.9 cm

OTHER HOT HEAD FEATURES

- Rotates 360° with Most Types of Film and Video Cameras
- Can Be Used with Film Magazines up to 1,000 ft. in Size
- Rotates a Continuous 360° Pan and Tilt with Lenses up to 10:1
- Smooth Pan and Tilt with Your Choice of Handwheel or Joystick
- Joystick Control System Offers One Man Pan/Tilt, Zoom and Focus
- F.I.Z. Controls Come with Witness Camera, Viewing Monitors and Mobile Control Cart
- Works on All Types of Crane Arms
- Smooth, Silent Performance
- Remote Head Technician Available upon Request
- Can Be Used with a Variety of Motion Picture and Video Cameras

*It is advised that the user of Chapman/Leonard equipment check with the manufacturer for the latest updates on *all* equipment.

Figure 149 Hot Head remote camera with Preston System.

POWER POD
(REMOTE CAMERA SYSTEM)

SPECIFICATIONS

Height (w/o Riser)	1 ft. 7 in.	48 cm
Width	11 1/4 in.	29 cm
Depth	1 ft. 4 3/4 in.	43 cm
Weight	40 lbs.	18 kg
Shipping Weight w/ Case for Complete System	492 lbs.	224 kg
Load Capacity (Recommended)	60 lbs.	27 kg
Voltage	12, 24 & 30 v DC	
Maximum Speed	3 sec per 360°	
Minimum Speed	16 min. per 360°	
Number of Slip Rings	4 rated at 9 amps	
Number of Limit Switches	1 Tilt Access	
Riser Size	300 mm & 150 mm	

OTHER POWER POD FEATURES

- Rotates 360° with Most Types of Film and Video Cameras
- Works on All Types of Arms
- Can Be Used with Film Magazines up to 1000 ft. in Size
- Smooth, Silent Performance
- Can Rotate a Continuous 360° Pan and Tilt with Lenses up to 10:1
- Smooth Pan and Tilt with Your Choice of Handwheels or Joystick
- F.I.Z. Controls Come with Witness Camera and Viewing Controls
- Trained Technician Available upon Request
- Can Be Used with Arriflex and Panavision 65mm Cameras

*It is advised that the user of Chapman/Leonard equipment check with the manufacturer for the latest updates on *all* equipment.

Figure 150a Power Pod.

POWER POD
(REMOTE CAMERA SYSTEM)

SPECIFICATIONS

Height (w/o Riser)	1 ft. 7 in.	48 cm
Width	11 1/4 in.	29 cm
Depth	1 ft. 4 3/4 in.	43 cm
Weight	40 lb.	18 kg
Shipping Weight w/ Case for Complete System	492 lb.	224 kg
Load Capacity (Recommended)	120 lb.	54.5 kg
Voltage	12, 24 & 30 v DC	
Maximum Speed	3 sec per 360°	
Minimum Speed	16 min. per 360°	
Number of Slip Rings	4 rated at 9 amps	
Number of Limit Switches	1 Tilt Access	
Riser Size	300 mm & 150 mm	

OTHER POWER POD FEATURES

- Rotates 360° with Most Types of Film and Video Cameras
- Works on All Types of Arms
- Can Be Used with Film Magazines up to 1,000 ft. in Size
- Smooth, Silent Performance
- Can Rotate a Continuous 360° Pan and Tilt with Lenses up to 10:1
- Smooth Pan and Tilt with Your Choice of Handwheels or Joystick
- F.I.Z. Controls Come with Witness Camera and Viewing Controls
- Trained Technician Available upon Request
- Can Be Used with Arriflex and Panavision 65mm Cameras

*It is advised that the user of Chapman/Leonard equipment check with the manufacturer for the latest updates on *all* equipment.

Figure 150b Power Pod.

WEAVER STEADMAN'S "ds Remote™"
CAMERA SYSTEM
(with Preston System)

SPECIFICATIONS

2-Axis Height (Minimum Configuration)	2 ft. 1 in.	63.5 cm
2-Axis Width (Minimum Configuration)	1 ft. 9 in.	53.4 cm
2-Axis Depth (Minimum Configuration)	1 ft.	30.5 cm
3-Axis Height (Minimum Configuration)	2 ft. 8 in.	81.3 cm
3-Axis Width (Minimum Configuration)	2 ft. 2 in.	66 cm
3-Axis Depth (Minimum Configuration)	2 ft. 1 in.	63.5 cm
2-Axis Weight	61 lb.	27.7 kg
3-Axis Weight	93 lb.	42.3 kg
2-Axis Payload Capacity (Recommended)	120 lb.	54.5 kg
3-Axis Payload Capacity (Recommended)	90 lb.	40.9 kg
Electronic Limit Switches (Both Directions)	Pan, Tilt & Roll	
Pan, Tilt & Roll Movement	360° Continuous	
Speed Range (Pan, Tilt & Roll)	3 sec. to 24 hr.	
Number of Slip Rings	120	
Mounting Base	Standard Mitchell	
Outputs at Camera	BNC 75 Ohm (x3)	
	12 volts @ 2 amps for video (x2)	
	12 or 15 volts @ 10 amps peak (x2)	
	24 or 30 volts @ 15 amps peak	
Lens Control Systems	Preston Fi+Z and Arri Lens Control	
Outputs Spare for Client's Use	Two Channels 2 amps	
	Five Channels 2 amps	
Link between Head & Controls (Single Cable Capability)	50 ft. - 800 ft	15 m - 244 m
Supply Voltage Range	48 volts DC, 90-240 volts AC	
Power for Head @ 48 volts DC	1.6 - 10 amps Peak	

OTHER WEAVER STEADMAN FEATURES

- Rotates 360° with All Common Film & Video Camera
- Can Be Used with All Common 1,000 ft. Film Magazines
- F.I.Z. Come with Witness Camera & Viewing Controls
- Can Be Used with Arriflex & Panavision 65mm Cameras
- Open Side Chassis for Tight Camera Positioning
- User Friendly, Quick, Simple Setup and Arrangement
- Pan, Tilt & Roll Movement in Any Direction
- Trained Tech Available upon Request
- Works on All Types of Arms
- Smooth, Silent Performance
- Powers Arriflex 435 at High Speed
- Instant Record and Playback
- Modular Components for Optimal Size & Camera Placement
- Can Rotate a Continuous 360° Pan, Tilt and Roll with Lenses up to 10:1
- Smooth Pan, Tilt and Roll with Your Choice of Handwheels or Fluid PTR

*It is advised that the user of Chapman/Leonard equipment check with the manufacturer for the latest updates on *all* equipment.

Figure 151 Weaver-Steadman's "ds Remote."

FLIGHT HEAD
(Third Axis Gyrostabilized Remote Head)

SPECIFICATIONS

Height	36 in.	91.5 cm
Width	22 in.	55.9 cm
Depth	30.6 in.	77.7 cm
Weight	55 lbs.	25 kg
Shipping Weight for Complete System	850 lbs.	386.4 kg
Payload Capacity (Recommended)	66 lbs.	30 kg
Range of Movement:		
Pan	Unlimited	
Tilt	75º Positive to 165º Negative	
Roll	95º Left or Right	
Maximum Usable Focal Length	250 mm	
Mounting Base	Standard Mitchell	
Dynamic Stabilization Error	No more than 3 Arc Minutes	
Maximum Angular Speed	120 Degrees / sec.	
Maximum Angular Acceleration	120 Degrees / sec. / sec.	
Regular Current	2.5 amps	
Operating Temperature	14º F to 122º F	
Power Supply:		
AC	110 / 220 v 50 - 60 Hz	
DC	22 - 32 v	
Regular Current	2.5 amps	
Operating Temperature	14º F to 122º F	
Setup Time	Approximately 1 Hour	

OTHER FLIGHT HEAD FEATURES

- The Flight Head Can Be Mounted on Lenny Arms, Super Nova & Apollo Mobile Cranes, for Increased Versatility in Camera Movement, Especially with Dual Axis Movements.
- The Flight Head Can Be Mounted on the Auto-Robot Crane. This Setup Can Be Mounted on Cars, Boats and Cranes.
- The Flight Head Offers Automatic Backpan Compensation to Simplify Tough Following Shots.
- The Flight Head Has a Unique Ability to Dutch, Pan and Tilt with a Single Operator. The Auto-Robot Crane Allows Remote Control of the Crane Arm.
- Gyrostabilized Head Corrects the Horizon, while Allowing Motion of the Head's Base.
- Operates with Gear Head or Joy Stick.

Figure 152 Flight Head three-axis gyrostabilized remote head.

On a personal note, I have always liked the Power Pod because it is pretty close to grip proof. It has one attaching nut like most remotes. It has very few cables, which are all bundled together in one jacket. Each connect is color-coded, different sized, and different pinned. It comes with a small remote control box called a zapper. It is virtually mistake proof—it either works or it doesn't. It is a great unit, and usually a technician is not required.

Another fantastic unit is the Cam-remote by Mathews. This remote can be built to a smaller overall size so you can go through a smaller opening, such as a car side window. This unit usually comes with a technician, which is an added cost, so you really have to watch your budgets. I say this like a company man. That's because I am. I'm a company in myself, and if I put the production company out

FLIGHT HEAD
(Three Axis Gyrostabilized Remote Head)
Maximum Payload: 66 lb. (30 kg)

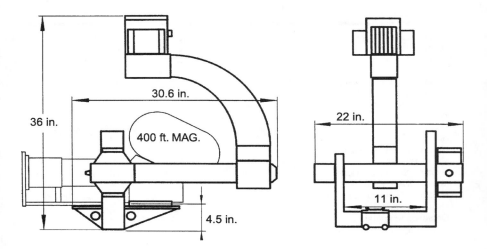

FLIGHT HEAD SYSTEM STANDARD PACKAGE AND ACCESSORIES
Joystick (Pan, Tilt, Dutch and Zoom) and Wheels Control (Pan and Tilt)
2 Monitors
Preston FiZ Lens System
8 Batteries (10 Hours)
Cables (up to 130 ft.)
3 Chargers -110 ac
Battery Maintainer
Shipping Cases
Wireless Intercom w/3 Headsets
Wireless Intercom Headset (w/ Item #8200)
Flight Head Shock Absorber - 3 Axis
Chapman/Leonard Battery Pack
Chapman/Leonard Battery Charger - 110v
Chapman/Leonard Battery Charger - 220v

*It is advised that the user of Chapman/Leonard equipment check with the manufacturer for the latest updates on *all* equipment.

Figure 152 *continued*

of business because of cost overruns, we both lose. So watch it. Discuss the issue. Figure out what's best for all. There is usually a happy medium.

When working with remote heads, you are usually on a crane, jib, or arm. This will take you away from the camera operator, unlike being close while on a dolly. You could find yourself anywhere from 25 feet to 100 feet away. I suggest you have your soundperson set up a one-way communication system for the operator and you and your helper grip on the crane or arm. Have the sound department wire an omnidirectional mike and transmitter. Wire you and your helper with a receiver and headset.

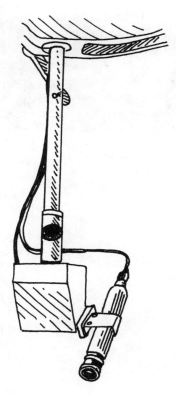

Figure 153a   Microshot head.

Figure 153b   Microshot head.

T.O.T

The following specifications are what was up to date at the time of printing, *but* things change. *Always* check with the manufacture or vendor to ensure that you are getting the latest specs. This book shows only some of the equipment that is available. New products are always being introduced and old products are constantly changing.

Microshot Head

Specifications

Height	3.5 ft./8.8 cm
Width	3.0 ft./7.6 cm
Depth	2.5 ft./6.3 cm
Weight	1.3 lbs./0.625 kg
Maximum load	3.3 lbs./1,500 kg
Maximum speed	360 degrees in 2.5 seconds
Minimum speed	360 degrees in 17 minutes
Voltage	12 volts DC
Temperature range	59 to 131°F/–15 to +55°C
Drive shaft	0.35 ft./0.8 cm
Control cable length (tested)	1,000 ft./300 m

T.O.T.

Use Speed-Rail as a track to get a Chapman dolly down a short staircase.

Hot Shot Head

Features

- Nodal camera position allows the camera to pan and tilt on the center axis of the lens.
- Pan slips rings allow continuous rotation of the Hot Shot.
- Tilt limit switches ensure that cables do not get snagged.
- A new breed of electronics offers the same sensitivity and control as the Hot Head.
- Fully adjustable speed controls allow 360-degree control of pan and tilt, in speeds ranging from 2.5 seconds to 17 minutes.
- The Hot Shot offers a choice of control system, either via the standard joystick console or via the "tracer" pan bar system.
- Reversing switches ensure that the operator has total and user-friendly control of the head and camera.

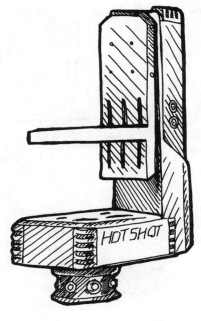

Figure 154   Hot Shot.

Specifications

Height	22 in.
Load capacity	50 lbs.
Width	7 in.
Voltage	24 volts DC, 100–240 volts AC
Upright width	5 in.
Maximum speed	2.5 seconds per 360 degrees
Depth	14 in.
Weight	38 lbs.

Mini Hot Head

Specifications

Height	17 in./43 cm
Width	12 in./30 cm
Depth	6 in./16 cm
Weight	11 lbs./5 kg
Load capacity	33 lbs./15 kg
Voltages	24 volts DC, 100–240 volts AC
Maximum speed	2.5 seconds per 360 degrees

Figure 155 Mini Hot Head.

Minimum speed	17 minutes per 360 degrees
Number of slip rings	24
Number of limit switches	2
Riser size	4 in./10 cm

Hot Head II

The Hot Head II can handle virtually any 35-mm, 16-mm, or video camera. The system comes with the Preston lens control system using Microforce and Micro-servo controls with Heden Motors for zoom, focus, and iris. The camera has full three-axis capability without danger of dropout via broadcast-quality slip rings.

Features

- 360-degree simultaneous pan and tilt
- Full slip-ring facility controls all functions of film and video cameras
- Broadcast-quality video pictures through slip rings
- Adjustable-height arm accepts all film magazines up to 1,000 feet
- Speed range of 2.5 seconds to 15 minutes for 360 degrees
- "Worral"-type handle controls
- Video console provides one-person operation of head, zoom, and focus
- Fully adjustable electronic limit switches
- Power supply: 110/220 volts or 24-volt battery

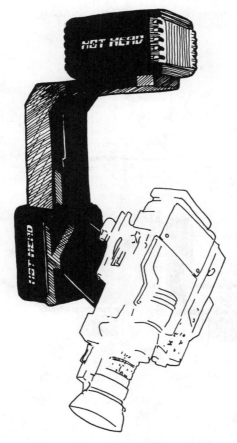

Figure 156a Hot Head II.

- Multi-core, digital, or radio link gives complete cable-free operation up to 1 mile
- Shot box facility allows all functions to be memorized and repeated in up to 99 user-defined positions

Hot Head II Package
- Hot Head II
- Preston Complete Lens Control System
- Lens Witness Camera
- Pan and tilt wheels
- 125-ft. Hot Head main cable
- Monitors
- Three-axis adaptors for video cameras
- Experienced technician

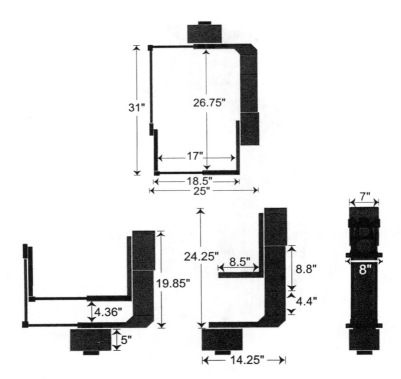

Figure 156b Hot Head II.

Specifications

Height	27 in./68 cm
Width	15 in./37 cm
Depth	11 in./27 cm
Riser size	4.4 in./11 cm
Weight	44 lbs./20 kg
Load capacity	154 lbs./70 kg
Maximum speed	2.5 seconds per 360 degrees
Minimum speed	17 minutes per 360 degrees
Voltages	24 volts DC, 100–240 volts AC
Type of mount	Mitchell
Number of limit switches	2

Hot Head II Plus

Specifications

Height	31 in.
Width	25 in.

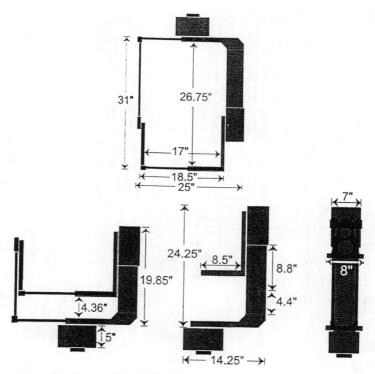

Figure 157 Hot Head II Plus.

Depth	19.85 in.
Riser size	8.8 in.
Weight	45 lbs.
Load capacity	120 lbs.
Maximum speed	3 seconds per 360 degrees
Minimum speed	16 minutes per 360 degrees
Diameter of tilt plane	19 in.

T.O.T.
Watch for the DP's hand moves during the shot and always float your move. Feather your starts and stops.

HD Hot Head

Specifications

Height	27 in./68 cm
Width	19 in./47 cm
Depth	11 in./27 cm

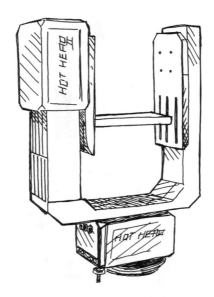

Figure 158 HD Hot Head.

Weight	48 lbs./22 kg
Load capacity	176 lbs./80 kg
Voltages	24 volts DC, 100–240 volts AC
Maximum speed	2.5 seconds per 360 degrees
Minimum speed	17 minutes per 360 degrees
Number of slip rings	34
Number of limit switches	2
Riser size	4.4 in./11 cm

Pee-Pod 1,000 Head

Features

- Lightweight construction
- Multiple slip rings with three-axis channel
- Precise smooth control at slow and high speeds
- Low noise levels
- Simple cabling
- Programmable
- Can be linked to a personal computer by RS 232
- Onboard intelligence
- Direct interface for zoom/focus with most broadcast lenses
- Operator link via cable, telephone, RF, microwave, or satellite

Figure 159a   Hot Head.

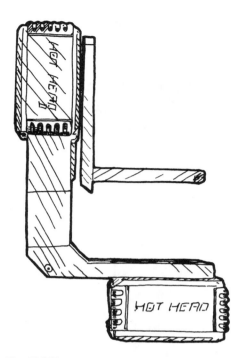

Figure 159b Hot Head NTS.

Power Pod System

The Power Pod is a sophisticated electronic pan and tilt head, much like the Hot Head II. Both the Power Pod and Hot Head II are designed to capture those dangerous shots that would otherwise be left behind by keeping the cameraperson and crew at a safe distance. By using these remote heads, you can capture those moments of danger and excitement without compromising vision or losing artistic inspiration. The Power Pod and Hot Head II also give the cameraperson that extra edge by allowing placement of the camera in unusual and precarious setups. Both heads are especially great for sporting events and special effects.

Figure 160a   Pee-Pod 1,000.

The Power Pod is a remote head system offering the director and the cameraperson a variable format that can be easily changed in minutes. The Power Pod can handle loads up to 60 pounds, giving smooth pan and tilt with low noise levels.

In its lowest profile, the Power Pod offers a minimum distance of 8.5 inches from the top of the leveler to the base of the camera, giving you a low-profile and rigid unit with plenty of torque.

In its tallest profile, the Power Pod can rotate the Golden Panaflex, Arriflex BL cameras, and Movie-cam, all with 1,000-foot magazines and long focal-length lenses. The Power Pod is also great for all video cameras.

Power Pod 2,000 Specifications

Weight of two-axis format	70 lbs./32 kg
Weight of three-axis format	125 lbs./56 kg
Maximum recommended load (two-axis)	200 lbs./90 kg
Maximum recommended load (three-axis)	150 lbs./68 kg
Pan, tilt, and roll movement	360 degree continuous
Electronic limit switches	Tilt and roll
Speed range of pan, tilt, and roll	2.5 seconds to 37 hours
Mounting base	standard Mitchell

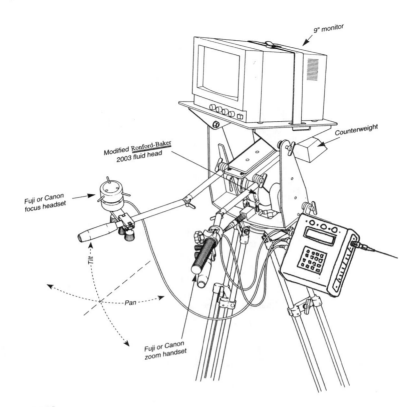

9" monitor

Counterweight

Modified <u>Ronford-Baker</u>
2003 fluid head

Fuji or Canon
focus headset

Tilt

Pan

Fuji or Canon
zoom handset

Figure 160b   Pee-Pod 1,000.

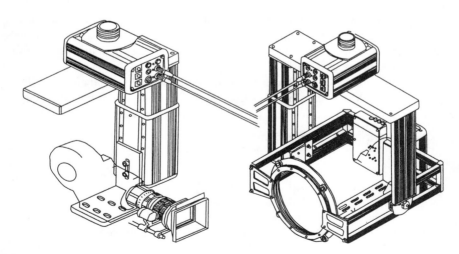

Figure 161a   Power Pod 2,000.

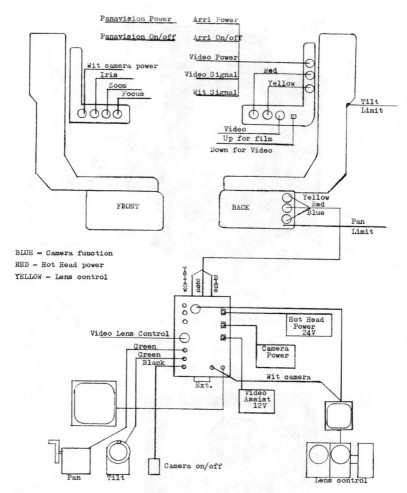

Figure 161b Cable system for the Power Pod.

A simplified control system reduces the number of cables needed to run the head, without any loss of response or sensitivity. Control handles are just one option offered; these are Worrel-type handles with adjustable fluid damping that gives smooth drag to the handles. A joystick control is another standard option available. As with all other Power Pod electronics, this unit is based on its own plug in a personal computer board, which can easily be mounted into other control panels. Both systems basically comprise three units:

1. *The Head*: This unit consists of two basic modules that, when used together or with other Power Pod accessories, can be rearranged in just minutes to produce many different geometric formats.

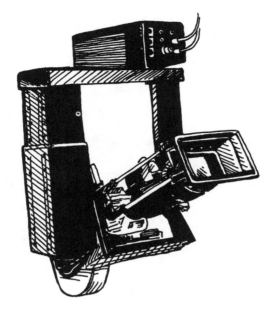

Figure 161c   Power Pod 2,000, two-axis.

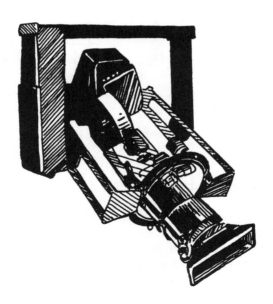

Figure 161d   Power Pod 2,000, three-axis.

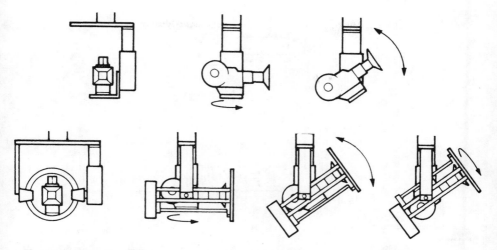

Figure 161e   Power Pod 2,000. *Top*, two-axis format. *Bottom*, three-axis format.

2. *The Electronic Control Module*: The Electronic Control Module (ECM) is a single unit that runs the head.
3. *The Command System*: Here we have a choice of ways that can control the head. These command systems are plugged into the ECM and tell it the movement the operator wants from the Power Pod. The most commonly used command systems are Worrel-type handles or joystick. These and other options are available for the Power Pod.

Cam-Remote Systems

Specifications

Camera cradle capacity	60 lbs./27 kg
Weight of unit (empty)	44 lbs./20 kg
Power requirements	110–220 volts AC or 18–27 volts DC
Pan speed (maximum):	1 revolution per 2.4 seconds
Tilt speed (maximum):	1 revolution per 2.6 seconds

Scorpio II

With the new Scorpio II remote head, 360-degree continuous rolls are now possible. The digitally controlled Scorpio performs flawlessly with heavy camera loads up to 176 pounds. All axis types (pan, tilt, and roll) are programmable and repeatable. Hand wheels, joystick, and pan-bar control systems are available, and the video monitor displays all camera data.

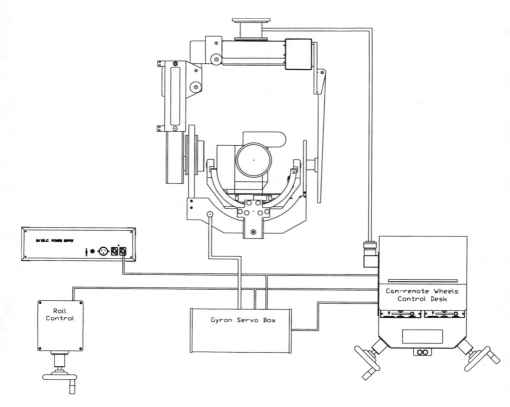

Figure 162a Cam-Remote system.

Specifications

Maximum weight at the head	176 lbs./80 kg
Two-axis head weight	62 lbs./28 kg
Three-axis head weight	86 lbs./39 kg
Pan, tilt, and roll	360-degrees continuous rotation

Libra III Head

The Libra III is a new generation three-axis remote camera mount. It is unique in that it can be operated in either direct mode (digital), or you can choose to stabilize one axis, two, or all three at the flick of a switch. Custom-designed motors give it the precision of a well-tuned geared head, complemented by the world of possibilities offered by stabilization.

Extremely unstable, wet, and muddy conditions are well tolerated. The Libra III excels in action on a boat, off-road, on a camera car, or on a long crane. When

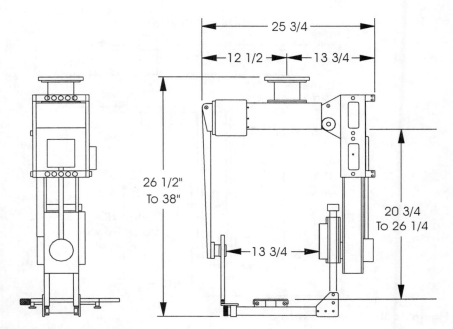

Figure 162b Cam-Remote system.

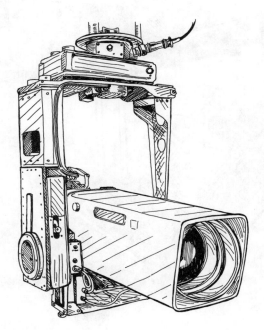

Figure 163a Mini-Mote system.

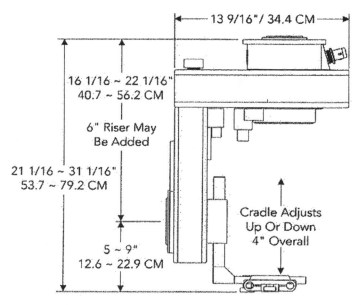

Figure 163b   Mini-Mote system.

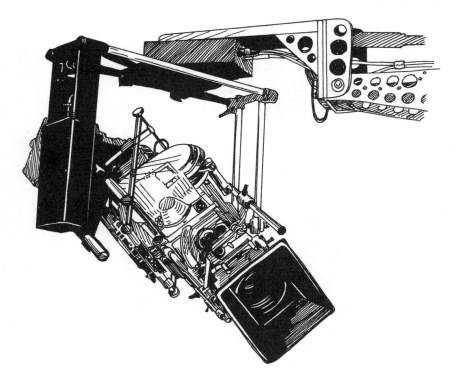

Figure 164   Scorpio II three-axis remote head.

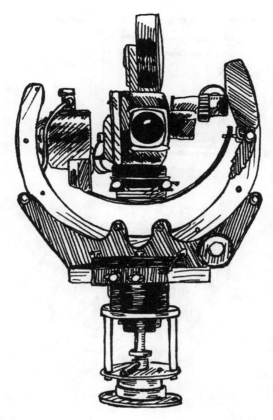

Figure 165a Libra III.

in stabilized mode, automatic back-panning on an arcing crane or dolly move is an added bonus. At the other end of the scale, precision moves are taken in stride. The Libra fits all industry-standard cranes and gripping equipment and can be either suspended or mounted upright. The onboard memory card can store moves of up to 40 seconds in length, and recording of longer moves or motion capture is available as an option.

Specifications

Pan rate	130 degrees per second
Power static	3 amps
Tilt rate	130 degrees per second
Power dynamic	8 amps
Roll rate	100 degrees per second
Memory	Ram card
Power	24–35 volts DC/AC
Pan	Travel 350 degrees

Figure 165b Libra III.

Weight	50 lbs.
Tilt	Travel 270 degrees
Width	20
Roll Travel	90 degrees
Height	20 in.
Mounting	Mitchell bracket

Flight

FLIGHT HEAD

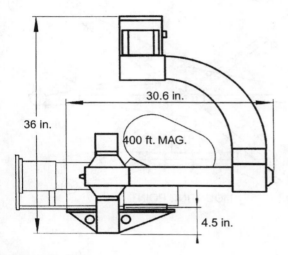
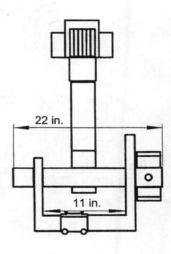

Figure 166a Flight head.

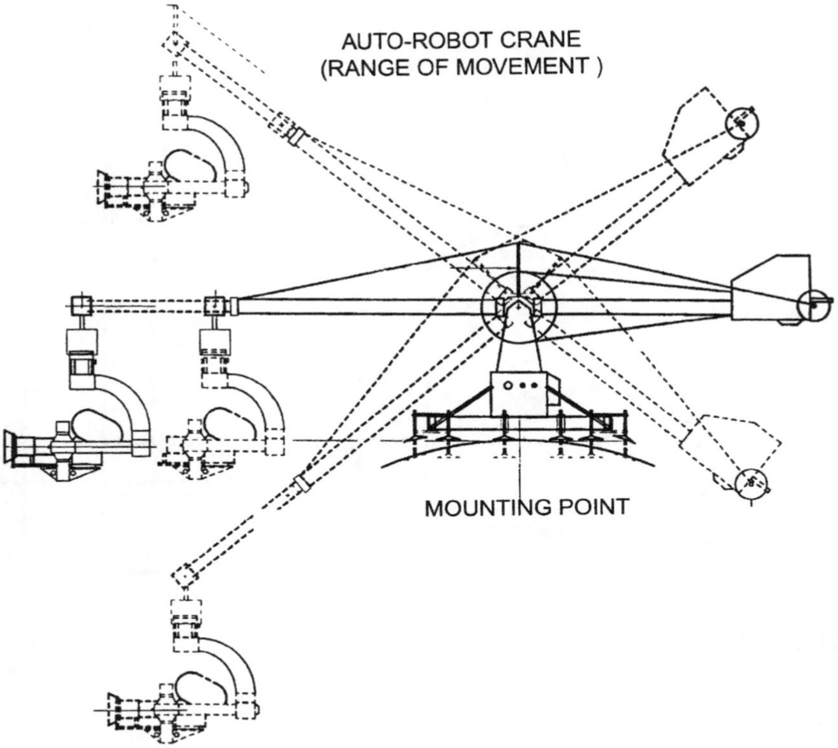

AUTO-ROBOT CRANE
(RANGE OF MOVEMENT)

MOUNTING POINT

*It is advised that the user of Chapman/Leonard equipment check with the manufacturer for the latest updates on *all* equipment.

Figure 166b Flight Head Auto-Robot crane.

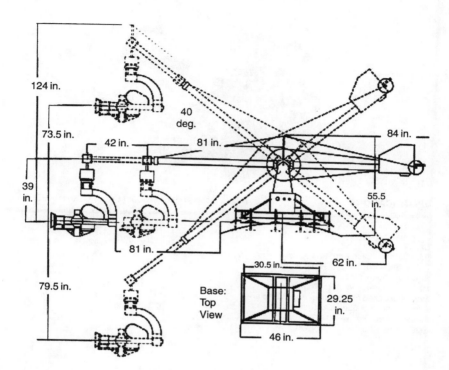

FLIGHT HEAD and AUTO-ROBOT CRANE
(Four Axis Gyrostabilized System)
Maximum Payload: 120 lb. (54.5 kg)
Unit Weight 1,500 lb. (681.8 kg)

FLIGHT HEAD AND AUTO-ROBOT STANDARD PACKAGE AND ACCESSORIES
Joystick (Pan, Tilt, Dutch and Zoom) and Wheels Control (Pan and Tilt)
2 Monitors
Preston FiZ Lens System
8 Batteries (10 Hours) - For Flight Head
4 Batteries (20 Hours) - For Auto Robot
Cables (up to 130 ft.)
3 Chargers -110 ac
Battery Maintainer
Padding Kit
Straps
Transport Cart
Shipping Cases·
Wireless Intercom w/3 Headsets
Wireless Intercom Headset (w/ Item #8200)
Flight Head Shock Absorber - 3 Axis
Chapman/Leonard Battery Pack
Chapman/Leonard Battery Charger - 110v
Chapman/Leonard Battery Charger - 220v

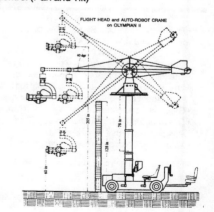

*It is advised that the user of Chapman/Leonard equipment check with the manufacturer for the latest updates on *all* equipment.

Figure 166c Flight head and Auto-Robot crane.

FLIGHT HEAD w/ AUTO-ROBOT CRANE
(Four Axis Gyrostabilized System)

SPECIFICATIONS   (Flight Head and Auto-Robot Crane - Item # 6020)

Unit Weight	580 lb.	263.6 kg
(Max. Configuration with Arri 453 camera and 70 mm Zoom Lens		
FIZ Wireless Control and Two Batteries)		
Shipping Weight for Complete System	1500 lb.	681.8 kg
Maximum Payload for Auto-Robot Crane	120 lb.	54.5 kg
Maximum Speed Approved for Base Vehicle	65 mph	100 kph
Angular Speed of Boom Control	25 deg./sec.	
Power (10 hour job w/ 216 Gel Batteries)	30 v, 7 A DC	
Setup Time	Approximately 1-2 Hours	

OTHER FLIGHT HEAD / AUTO=ROBOT FEATURES

- The Flight Head Can Be Mounted on Lenny Arms, Dollies, Super Nova & Apollo Mobile Cranes, or Any Standard Mitchell Mount.
- The Flight Head Can Be Mounted on the Auto-Robot Crane or Shock Absorber System. This Setup Can Also Be Mounted on Cars, Boats and Cranes.
- The Flight Head Offers Automatic Backpan Compensation to Simplify Tough Following Shots.
- The Flight Head Has a Unique Ability to Dutch, Pan, Tilt and Zoom with a Single Operator. The Auto-Robot Crane Allows Remote Control of the Crane Arm.
- Gyrostabilized Head Corrects the Horizon, while Allowing Motion of the Head's Base.
- Operates with Hand Wheels or Joy Stick.
- Can Be Used with a Variety of Motion Picture and Video Cameras, Including Panavision 65 mm Cameras
- Trained Tech Necessary with Every Rental

*It is advised that the user of Chapman/Leonard equipment check with the manufacturer for the latest updates on *all* equipment.

Figure 166d   Flight head and Auto-Robot crane.

Fluid Heads

Weaver/Steadman

The Weaver Steadman balanced fluid head has a modular design and unique tube frame versatility to deliver 360 degrees of tilt with only light finger pressure.

Features

- A tube is inherently rigid. The design offers maximum stiffness for all cameras up to 80 pounds.
- Four lengths of tube are supplied with the head to allow for extreme tilt angle or minimum profile.
- The camera can be supported conventionally from below to be suspended from above.
- Extreme low camera angles can be obtained.

New Features

- A lead screw leveler simplifies camera balancing.
- Heavy-duty axles and a drop safety collar are included.
- Dutch angle bracket allows mounting a Weaver/Steadman tilt mechanism on a traditional head for a roll axis.

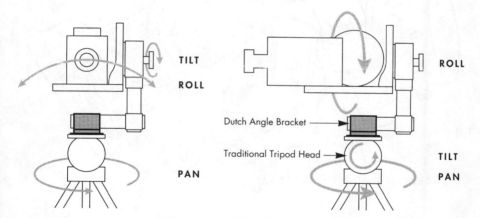

Figure 167a Balanced fluid head. Dutch angle bracket configurations.

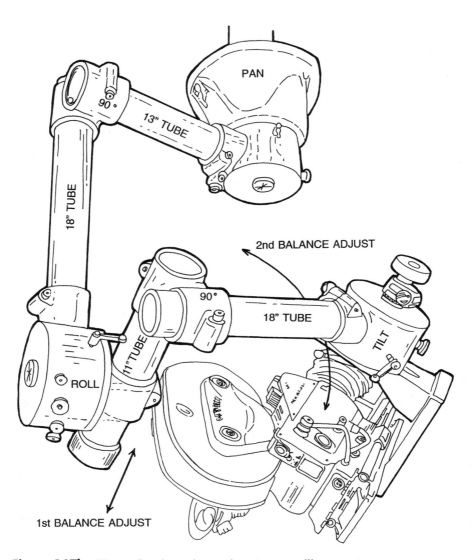

Figure 167b Weaver-Steadman three-axis system on ceiling mount.

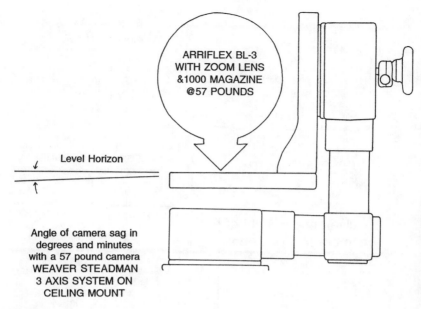

Figure 167c Arriflex BL-3.

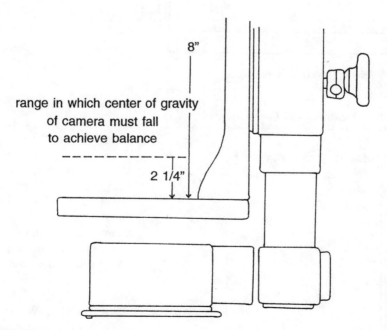

Figure 167d Standard mounting.

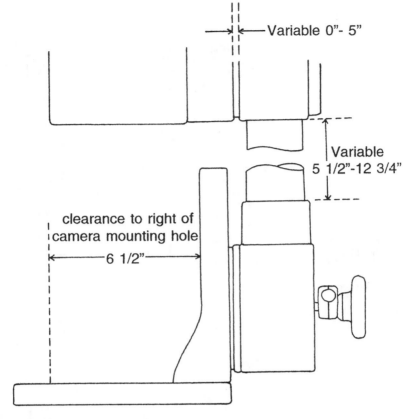

Figure 167e Inverted mounting.

Specifications and Components

Weight	18 lbs.
Maximum camera weight	80 lbs.
Mounting	Mitchell base standard
Tubes	4 supplied
Camera plates	3 supplied for Panavision, Arriflex, and video cameras
Contact	Weaver/Steadman for sales and rental information Weaver/Steadman Camera Support Systems 1646 20th St., Santa Monica, CA 90404 310/829-3296, fax 310/828-5935

> **T.O.T.**
> Although normally not a grip job, I have personally ordered this piece of equipment after speaking with the DP. It will solve several unforeseen problems.

Balanced Fluid Heads

Comparison of Three-Axis System on Ceiling Mounts

Feature	Weaver/Steadman	Ronford 7
Center of gravity design	Yes	Yes
Weight	18 lbs.	24 lbs.
Camera sag with 57-lb. Arriflex	0 degrees 21 minutes	1 degree 26 minutes
Dampening increments	5	4
Arri BL-3 compatible	Yes	Yes
Panaflex compatible	Yes	No
Variable geometry	Yes	No
Camera to deck clearance	$1\frac{1}{16}$ in.	$1\frac{9}{16}$ in.
Level for inverted mounting	Yes	No
Dual brakes on pan and tilt	Yes	No

Pearson Balanced Fluid Heads

All Pearson balanced fluid heads are designed for the professional film and video cameraperson who demands the ultimate in smoothness and versatility in a camera head. The A4000 Pearson head is supplied complete with the basic sealed fluid units, handle, and controls, and is ready for mounting on the Pro Jr. Tripod top plate. The A4000 requires the addition of a camera mounting assembly to complete your fluid head.

Features

- Model A camera mount assembly for Arri 35IIC
- Model E-V camera mount assembly for lightweight video, Arri and Eclair 16 mm cameras
- Model BL-V camera mount assembly for larger video cameras and Arri 35BL and Arri III

Specifications, A4000

Body casting	Lightweight magnesium
Other hardware	Stainless steel or chrome plated for corrosion resistance
Handles	One 22-in. control handle of stainless steel. Handles

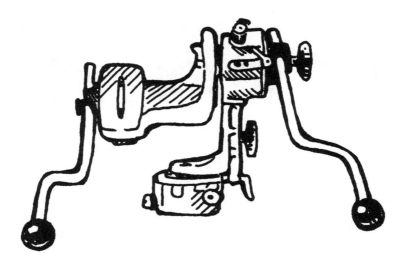

Figure 168   Pearson A4000 balanced fluid head.

	adjust to 360-degree rotation. The A4000 head provides for two control handles; the second handle and mounting bracket are optional.
Weight	20 lbs.
Mounting	Any Pro Jr. tripod with optional adaptor on Mitchell Tripod or high hat. No additional accessories are necessary to mount the head upside down on a crane or jib-boom arm.
Operational range	+140 degrees to −40 degrees
Maximum distance between two control handles	22 in.
Pivots	Ball bearings for pan and tilt action pivots
Control	All adjustable fluid tension control, allowing three stages of control
Leveling	Spirit level
Tilt	Capable of full tilt with many models of cameras

The Pearson Dual A4000 is supplied complete with three sealed fluid units, two control handles, and ready for mounting on any Pro Jr. top plate. The Dual A4000's design eliminates the need for a separate camera mounting assembly and easily accommodates a wide range of camera sizes.

Specifications, Dual A4000

Body casting	Lightweight magnesium
Other hardware	Stainless steel or chrome plated for corrosion resistance
Handles	Two 22-in. control handles; handles adjust to 360-degree rotation
Weight	35 lbs.
Mounting	Any Pro Jr. tripod or with optional adaptor on Mitchell tripod or high hat. No additional accessories are necessary to mount the head upside down on a crane or jib-boom arm.
Operational range	+140 degrees to –40 degrees
Maximum distance between control handles	22 in.
Pivots	Ball bearings for pan and tilt action pivots

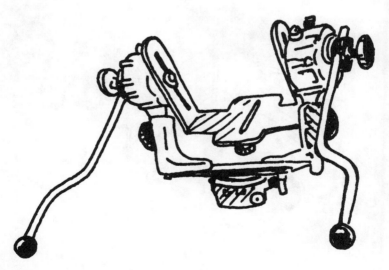

Figure 169   Pearson Dual A4000 balanced fluid head.

Control	All adjustable fluid tension control, allowing three stages of control
Leveling	Spirit level
Tilt	Capable of full tilt with may kinds of cameras

Other Camera Mounts

- Model A Camera Mount: Assembly for Arri 35IIC with $^3/_8$-16 captive tiedown screw.
- Model E-V Camera Mount: Assembly for lightweight video, Arri, and Eclair 16-mm cameras with $^3/_8$-16 captive tiedown screw.
- Model BL-V Camera Mount: Assembly for larger video cameras and Arri 35BL and Arri III with $^3/_8$-16 captive tiedown screw for video, 35-mm, and 16-mm cameras.

These mounts are for video, 35-mm, and 16-mm cameras. The Pro Jr. to Mitchell adapter assembly has a shaft, washer, and lock-off knob. The unique design of the Pearson head allows it to be mounted upside down (underslung) on a boom or crane, providing a low optical axis for ground level and table top filming.

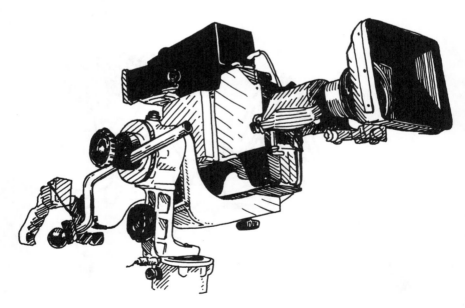

Figure 170   Pearson A4000 with video camera.

> ### T.O.T.
> The Pearson head is great for low-angle shots. I suggest you look at the storyboard and talk to the DP to determine whether such a head can be used. The camera department usually orders this piece of equipment.

Mini Seven Head

This new lightweight head is designed for use with film or video cameras with a maximum weight of 26.4 pounds or 12 kg. The camera screw and platform adjust vertically and horizontally to put the camera on its center of gravity, which allows the camera to remain in any given position without using balance springs. The amount of "feel" required is selected from one of the three positions within the patented fluid system. The head is designed to be as lightweight as possible without sacrificing strength or reliability.

Technical Specifications

Design	Fluid-cushioned free head
Control	Sealed fluid system gives 360 degrees of control in both pan and tilt; smooth, accurate braking on pan and tilt.
Leveling	Circular spirit level
Pivots	100-mm ball base; other fittings possible to order
Assembly	Thrust races and ball bearings throughout; camera screw and platform

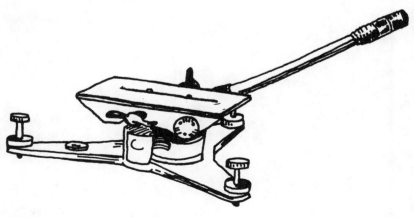

Figure 171 Movie Tech rocker plate.

adjust for vertical and horizontal balance; second pan bar and ratchet pan bar available

Operational temperature range	+150°F to –40°F/+60°C to –40°C
Weight	6.6 lbs./3 kg

T.O.T.

Put the back lifting bars in Fisher #10, then stand on them; this will offset the weight enough to lift up the front of the dolly to get up a curb.

Movie Tech Rocker Plate

Advantages

- 360-degree panning of the camera on its own axis
- Infinitely variable panning friction
- Tilt locks allow the camera to be fixed at any position within tilt range
- Base with integrated water level for leveling on uneven surfaces
- Left-handed or right-handed operation possible
- Camera fitting: $^3/_8$-in. screw

Technical specifications

Tilt plate height	110 mm/4 ft. 3 in.
Tilt range	43 degrees
Weight	5.5 kg/12 lbs.
Max. Payload	40 kg/88 lbs.
Transport case (dimensions)	50 by 40 by 15 cm/18 ft. by 14 ft. 6 in.

Stinger Arm

STINGER™ ARM WITH GLIDING FLUID HEAD
(Jib Arm with 2 Axis Gliding Fluid Head)

Stinger™ Arm Adapts to
HD Video Cameras

Stinger™ Arm Adapts to Larger Film
Cameras with Magazines of up to 1000'.

SPECIFICATIONS

STINGER™ ARM **MOUNTED ON SUPER PEEWEE® IV

Maximum Camera Mount Height above Ground (Head Overslung)	9 ft. 7 1/2 in.	2.9 m
Maximum Camera Mount Height above Ground (Head Underslung)	67 1/2 in.	1.7 m
Minimum Camera Mount Height above Ground (Head Overslung)	26 1/4 in.	67 cm
Minimum Camera Mount Height below Ground (Head Underslung)	22 in.	56 cm
Maximum Reach (Stinger™ Glide Slide out)	60 in.	1.5 m
Maximum Reach w/ Panavision Fraser Lens System (Stinger™ Glide Slide out)	63 in.	1.6 m
Minimum Reach (Stinger™ Glide Slide in)	32 in.	81 cm
Full Arm Length	87 in.	2.3 m
Stinger™ Arm Travel	56 in.	1.4 m
Stinger™ Arm Travel on Super PeeWee® IV	89 1/2 in.	2.3 m
Stinger™ Arm Glide's Travel	24 in.	61 cm
Balance Ratio	2:1	2:1
*Maximum Camera Load	70 lb.	32 kg
Carrying Weight (w/o Fluid Head and Counter Balance Weights)	108 lb.	49 kg
Minimum Standard Operational Weight (w/o Camera Load)	125 lb.	57 kg
Maximum Operational Weight (w/o Camera Load) With Max. Counter Bal. Weight	390 lb.	177 kg

STINGER™ 2 AXIS FLUID HEAD

Maximum Height	25 7/8 in.	66 cm
Width	19 1/4 in.	49 cm
Depth	4 in.	10 cm
Weight	17 lb.	8 kg
Load Capacity	70 lb.	32 kg
Maximum Camera Magazine Size Capability	1000 ft.	1000 ft.
Pan and Tilt Movement	360°cont.	360°cont.

OTHER STINGER™ ARM FEATURES

- Compact and Lightweight Arm
- Stinger™ Arm Glide System Allows up to 2 ft. of Horizontal Travel
- Accurate Horizontal Marker System for Stinger™ Arm Glide
- Stinger™ Arm Glide System Allows Continuous Vertical Travel for up to 60 in.
- Black Anodized Arm for easy Maintenance

Stinger™ Arm
Glide System
Allows up to 2'
of Horizontal Travel.

*Payload Includes Camera and Film on Arm.
**Check Specifications Book for Added Measurments from Super PeeWee® IV Specs

Figure 172 Stinger Arm System (mounted on Super Peewee IV).

OTHER STINGER™ ARM FEATURES (continued)

• Works on Super PeeWee® IV and Hybrid Camera Dollies along with a Variety of Bases.
• Precision Design for Rigidity without the Need for Cabling System.
• A Variety of Counter Balance Weights Available from 2 1/2 lb. to 25 lb.
• New Anvil Case for Easy Transportation and Quick Setup.
• Comes Assembled and Ready for Use Allowing Quick Setup.
• Stinger™ Arm Glide System Has Drag Control.
• Cushioned Stops with Dampening Points at Top and Bottom Travel of the Arm.
• Fluid Dampening System Resulting in Zero Backlash.

Stinger™ Arm Glide System Has Drag Control

• 360° Continuous Pan Travel.
• Works with a Variety of Heads (Including Remote Camera Systems) .
• Designed to Work within Tight Areas.
• Precision Design Weights Are Contoured and Shaped on a Radius to Follow the Arc of the Arm.

STINGER™ ARM GLIDING FLUID HEAD FEATURES

• Head Can Be either Overslung for More Height or Underslung.
• Black Anodized Head for Easy Maintenance.
• 360° Continuous Pan Travel.
• Markers for Tracking Glide System on Fluid Head for up to 2 ft. of Horizontal Travel.
• Glide System Has Drag Control.
• Added 6 in. of Clearance to Handle Camera Magazines of up to 1000'.
• 2 Axis Head - Pan and Tilt with Fluid Dampening on Every Axis.
• Precision Bubble Level Conveniently Located on Head.
• Camera Mounting Plate with 3/8 in. Bolt Pattern.

Stinger™ Arm Fluid Head can be Overslung or Underslung as pictured

Stinger™ Arm Fluid Head Has Pan and Tilt Capabilities with Dampening on Every Axis.

Figure 172 *continued*

STINGER ARM SYSTEM
(mounted on Super PeeWee IV)
MAXIMUM CAMERA LOAD: 70 lb. (32 kg)
MAXIMUM OPERATING WEIGHT (w/o payload) 390 lb. (177 kg)

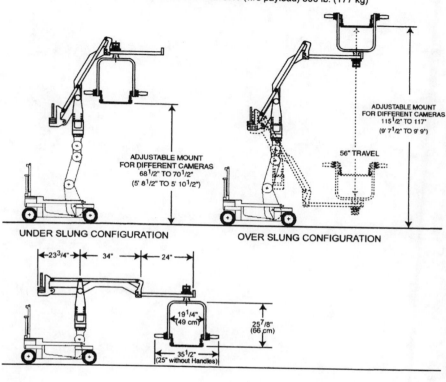

ADJUSTABLE MOUNT
FOR DIFFERENT CAMERAS
115$\frac{1}{2}$" TO 117"
(9' 7$\frac{1}{2}$" TO 9' 9")

56" TRAVEL

ADJUSTABLE MOUNT
FOR DIFFERENT CAMERAS
68$\frac{1}{2}$" TO 70$\frac{1}{2}$"
(5' 8$\frac{1}{2}$" TO 5' 10$\frac{1}{2}$")

UNDER SLUNG CONFIGURATION   OVER SLUNG CONFIGURATION

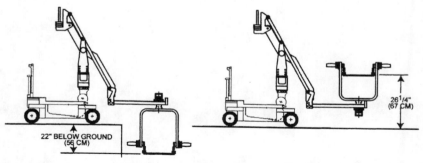

*It is advised that the user of Chapman/Leonard equipment check with the manufacturer for the latest updates on *all* equipment.

Figure 172 *continued*

Glossary

Here are some terms or words that you might hear daily in the course of your stay in the film and television business. A few of these words may be exclusive to the grip department, but for the sake of understanding the overall flavor of a working set, you should be aware of some general words that are used almost daily. Here is an example: You're a grip who was asked to work the *sticks* for the camera department. The AD yells "tail slate," or your may hear, "grab a Gary Coleman, with a postage stamp, and put an ear on the third zip light," or "lamp right next to the egg crate, then drop some beach on that hog trough before they pull the buck." "Say what?" you ask.

ABBY SINGER   The shot before the last shot.

AGE   This technique is used to make a new object, such as a mailbox, look older and to create a used look, such as old clothes, a sign, etc.

AMBIANCE   Sound recorded in the area that filming was done. This "quiet" sound that is recorded is added to set the mood of a scene.

BABY   A 1,000-watt lamp.

BACKING   A scenic piece behind a set window or open door. Also called a *drop*. A photographed or painted canvas background used on movie or video sets seen outside windows or doors.

BACK TO ONE   Go to your start position.

BAIL   The U-shaped metal arm that a movie lamp sits on. The bottom of the U has either a male pin or female receiver for attachment to a stand or hanger device.

BASE CAMP   The place where all the production vehicles are located—sort of like a mobile headquarters.

BASTARD SIDE   A term used for stage right.

BATTENS   When a cloth drop or backing is held up (or flown) using two pieces of wood (1 inch by 3 inches or 2 inches by 4 inches) by the length in a sandwich configuration attached to the top of the drop.

BEACH   Slang for a sandbag.

BEAVER BOARD   Usually a one-eighth apple box with a baby plate nailed onto it, for placing a lamp at low angles; also called a *skid plate.*

BECKY   A fixed-length mount bracket much like a trombone. The wall attachment has feet that are the only thing that adjust. The receiver is a fixed height (about a foot down using the bottom pin).

BELLY LINES   Ropes strung (usually about 10 feet apart) under a large silk, grifflon, or black.

BLACKS   Drapes used to hide or mask areas not to be shown on film or stage.

BLOCK AND FALL   A rope-and-pulley system that allows you to lift a heavy object with less pulling force.

BLOCKING   A rehearsal for actors and camera movement.

BOGGIE WHEELS   Wheels that do not usually come standard with each dolly. They are used to adapt a dolly to a specialty track, such as a pipe dolly, sled dolly, or tube track. There are several types or sets of boggie wheels.

BOOTIES   Surgical-style paper shoes put on over your street shoes before walking on a dry painted surface—prevents a mar or a scuff.

BOSS PLATE   A metal plate attached to the stage floor of a set to hold a set wall or scenery in place.

BOTTOMER   Flag off or block unwanted light from the bottom of a light source; also called a *bottom shelf.*

BOUNCE   Light that has been redirected first. It is shone onto a foam core, a show card, or any surface, and redirected (bounced) onto the subject. (See *fill light.*)

BRANCHLORIS   When a limb or branch from a tree is placed in front of a light to cause a pattern.

BROWNIE   A nickname for the camera.

BRUTE   A carbon arc lamp that runs on 225 amps.

B-TEAM   The stand-ins used for blocking and lighting a scene.

BUCK   Usually means a car that has been cut in half or the roof cut off for filming the inside of the vehicle, such as showing a center console or dashboard.

BULL PEN   Slang word used for the area where all the grip equipment is staged (set up). Also called the *staging area*. The place is usually as close to the set as possible and ready to work.

BUTTERFLY KIT   Assorted nets, silks, solids, and grifflons used for light control usually 5 feet by 5 feet or 6 feet by 6 feet frame sizes, but a general statement only. Commonly, a 12 feet by 12 feet or 20 feet by 20 feet is also called a butterfly kit. (It should be called an *overhead kit*.) The term *butterfly* now generally means a kit containing one each of a single, double, silk, solid, frame, and grifflon.

CAMERA LEFT   A direction to the left of what the camera sees.

CAMERA RIGHT   A direction to the right of what the camera sees.

CANS   Headsets used to hear what is being recorded for the film.

CEILING PIECE   A frame built from flat 1 inch by 3 inch lumber with a luan gussets covered on one side with muslin cloth (usually seamless).

CELO   A cucoloris made of wire mesh material used to give a pattern of bright and dark spots when used in front of a light.

CHARLIE BAR   A 1-inch to 6-inch-wide by 3-foot-long strip of wood with an attached pin used to create shadows on an object (thin long flags, gobos).

CHEATED   Avoiding an object for a better shot—moving it from the camera's view.

CHECKING THE GATE   This means to check the pressure plate in the camera that holds the film in place for any film chips, dirt, or debris. This task is accomplished after each scene.

CHERRY-PICKER   See *condor*.

CHROMATRANS   Looks like a giant slide that is lit from the back. Chromatrans come in all sizes from small to 30 feet by 100 feet or larger. They are usually pictures of city landscapes, but they can be countrysides, airports, whatever. There are daytime and nighttime chromatrans/translights. They are usually transported rolled up in a large cardboard tube. They usually are hung from grommets.

CLAPPER/LOADER   Another name for a camera assistant.

CLEAR LUMBER   Lumber without knots in it. It is normally used for dolly track.

CLEAT   A point to tie off a rope, usually an X-shape or a cross-shaped piece of wood nailed to a stage floor.

CLOTHESLINE   When a rope or cable is strung about neck height (like the old clothesline days). If a clothesline is needed, always hang some tape from it to mark it visually so that no one gets hurt.

COLOR TEMPERATURE   The warmth or coolness of a light is measured in degrees Kelvin. 5,600 K is considered daylight (blue) and 3,200 K is a tungsten (or white light)

COME-A-LONG   A hand-crank cable that can pull heavy objects closer together, like a wrenching block and fall.

CONDOR   A machine with a telescoping arm on it. The arm will also boom up, down, left: or right. Used a lot for lighting platforms. Also called a *cherry-picker*.

COURTESY FLAG   A flag set for the director, DP, talent, agency, or anyone who needs shading.

COVE   When you tent a window or doorway to make it night during the day.

CRAFT SERVICES   A table of food and sweets set out for the entire film cast and crew.

CROSSING   Spoken (yelled out) when crossing in front of a lens if there is not any filming going on, but the cameraperson is looking through the eyepiece. A courtesy to them.

CUT   The term used when setting a flag in front of a light to cut or remove the light from an object. There are two types: (1) a hard or sharp cut, which means making a hard shadow, close to the object, and (2) a soft cut, where you hold the flag or scrim closer to the light source.

CYC-STRIPS   A single lamp to several lamps placed in one housing fixture.

DAILIES   Usually film shot the day before shown to the director, cameraperson, and crew. A review of that day's work to ensure there are no reshoots. Sometimes called *rushes*.

DAPPLE   Can be shadows made by a branch with leaves on it.

DEAL MEMO   A written paper describing what money you have accepted for your service.

DECK POLE   A pointed stick about 4.5 feet long that sticks in the holes along the green beds, to which an arm and flag is attached.

DINGO   A small branch-a-louris.

DOWN STAGE   Means closer to the camera or audience.

DP   Director of photography.

DUTCH ANGLE   Usually means to lean the camera sideways either left or right to film in that position.

EAR   Put a flag up on the side of a light to block light; also called a *sider*.

EARS ON   Turn your handheld walkie-talkie on.

EASY-OUT Looks like a reverse drill and is used to get out broken bolts. Drill with a small bit and then put the easy-out in the hole and twist out.

EGG CRATE A soft light control frame that directs light without it spilling off the subject. Looks sort of like a rectangle box with several dividers spaced evenly in it.

EYE LIGHT The eyes are given a sparkle light (also called an *obie light*).

E-Z-UP A popup-style tent that usually comes in an 8 feet by 8 feet or a 10 feet by 10 feet size. (Larger and smaller sizes are available.)

FEATHER When a flag is set in front of a light source and you get closer to or farther from the source with the flag, this will feather, soften, or harden the shadow on the surface of an object.

FILL LIGHT Light added to the opposite side of a subject to "fill in" the shadows made from the *key light*.

FIRST TEAM The talent, the actors that will be filmed, the A-team.

FLARE When a light shines into the camera lens, it will flare or cause a glare to form on the film. This unwanted light on the lens causes a distortion or distracting light on film.

FLASHING Called out before someone takes a flash photo. This lets the gaffer know that one of his lights has not burnt out.

FLOAT A FLAG To handhold a flag as the camera is moved, to float with the camera, blocking unwanted light flares. Floater also refers to a handheld flag or net that moves with an actor during a take.

FLOOD Spreads light to the overall subject.

FLY IT OUT Pull it out of the scene.

FLYING IN The object asked for is being fetched in an extremely quick manner.

FLYING THE MOON A bunch of lights hung on pipes shaped into a box frame. Then a muslin (rag) cover is wrapped around it, and it is flown over an exterior location by a cable on a crane.

FRAME LINE The edges (top or bottom or sides) of what the camera will pick up.

FREEBIE (or public service announcement, PSA) A film project for which the crew usually receives no pay. (It's a way to give something back to the industry for being so good to you.)

FRESNEL The glass lens in front of a movie lamp used to spread or focus the light.

F-STOP   A measurement of the lens aperture. Lenses are rated by speed (how much light they can gather); a lens that can film with a minimum of F/1.4 is considered faster than a lens that films with a minimum of F/8. Example: F/1.4 equals less light needed for correct exposure and F/8 equals more light needed for correct exposure.

FULLER'S EARTH   Used to make blowing dust in the background or to dust down or age a person or object.

GAFFER   Head electrician.

GAFFER'S TAPE   Adhesive tape similar to duct tape; also called *grip tape* or *cloth tape*.

GARY COLEMAN   A short 20-inch-high C-stand.

GEL   Usually a transparent cellophane material used for changing the color of a light, either for visual effect or for film exposure correction.

GHOST LIGHT   A single large lightbulb mounted on its own wooden stand. Usually left on a stage that's not being used because it is believed to keep friendly spirits illuminated and evil spirits away and because it helps people see the set objects laying on an unlit stage.

GOBO HEAD   Also called a *grip head* or *C-stand head*, used as a clamping device for holding equipment.

GRAZE   Go to the craft services food table.

GREEK IT OUT   To disguise a word to make a logo unrecognizable. For example, Coke might become Ooko AA Cola.

GRIP TAPE   Adhesive tape similar to duct tape; also called *gaffer's tape* or *cloth tape*.

GRIP RADIO TALK

10–100	to the restroom
10–4	I understand
what's your 20?	where are you?

GRIP HEAD   A C-stand head, used as a clamping device; also called a *gobo head*.

HAIR IN THE GATE   This is when a piece of debris or film chip is lodged in the corner of the pressure plate gate. This also means that as protection against that chip or debris that may have scratched the film emulsion, the last shot must be reshot (sort of like insurance).

HAND SHOES   Leather gloves.

HARDMARKS   Permanent objects or tape marks placed by the camera assistant.

HEADACHE   Duck, something has fallen from over head.

HEMP   Rope from $\frac{1}{4}$ inch to 1 inch usually.

HERO   Usually means the product of the commercial, such as a perfectly prepared hamburger, a toy, or a color-corrected label. Whatever it is, it is perfect (hero) for the shot for filming a commercial.

HIGHLIGHT   Used to brighten an area of an object or to emphasize an interesting part with light.

HISTORY   Remove it from the set, lose it, only a memory, gone, vapor.

HMI (Hydragyrum Medium Arc)   Length Iodid lamp that usually burns at 5,600 degrees kelvin (also known as *blue light*).

HODS   A bead board, three-side bounce, usually made from polystyrene (bead board). About 18 inches long by 12 inches wide, with a 12 inch by 12 inch cap on one end.

HOG TROUGH   When you use nails, screws, or glue two sticks of 1 inch by 3 inches lumber to make an L-shape or V-shape brace. This process makes the otherwise flimsy piece of 1 inch by 3 inches board stronger by giving it a backbone.

HOT SET   Don't move anything because more filming is to be done.

IDIOT CHECK   This means to send a grip out searching the set for any equipment that may be left behind after you have finished the shoot before leaving the location.

INCANDESCENT LAMP   A lamp with a 3,200 degree kelvin temperature (also called *white light*).

JUICER   Electrician, sparks.

JUNIOR   A 2,000-watt lamp.

KICK   A sparkle off an object or person—may be desired or required to be removed. This term can also be used when an object has shine on it or a shine is to be redirected on it from another object—sort of like a reflection.

KILL THE BABY   Turn off the 1-kilowatt lamp.

KNEE CAPS   Means heads up, equipment coming through.

KODAK MOMENT   A chance to take a picture with the talent (actors and actresses). Same as a *photo op*.

LACE-OUT   Means to lay it out so it can be easily counted. Such as a prep or wrap day on a stage or returning from a show.

LANYARD   Cord on tools for working high in overhead perm.

LEAK   Means that a small amount of light has gotten past the flag or gobo.

LEGAL MILK CRATE   Not stolen from a store, they are rented or bought outright.

LENSER   This is a term to shade the lens, such as with a flag, or using a camera-attaching shade called an *eyebrow*, or even using a handheld flag.

LEXAN   We use this plastic sheet material that comes in a 4 feet by 8 feet sheet in many different thicknesses (e.g., $\frac{1}{8}$ inch, $\frac{1}{4}$ inch, $\frac{1}{2}$ inch, 1 inch) to protect the camera and personnel from explosions. It is optically clear and highly recommended.

LIMBO TABLE   This table has a 90-degree sweep, usually used for product shots. The back part stands straight up and then curves 90 degrees to form a table, which the product is placed on.

LINE OUT   Called out from overhead when a rope or line is let out.

LOSE IT   Remove it from the set, or from the surrounding area; no longer needed.

LUAN   Plywood-like material that starts at about $\frac{1}{8}$ inch thick, which is used to make set walls. Can be a three-ply timber, which is still lightweight, paintable, and stainable. It is sometimes called Philippine Mahogany.

MAKE IT LIVE   Set the object in place.

MARTINI SHOT   Last film shot of the day. Slang for the next shot will be "in a glass," the wrap shot.

MICHAEL JACKSON   Taken from his song "Beat It," means get out of the way.

MICKEY MOLE   A 1,000-watt lamp.

MICKEY ROONEY   A nickname for a little creep of the dolly, a slight, little, slow movement.

MIGHTY MOLE   A 2,000-watt lamp.

MOLELIPSO   A 1,000-watt to 2,000-watt lamp mainly used for performances. The spotlight.

MOS (Mitt Out Sound)   Not a sound take or recording.

MOUSE   The shadow of the microphone.

MULLIONS   The boards that hold each pane of glass in that give you a French window effect.

ND   Neutral density filter is a soft-rolled gel. It also comes in large plastic sheets as well as small glass. It is used to reduce the brightness of a lamp or light source—sort of like sunglasses.

NECK DOWN   Slang term for being hired from the neck down. (Means don't think, just do.)

NEGATIVE FILL   A black surface used to remove unwanted light close to the actor.

NET   This is when you use scrims (nonelectrical dimmers) to reduce the light on an object in small amounts.

NEW DEAL   When this scene is over we are starting on a new setup.

NG   No good.

NODAL POINT   The dead center of the camera lens if the camera was to rotate in a 360-degree twisting motion.

NOOK LIGHT   A light of 650 watts to 2,000 watts on an average.

OBIE LIGHT   A small light placed just on top of the camera to add a sparkle to the talent's eyes or used as a fill light.

ONE-LINER   A breakdown of the script that will inform the crew what scenes will be shot that day. It will have the scene number and a bit of the story line or action that will occur.

ONSTAGE   Means move toward the center of the set or stage.

OPERATOR   Camera operator; can also be the director of photography (DP), but does not have to be. Mostly two different people on movies.

OVERCRANKING   Speeds up the frame rate of film through the camera. When processed and projected at normal speed (24 frames per second [FPS]), the action appears in slow motion.

OVERHEAD KIT   Usually means a kit of a 12 feet by 12 feet or 20 feet by 20 feet set of one each of a single, double, silk, solid, frame, and grifflon. Commonly referred to as a *butterfly kit*, although overhead kit is more descriptive.

OZONES   The open area between the wood beams that make up the perms. This is the area that we throw ropes over to rig either lights, greenbeds, or set wall tieoffs or whatever from.

PAN   Rotate the camera left or right.

PARABOLIC REFLECTOR   The part of the lamp behind the glove (lightbulb) used to gather and reflect the light onto a subject.

PHIL-LOPPY   A 4 feet by 4 feet floppy-type flag made of a white-out bounce material. Excellent for bounce/fill (contributed by Phil Sloan, local 80 Key Grip).

PHOTO OP   A chance to take a picture with someone you would like to be seen with, such as an actor or actress.

PHOTO FLOOD GLOBES   Normal-looking lightbulbs that give off a brighter light (they have a short useful life).

PIPE GRID   A series of pipes, most often connected together for rigidity, that are usually hung by chains above a movie set.

PLAYBACK   The video recording of the scene just shot.

POOR MAN'S PROCESS   Can mean filming a stationary vehicle by passing a light, shadow, or background object by it, giving the impression that the vehicle is in motion. Also a slight shaking or a lever under the frame of the car, giving it a small jolt every so often works well.

POV (Point of View)   What a person sees.

PRACTICAL   A fixture (light) in frame such as table, floor, or wall lamp.

PREP   To prepare for a job. For example, to check out the equipment or camera to ensure that they are in good working order for the job that you are going to begin.

P-TON   A sharp, flat peg with a ring welded to it for a rope to tie off to. It can be hammered into small cracks in cement or asphalt without much damage.

RAGS   Any one of the following is referred to as a rag because they do not usually have a permanent frame affixed to them: muslin (bleached or unbleached), nets (single or double), silk, solid, or grifflon.

REEFING   A way to properly fold a large rag (i.e., grifflon, black, or any material that requires folding).

ROPE WRENCH   A knife to cut the rope.

SAIL BOATS   Used to hoist/fly a backing or translight, making it mobile.

SCAB PATCH   For example, two 2 feet by 4 feet by 16 feet pieces of lumber are laid end to end to total 32 feet long, and a third equal-length piece of lumber is laid equally on both ends and nailed together. Also a patch laid over a hole like a Band-Aid. Both examples are called *scabbing*. A *sandwich* is the same as a scab patch, except that it's nailed on two sides with two pieces of scab lumber.

SCENE DOCK   A storage place for several wall flats. You can also "temporarily" store a removed wall on set next to a working wall with hog troughs or set braces.

SCOUT   To go to different places or locations to check out an area.

SCRIMS   These are made from net material as well as wire mesh that fits right in front of a light.

SEAMLESS PAPER   A wide roll of paper used for a background, such as that used in a portrait shot.

SET CONSCIENCE   Be aware of what is where on the set. (This will make or break you. If you are not aware of where your equipment is when called for, you can look pretty bad.)

SET DECORATOR   The person who actually decorates the set with the right objects for the storyline. This will make a scene look real to the viewing audience.

SHEAVE   The wheel in the pulley, which allows the rope or wire to ride on.

SIDER   Put a flag up on the side of a light to block light; also called an *ear*.

SKID PLATE   Usually a one-eighth apple box with a baby plate on it, used for setting lamps at low angles. Also called a *beaver board*.

SLEEPER TRACK   Framing track made from 4 feet by 8 feet frames made from straight kiln-dried lumber (no warping),which is used under the dolly or crane track to reinforce the foundation of the track for the dolly.

SLOW IT DOWN (take it down, knock it down)   All mean to "reduce" it. It usually refers to bringing down the intensity of a light.

SNOOT   A device shaped like a funnel or coffee can hooked on the front of a lamp.

SOFFIT   The outcropping of a set wall or header where a movie light can be set.

SOFT   A gentle, pleasing light.

SOFTLIGHT   A range from 650-watt to 4,000-watt on an average, also known as a *zip light*.

SOLDIER-UP   This means to set up more stands in rows ready for action.

SPAN SET   A loop of extremely strong material wrapped around a frame or beam being hoisted up by a wench or crane. Comes in 1-foot to 20-foot loops and can be larger upon request.

SPARK   Electrician, juicer.

SPEED   The camera or the soundperson may call out when they have their equipment running at the desired speed or operating RPM for filming.

SPILL   When you set a light or you are using the natural sunlight. You will be directing the light onto an object, and you will allow the light to spill or leak off the one object onto something else.

SPOT   Direct all light to one point on subject.

SQUEEZER   An electrical dimmer.

SQUIB A small explosive device (which can be activated "accidently" by pressing the talk button on your walkie-talkie). Used to make a bullet hole or wound during a scene. Used by the special effects crew.

STEVADOR A hand truck.

STORYBOARDS Cartoon-like drawings used as a representation for the shoot, indicating the camera angles or framing.

TABLE IT Means to lay flat or parallel to the ground, such as a reflector or 12 feet by 12 feet frame.

TAG LINES Ropes usually made of $\frac{1}{4}$ inch hemp, tied to a lamp hanger (trapeze) used to pan or tie off a lamp. They are also used to tie off rags on frames.

TAIL SLATE To hit the camera sticks after the scene has been shot. The slate is turned upside down, with the wording facing the lens, and then the hinged sticks are slapped together; also called *tail sticks*.

TAKE DOWN Means to reduce the light on an object by use of nets, scrims, dimmers, or wasting/spilling some of the light.

TAKE When a scene is shot.

TALENT A term used for actors.

TEASER Used to cut light, like a flag.

TILT Move the camera up and down in a tilting motion.

TOENAIL To put either a nail or screw in the edge of an object to secure it temporarily in place.

TOPPER Flag off or block unwanted light from the top of a light source; also called a *top shelf*.

TRACK SYSTEMS A track that can be used to hang a backing on that can be easily moved and replaced with a different backing.

TRUSS A triangle metal structure used to span a large area. Sometimes called a *rock-and-roll truss* for hanging lights on.

TURN ON TWO BUBBLES Turn on two lights in the same lamp.

TWEENIE A 650-watt lamp.

UPSTAGE Means move toward the back of the set or stage. (Comes from older stages that were built with a higher or raked upward incline toward the rear or back wall, away from the audience.)

WAFF To lightly fan, smoke, or move a curtain sheet (as if to make a breeze).

WALL BRACE A metal rod flattened on each end with holes drilled through it to attach a set wall to the wood-slatted floor. Also a hog trough can be used (see hog trough).

WALL FLAT A scenic covered wall usually made from 1 feet by 3 feet cover in thin plywood-type material.

WALL JACK A two-wheeled brace/jack used to transport a large set wall.

WALL SCONCE A lamp hung on a wall, a practical fixture.

WARNER BROTHERS A term used for an extreme closeup of a person; means to crop a little off the top of an actor's head with either a shadow or through the lens.

WASTE This is when you shine all the light on an object, then slowly turn the light so that some of the light will miss or fall off the object.

WATCH YOUR BACK Usually means that someone with equipment is coming from behind you to pass and get the equipment to or from the set.

WHIP-PAN A fast pan of the camera causing a blur in the motion.

WIG-WAG The red flashing light outside of a stage indicates that filming is going on.

WILD CEILING or **WILD WALL** Walls that are made to move individually from each other for filming.

WING When an object such as a flag is set in front of a light and then moved away or closer in a semicircular motion.

WIPE An image that moves across the frame during filming used to hide a cut during editing.

WRAP Means to put away all equipment or quit for the night. Go home.

ZIP CORD A lightweight cord that looks like an extension cord. It comes in different gauges, usually black, white, or brown but can be ordered in other colors.

Index